DECORATIVE ROUTING JIGS & TECHNIQUES

Cox, J.
Decorative routing.

PRICE: $46.95 (3559/br   )

DECORATIVE ROUTING

Jigs & Techniques

Jack Cox

STOBART DAVIES

STOBART DAVIES LTD.
Publishers & Booksellers
STOBART HOUSE, PONTYCLERC
PENYBANC RD, AMMANFORD SA18 3HP
Tel: 01269 593100 Fax: 01269 596116
www.stobartdavies.com

British Library Cataloguing in Publication Data

A catalogue record for this book is available from the British Library.

ISBN 0–85442–068–1

Published 1997 by
Stobart Davies Ltd, Priory House, 2 Priory Street, Hertford SG14 1RN.

Set in 10½ on 13½pt Garamond by Ann Buchan (Typesetters) Shepperton.

Printed in Great Britain

ACKNOWLEDGEMENTS

I have been extremely fortunate in receiving a great deal of help with the preparation of this book. To begin with, I am grateful to the management and staff of the Trend Company. In addition to much helpful advice, their assistance has taken the highly practical form of the loan of some of the equipment described and illustrated. In view of the fact that I am not an employee of the Company – my relationship is rather that of a long-standing satisfied customer - I consider their help to be exceptionally generous.

My thoughts on the subject of the odd effects produced on ellipses by router cutters are essentially based upon observation; my schoolboy-level mathematics could not possibly cope with a more rigorous approach. However, my good friend Dr Jeff Bourne, who also happens to be a professional mathematician, has provided me with several pages of mathematical analysis which, despite the fact that I am only just about capable of following them, have endowed my thoughts with a substance and authority which they would otherwise not possess. I am exceedingly grateful to him for removing my slight unease in respect of their validity.

My own expertise, if I may presume to employ such a word, is confined essentially to technical matters. In other respects, I am scarcely fit to be allowed out alone. For this reason, I am indebted to my publisher, Brian Davies, not only for his interest in my work, but also for his advice on matters of presentation and appeal.

Finally, to my wife Betty, I offer my very special thanks. Wives can afford to be honest in their criticism (well, some of the time anyway) and, on many occasions, her timely comments on the design of this or that piece have served to bring to the surface identical doubts of my own. In addition, she has been part-time typist, proof reader, photographer, photographer's model and general administrator. Not least, I am grateful for her tolerance with regard to the trail of bits of paper and wood shavings that I leave behind me everywhere I go.

CONTENTS

PROJECTS

INTRODUCTION

One of the commonest descriptions applied to the router is that it is a 'versatile' device. True enough, but the versatility comes from the range of commercial or home-made devices which may be attached to it. There are relatively few applications where the router is used as a freehand 'stand-alone' tool; most require the path of the router to be constrained in some way, by the use of an added jig or fixture. Attachments can range from simple fence or ski devices, to highly complex systems, including the complete computerised 'NC' package.

The purpose of this book is essentially to offer a number of jigs and projects which enable the versatility of the router/jig combination to be exploited in a particular way – that of producing decorative items which are primarily intended to be looked at, and which may or may not have some additional function. Most people are aware of the term 'ornamental turning' – a description of work essentially carried out on a lathe, bearing a degree of ornamentation and complexity sufficient to tax the imagination and ingenuity of some of the world's best engineers, but which is nevertheless based upon geometry. Much of this work is quite simple and involves straight lines, circles and, in some cases, ellipses. It is my hope that this book might be considered as an attempt to apply the more elementary principles to the concept of 'ornamental routing', and perhaps to introduce one or two new jigs to the router fraternity along the way. I would like to think also, that the bulk of the content is new, original work; certainly this has been my intention throughout.

No book of this type would be complete without some reference to workshop safety. I consider myself privileged to be in a position to demonstrate the use of the router to the general public from time to time, and also to supervise 'hands-on' use of the machine. The overwhelming impression I gain from beginners in particular is that they consider the router to be decidedly dangerous. This is by no means the case; if treated with due understanding and respect, it is not only safe, it is a positive joy to use. I do in fact derive a great deal of personal satisfaction, after a successful first-time use by an exhibition visitor, to share in his or her pleasure at having managed, not only to use such a 'nasty, dangerous machine', but to find it really rather easy. I can only hope that this book will help inexperienced readers along the way to the same viewpoint.

Most handbooks on routing provide 'rules' for safe operation. These generally deal with overloading, direction of movement and so on, and reflect the understandable concern of the makers of routers or jigs for their safe use. I have no quarrel with these – indeed I support them without reservation. I do however believe that it is equally important for the user to understand the underlying reasons for these rules, rather than simply attempting to apply them slavishly. Rules, however carefully formulated, are unlikely to cater for every possible situation and, without understanding, the user may thus face a dilemma. For this reason, I have devoted an entire chapter to the safe use of the router. This is positively *not* because I believe that the router in particular requires a massive dissertation on safety, but rather because I am firmly convinced that the use of *any* piece of woodworking machinery is materially assisted by some knowledge of how it actually performs its task (this is not always immediately obvious). For this reason, I have attempted to give the reader an understanding of the geometry underlying the behaviour of the cutter on the workpiece. Safety is not, by the way, confined entirely to the user. That of the workpiece can also be a problem; it is quite easy to mangle a piece of wood beyond salvation, without placing oneself at any risk whatsoever. In this connection, the reader will notice throughout the book, photographic and written evidence of some of my many mistakes, included for the purpose of demonstrating lessons which I believe to be valuable. I can't say that I am proud of them; indeed I like to think that bad luck played a part on occasion, but this sort of luck can, if one is honest about it, usually be ascribed to carelessness or lack of forethought.

I have a very great interest in woodworking of all kinds, with particular emphasis perhaps on woodturning and routing. I believe that the two are complementary, in that it is often possible to manage with one, that which cannot be managed with the other. For example, it is quite easy to make a complex assembly of segments and inlays with a router, of a form which would be extremely difficult to produce on a lathe, and then to (literally) turn the result into a bowl (quite difficult for a router). Although woodturning does not form any significant part of the content of this book, the reader additionally blessed with a lathe might well bear the thought in mind. In any event, within both disciplines, I have a personal passion for accuracy (a constant source of amusement and leg-pulling among my woodworking friends). On one occasion, the well-known woodturner Stuart Mortimer, whom I am privileged to regard as a friend, described my woodturning approach as 'engineering in wood'. The idea gave me some amusement at the time but, on reflection, I think it isn't at all a bad description. Certainly, if true of my woodturning, it is even more so of my routing; this will doubtless be found

evident in the following pages. Many of the projects require either jointing, or inlay, or both. In all cases, a few thousandths of an inch gap in any joint region will render that joint quite obviously second-rate in terms of appearance, even though it may succeed in holding the relevant parts together; I therefore make no apology for my obsession. In any case, routing with jigs should not normally demand a high degree of manual skill on the part of the user, since the jigs themselves take care of the accuracy problem, once they have been set up appropriately (setting them up can be the difficult bit).

Readers will notice that one or two of the photographs show that I am using the router whilst comfortably *seated* at the workbench and also, on occasion, with one hand only. This is one of the advantages of trammel work in general, since the router path is totally constrained and requires no effort from the operator to keep it 'on track'. This is of course a blessing to those of us euphemistically described as 'of advanced years' (whether we actually *feel* old or not) but, far more importantly, may be of very great benefit to disabled workers, who thereby needn't feel 'left out' of work of this kind.

I have found this book far easier to write and illustrate than to organise sensibly. For example, it is inevitable that a particular technique or style of jig may be employed in more than one project, leaving me with three possibilities open: I could indulge in a good deal of wasteful repetition of the same information. I could scatter the information about the book and leave readers to sort things out for themselves; I personally find this form of discursive 'buckshot' approach irritating, and I imagine that others would find it equally so. I have therefore taken my third option, that of making a description once only (I hope), and making references to it elsewhere as necessary. This too can be overdone and, if I have failed, I ask the indulgence of the reader.

A quick word about the projects: I find it flattering on occasion to hear my work described as 'difficult'. I am also bound to say that, for my competition entries, I deliberately attempt to convey that very thought, in the hope that the judges will be duly impressed. Of course, the whole thing is a complete 'con trick'; the work is almost totally managed by the jigs and the router. There is no way that I can prove this by the written word or, for that matter, by the illustrations provided; I can only urge the reader to put it to the test. In this context, the projects are arranged as far as possible in ascending order of 'difficulty'. They represent but a small part of my own output. I could easily fill another book of this size with projects alone, and maybe I will one day. Those presented here have been chosen because they illustrate particular jigs and techniques, and can be easily modified to choice. They can also be used as starting points for projects designed entirely by the reader.

I feel obliged to add a few words on the subject of metric vs. imperial measurements. Despite twenty-odd years of 'metrication', the UK remains an uneasy mix of both systems (for example, an 'eight by four sheet of six-mil plywood'). To this may be added that many older people, such as myself, although they may be able to handle metric dimensions (they are, after all, just numbers like any others), find it difficult to *visualise* sizes specified in this way. I have therefore taken the decision to stick with imperial measurement, except in very rare cases where no system other than metric will do – for example M6 studding, which specifies both a dimension and a screw-thread. I offer my apologies to (particularly) younger readers, brought up on the metric system, but this particular problem really does illustrate that it is not possible to please everybody.

Finally, it gives me great satisfaction to record that two project designs in my earlier book 'Beyond Basic Turning' were adapted by readers, each of whom won an award (one silver, one gold), at major national exhibitions. It is my hope that something of the kind occurs as a result of the appearance of this book. If this does happen at some future date, I will consider myself well rewarded.

1

TRAMMEL WORK

A substantial portion of this book features trammel techniques of one kind or another. In its simplest form, the router is arranged to swing about an external pivot point, constraining the cutter to traverse a circular path. Fig.1(a) shows the idea as a simple diagram. Fig.2, which demonstrates a practical application, shows the router raised above the workpiece by a plain block at the pivot point, and a ski at the other end. The workpiece is held to the worktop, and is contacted by the cutter only. Clearly, the minimum available radius is determined by eventual contact between the pivot and the router base. Nevertheless, this simple arrangement is capable of a wide application range, particularly where large radii are required. However, it is at a disadvantage where the

radius demands that the pivot point disappears below the base of the router, as shown in Fig.1(b). It is not particularly difficult to devise a jig to which performs this function. A very simple jig is shown in Fig.1(c); others might well make use of the router base itself. Such devices have their problems however. They may be difficult to adjust precisely, particularly where adjustment is required part-way through a multi-stage machining process. There may also be problems with control of the 'ride height' of the router above the workpiece, leading to possible tipping of the router. However, the real bugbear with such systems arises from the necessity for the pivot point to be on the workpiece itself – not a great deal of help where this particular area is required to be machined away.

Problems of this nature are easily dealt with by the Pivot Frame jig in its most fundamental configuration, termed the 'mini-pivot' mode. This device, initially an invention of mine, was taken up and marketed by the Trend Company who, in addition to making improvements to the design, also spotted a number of additional applications. These are featured elsewhere in the book. The jig performs its function by creating an artificial or 'imaginary' pivot point which is quite independent of the router itself. It remains necessary of course, to hold the work down in some way, but apart from this there is no contact with the workpiece by any part of the equipment other than the cutter. The maximum

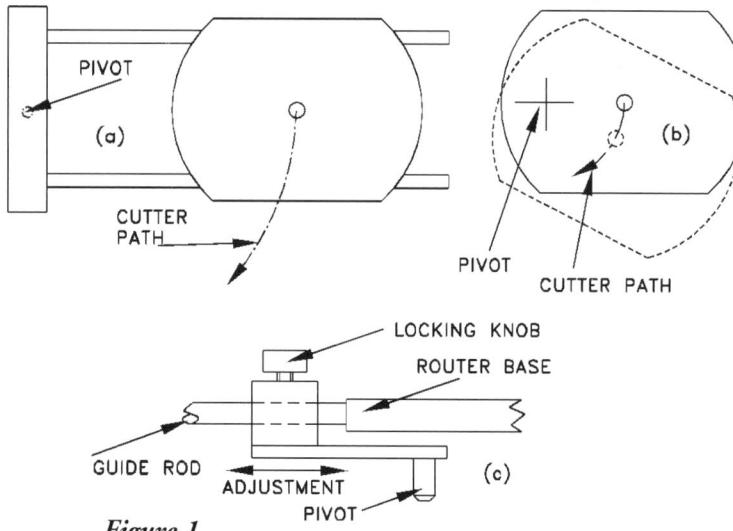

Figure 1

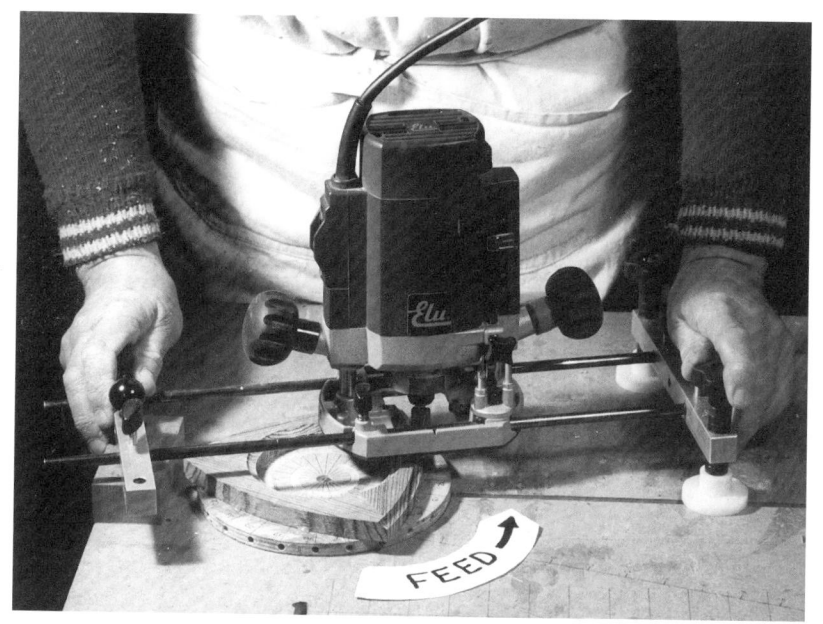

Figure 2

diameter of circle which may be cut is limited only by the length of the router guide rods, beyond which the beam trammel mode can normally take over. The minimum diameter may actually become zero or, in practice, as small as the user cares to make it. Essential features are shown in Fig.3(a). The router is fitted, via its guide rods, to a pair of light alloy 'pivot bars' which can be locked on to the rods. Each bar carries a pair of turned, shouldered nylon shoes. The assembly is mounted on a large circular disc; this is referred to as the 'primary disc' for reasons which will become clear later. The smaller diameter of the shoes bears against the rim of the primary disc, and the flange formed by the larger diameter sits on its top face. Thus, the entire assembly is free to rotate about the disc, with the router sitting at a fixed distance or 'ride height' above it, as Fig.3(b) shows. The ride height can actually be varied in a series of steps, by means of spacers inserted between the pivot bar and the shoes. There is some advantage in most cases, in fitting long guide rods to the assembly, since they allow a larger primary disc to

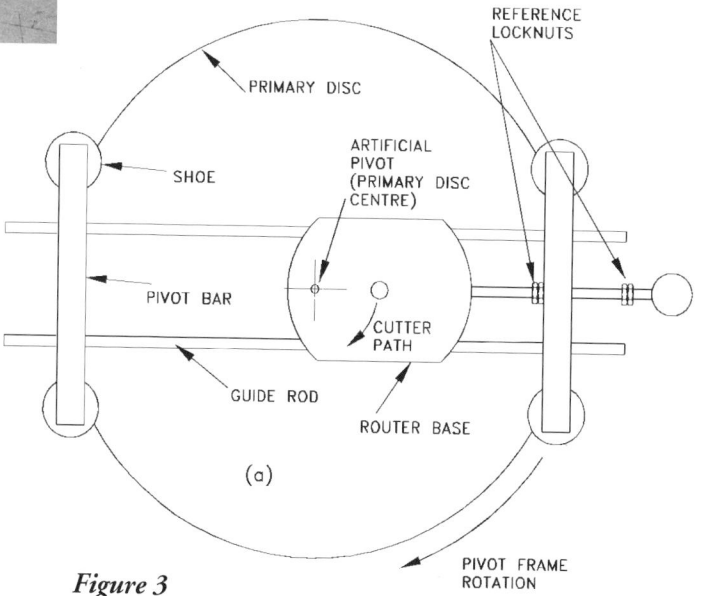

Figure 3

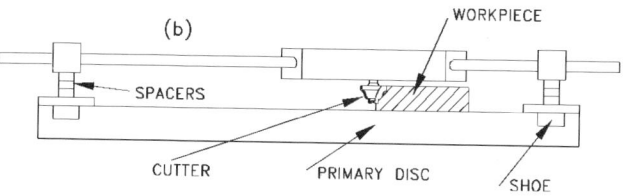

Figure 4

be used, thus increasing the range of the device; long rods are usually commercially available as a router accessory. The router is free to slide along the guide rods, but may be locked in any position with the standard router locking knobs, thus enabling any desired diameter of circle to be cut. The adjustment may be made either freehand, or by means of either of the two threaded micro-adjusters supplied with the kit. The micro-adjusters will be found extremely useful, apart from their obvious function of 'micro-adjusting'. With the aid of two pairs of locknuts, used as shown in Fig.3(a), the cutter operating radius may be preset in either one or two positions. To use either, the router is simply slid along the rods until the nuts contact the pivot bar, and is then fixed by means of its own locking knobs. I call this the 'reference locknut system' for convenience, since it is used extensively throughout the book. The shoes operate on the 'centre-finder' principle, and thus ensure that the cutter traverses the diameter of the primary disc, and may

therefore be positioned at dead-centre if necessary. Machining is carried out simply by setting the depth of cut and rotating the Pivot Frame assembly about the disc. A typical operation, that of cutting a circular recess in a small mirror frame, is shown in Fig.4.

Primary discs are not supplied as part of the basic kit, partly because requirements can vary widely, even for a single individual user, and partly because they are so easily home-made that it is scarcely worth the trouble of supplying them commercially. They may be made with the Pivot Frame jig itself in the simplest of its three possible 'beam trammel' modes. This is effected by removing the shoe assemblies from one pivot bar and replacing them with the central pivot stud and knob supplied with the kit (Fig.5). The other pivot bar assembly is removed entirely, allowing the base of the router to be supported by the workpiece itself. It is very important for best accuracy, that the base of the router sits flat against the surface of the workpiece. Dependent upon the make and model of the router used, it may therefore be necessary to fit one or more washers or spacers beneath the pivot bar. Primary discs are best made from a 'man-made' dimensionally stable material, such as MDF or plywood which, to obtain best accuracy from the system, should be not less than $\frac{3}{4}$" thick. This allows the bottom of the Pivot Frame shoes to ride well clear of the supporting worktop. Moreover, given accurate drilling, the thickness helps to ensure that bolts or rods passing through the disc (there will be plenty of these) are at right angles to the face; an essential requirement for accuracy.

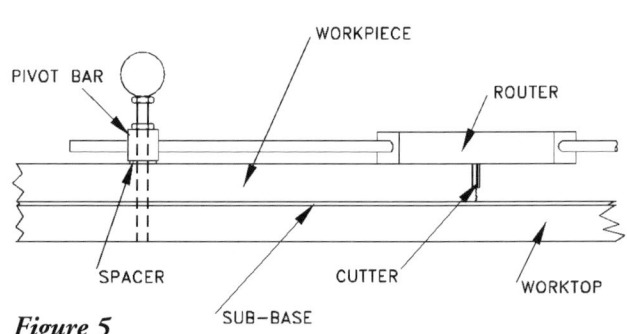

Figure 5

Two major problems with MDF are dust generation and the blunting effect on cutters. For these reasons, and where time is not an overwhelming consideration, it is sensible to reduce the router workload by sawing the blank to a slightly oversize circular form, and use the router to trim to final profile only, as shown in Fig.6. In the absence of suitable drawing equipment, discs of relatively large diameter may be marked out accurately enough for preliminary sawing, with a pin, a pencil and a loop of string.

The actual diameter of a given primary disc is not particularly important – near enough is good enough. The truth and continuity of its circular profile are, on the other hand, of the utmost importance, since any irregularities will be transferred to the workpiece in some way, when the jig is put to use. Accuracy of the primary disc commences with the pivot point. That supplied with the Pivot Frame kit is actually a length of 6mm. diameter steel threaded rod (commonly known as 'studding'). This is intended to fit a hole of this size

drilled or bored in the centre of the workpiece (Fig.7(a)). A pivot point of the type shown in (b), working in an indent in the workpiece, is not recommended, since it would be difficult to guarantee that the base of the router is flush with the face of the workpiece. Moreover, any wear and tear on the indent would impair accuracy and, in the worst case, the pivot point could actually jump out of the indent during machining. The studding must be a 'push fit' in the hole, for best machining accuracy. If available drill or cutter sizes result in free play of the studding in the hole, this may be taken up by wrapping thin plastic adhesive tape around the studding until a firm fit is obtained. This procedure will only cope with very small differences of diameter, but is worth doing where necessary, despite the fact that the tape will be found very difficult to remove from the threads of the studding afterwards.

It may be difficult to use a drill press to drill the central hole in discs of large diameter since the throat of the press may not accommodate the requirement. The

Figure 6

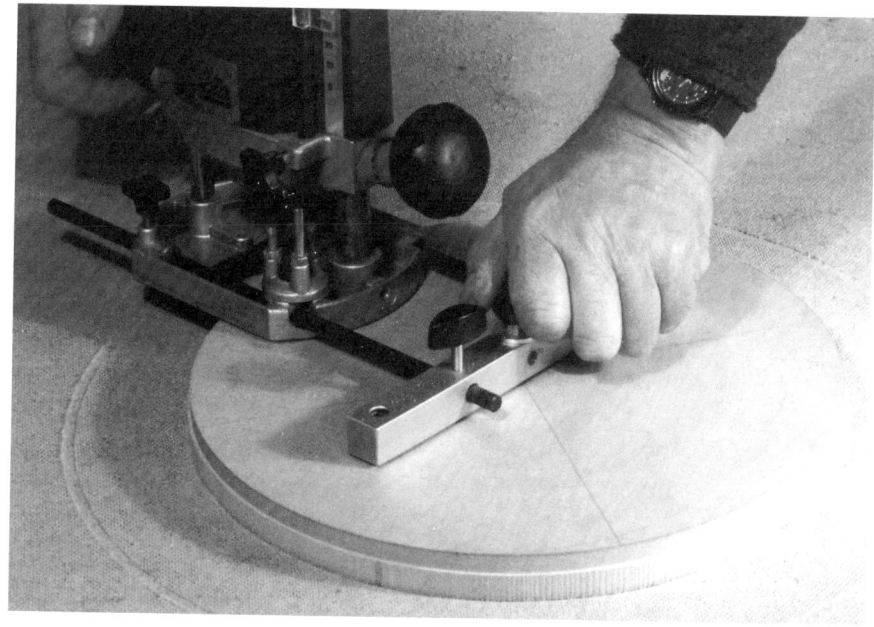

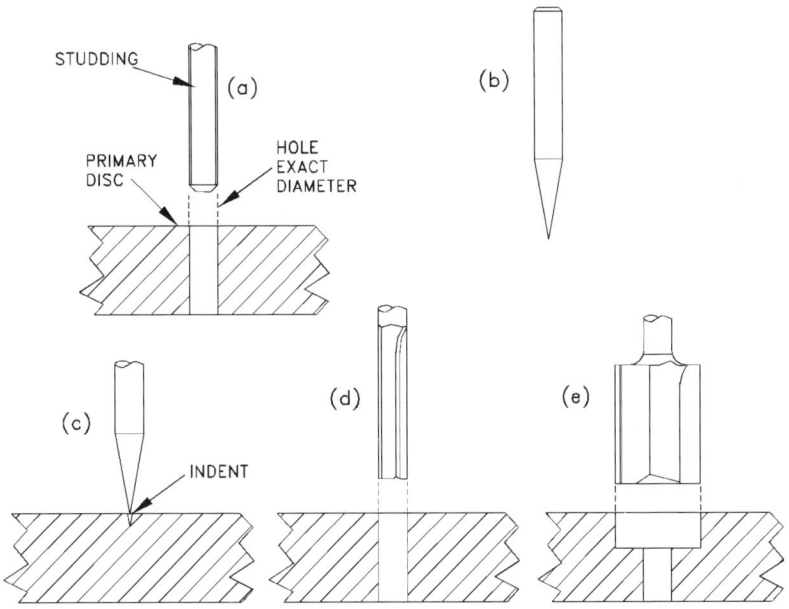

Figure 7

router may be used for this purpose however, provided that the router is located and retained in the required position. One of the simplest ways of providing location is with a jig made from an offcut of MDF or plywood, with a rectangular cutaway at one corner. The router is placed in the desired position, and the jig pushed firmly against it (Fig.8) and cramped in position. The hole may now be plunge-cut with no risk of the router drifting out of position, provided that slight sideways pressure is maintained to keep the router firmly in

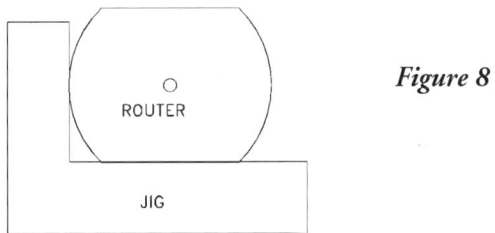

Figure 8

position. The jig has a further use in that it may be used to provide counterbored holes in precisely located positions. For this purpose, in addition to the router cutters, a 'pointer' device is required. This may take the form of the 'undesirable' pivot point shown in Fig.7(b) but, in this application, it is used for initial location only. It is placed in the router collet thus enabling the axis of the machine to be placed precisely over the required position. It helps if the position itself is initially established manually in the workpiece with an indentation from a hand-held scriber. This enables the pointer to be located firmly in the indentation (c) and held there by locking the plunge knob; the jig is then brought up to the router base and cramped in position. With the position of the router thus established, the necessary boring and counterboring cutters may be fitted in turn (d) and (e).

The primary disc profile may now be machined (Fig.6). The disc is placed on a sacrificial sub-base of hardboard of slightly larger size, to enable the cutter to machine the full depth of the disc without damaging the worktop. Both the disc and the hardboard should however, be held down in some way (preferably by a couple of screws) to prevent unwanted rotation of the work whilst machining. If these screws are located at some personal 'standard' dimension along a diameter of the disc, the holes left afterwards may well be found convenient for other uses, such as subsequent attachment of the disc to a worktable or batten. When machining, the router must be rotated on the pivot in an anticlockwise direction, viewed from above. This is an essential safety measure for this particular task. To complete the disc, a small relief chamfer is provided at its top outer edge. This is to assist rapid placement of the pivot frame shoes over the disc and may be done, either with a 45° cutter, or more or less any ovolo cutter, suitably placed (Fig.9).

Some applications are materially assisted by providing a primary disc of annular form, either by itself or fitted to a solid disc. These will be dealt with in due course but for the moment only the cutting of the disc

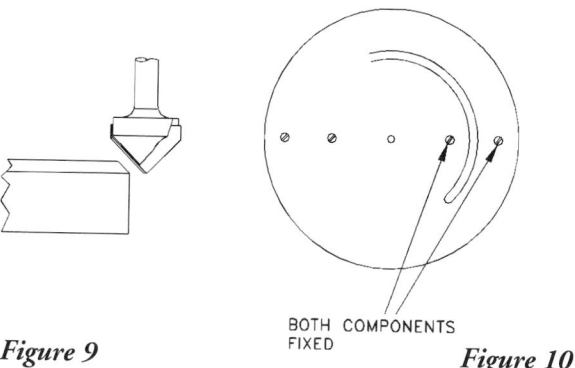

Figure 9 BOTH COMPONENTS FIXED *Figure 10*

itself is discussed. It is convenient to cut the inner and outer diameters at the same setting, using the same pivot hole (Fig.10). Both the annulus and the central waste must be firmly fixed to the worktop prior to cutting, since movement of either on final breakthrough is to be avoided. If the pivot bolt is held with a nut on the underside of the main worktop, it will allow both hands to be used on the router itself (Fig.11). Since the annular cut is necessarily performed entirely with the router (ie. no preliminary sawing-away of waste), it is as well, particularly with MDF, to limit the width of 'kerf'. The cutter should therefore be no larger than $\frac{1}{4}$" diameter.

The foregoing describes the basic Pivot Frame system. Were this the only possible configuration, the device could be considered as useful for cutting circles and nothing more – and much the same would apply to the beam trammel. Both devices are capable of far more than this however, and it is now appropriate perhaps, to discuss the ways in which their capabilities may be extended. It is quite possible to machine pieces which have regular profiles formed by groups of circular arcs, either convex or concave. Two simple forms are shown in Figs 12 and 13, together with the Pivot Frame configurations which generate them. Fig.12(a) shows an equilateral triangle convex design, a shape which is a particular favourite of mine, as will become evident. It is achieved by offsetting the workpiece from the centre of the primary disc, and setting the Pivot Frame cutting radius to the desired position (b). Three separate cuts are made, rotating the workpiece by 120° between each.

The cuts may of course be profiled in elevation also, using cove or ovolo cutters for example. A concave eight-sided design is shown in Fig.13(a). This is dealt with in much the same way, but requires a much greater offset (b), from which it can be seen that, under some circumstances, the combination of offset and workpiece size may cause the workpiece to impede the progress of the nylon shoes on the primary disc. /This can be handled

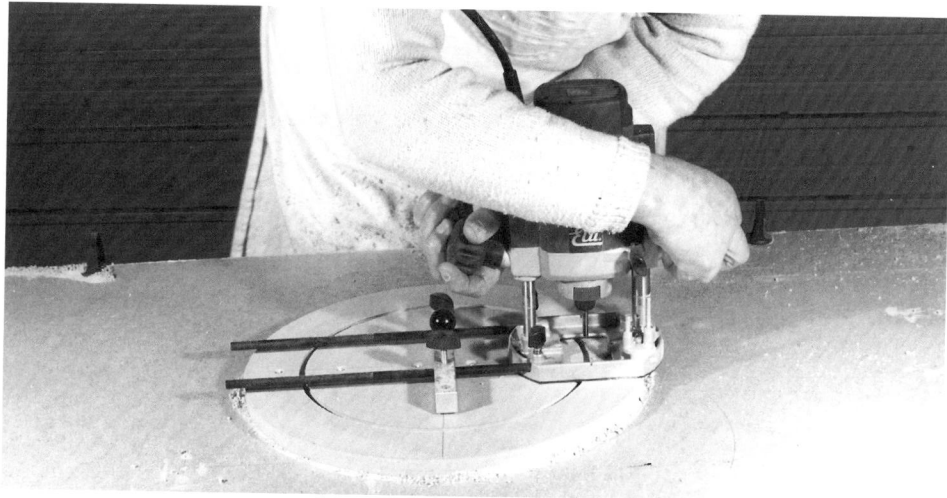

Figure 11

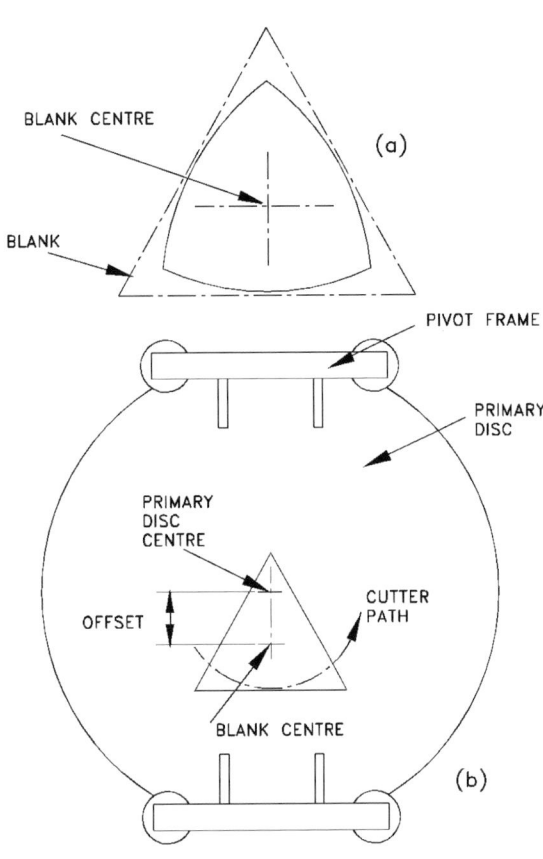

Figure 12

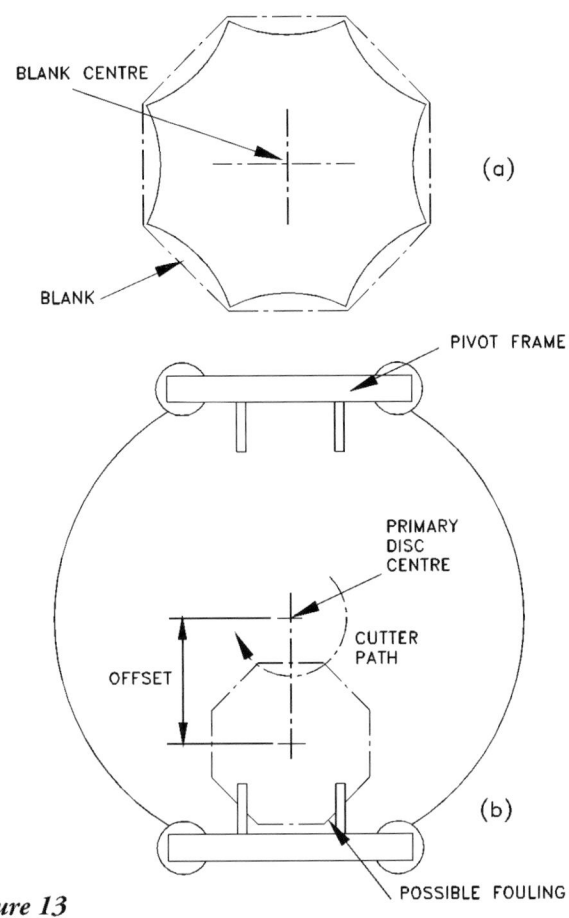

Figure 13

with an annular primary disc, and will be discussed later, but it is also quite easy to use a similar offset technique with a beam trammel set-up, as shown in Fig.2, an arrangement which complements the mini-pivot system extremely well.

The position of the workpiece in terms of angular position and offset can be handled simply by marking out its required stations on the primary disc with a pencil, and using hot-melt glue or double-sided adhesive tape to hold it. This will rapidly make a mess of the face of the disc, and there is a much better way: the extra fitment required is a further, smaller disc, termed a

'secondary disc' (Fig.14(a)). This is drilled (or routed) with a central hole, to take a bolt or length of studding, which is also free to slide in a slot on the primary disc (b), and to be locked in position by means of a nut on the underside. It is important that both the hole and slot are at right angles to their respective faces and that the fit of the bolt is not sloppy in either. The secondary disc is indexed around its rim with a number of equally spaced holes. A great deal of flexibility is given by the choice of 24 holes, since this number can be used to give equal angular offsets of 3,4,6,8,12 and 24 stations (another disc comprising 20 holes will give 5,10 and 20 stations).

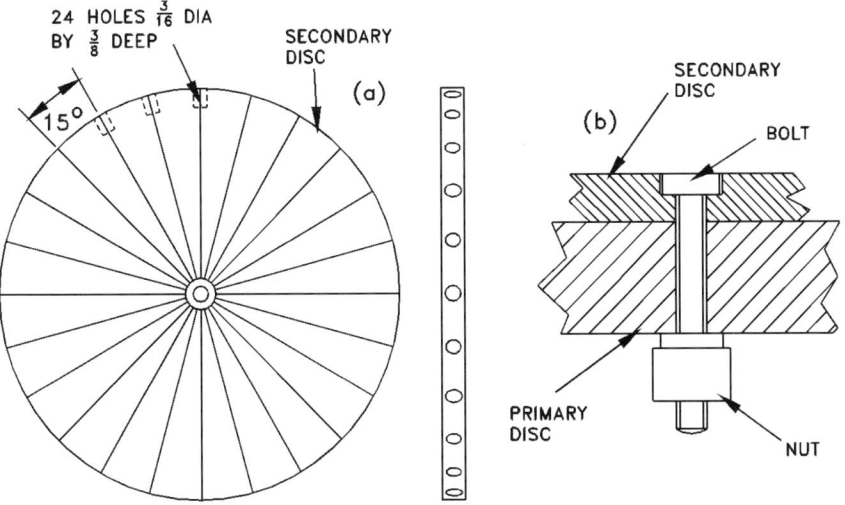

Figure 14

The angular position of the disc is fixed by means of a simple adjustable stop mounted on the primary disc; this also serves to determine the amount of offset given to the secondary disc (Fig.15). It is still necessary of course, to mount the workpiece on the secondary disc, usually with the centre of the workpiece over the centre of the disc, but this operation needs to be performed once only, regardless of the number or complexity of the operations to be executed on the workpiece.

The adjustable stop can be made entirely in metal, for maximum accuracy, as shown in Fig.16(a); this particular version, which features locating dowels in addition to

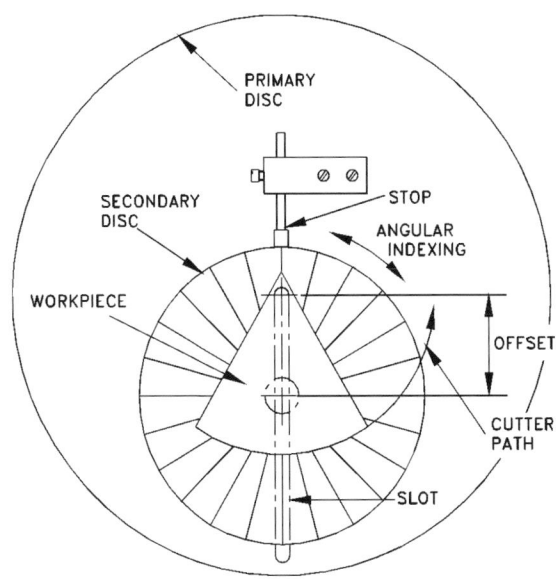

Figure 15

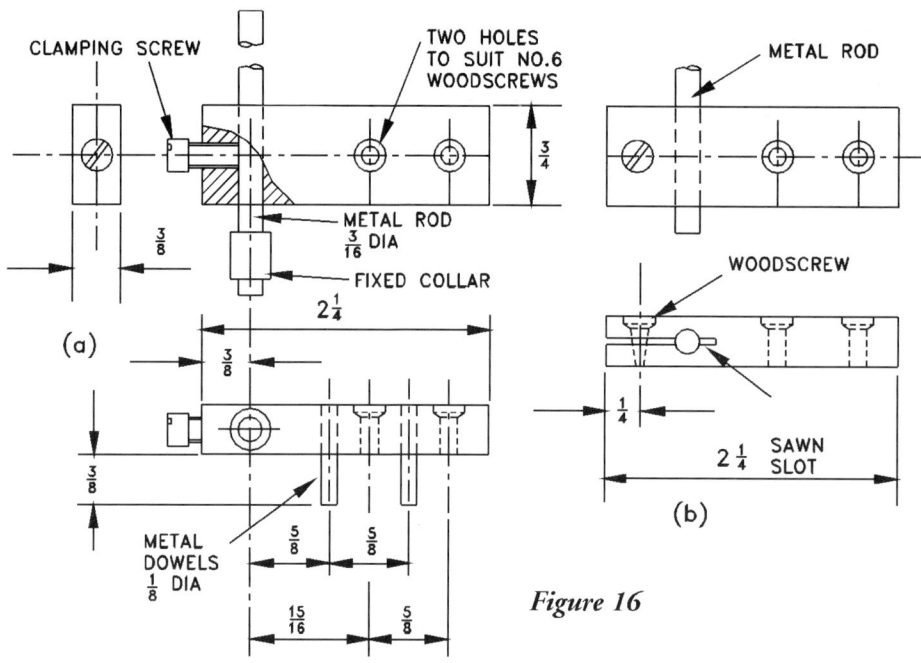

CLAMPING SCREW

TWO HOLES
TO SUIT NO.6
WOODSCREWS

METAL ROD

$\frac{3}{4}$

METAL ROD
$\frac{3}{16}$ DIA

FIXED COLLAR

$2\frac{1}{4}$

(a)

$\frac{3}{8}$

$\frac{3}{8}$

$\frac{3}{8}$

METAL
DOWELS
$\frac{1}{8}$ DIA

$\frac{5}{8}$　$\frac{5}{8}$

$\frac{15}{16}$　$\frac{5}{8}$

WOODSCREW

$\frac{1}{4}$

$2\frac{1}{4}$ SAWN
SLOT

(b)

Figure 16

Figure 17

fixing screws, does however require access to metalworking equipment. A more rudimentary version is shown in (b). This will serve well enough, but is hardly as accurate as the dowelled metal version. It is best made in hardwood since, if made in MDF for example, the woodscrew will eventually wear away the thread in the material and lose its cramping action. Both types are shown also in Fig.17. Regardless of which version is chosen, a metal stop-rod is strongly advocated. For a plain rod, the holes in the secondary disc must all be of the same depth. For the shouldered rod shown in Fig.16(a), the precise depth of hole is not important provided it is deep enough. The brass version will be encountered many times in the book; the simpler version is shown in a Pivot Frame set-up in Fig.18.

Figure 18

Figure 19

Generally speaking, the machining of any regular pattern on the mini-pivot system will require (apart from cutter style and depth of cut) only two settings, those of cutter path radius and offset (Fig.15). For some applications, a further setting will be required, that of limitation of rotation of the Pivot Frame about the primary disc for 'stopped' work. This idea is not developed as a project, although I have actually made a mirror frame embodying the idea (Fig.19). As a starting point for readers wishing to pursue this particular line, the general nature of the set-up is shown in Fig.20. The stop setting is determined by trial and error on a sacrificial workpiece and implemented by means of a batten cramped to the main worktop such that it impedes the path of the Pivot Frame shoes.

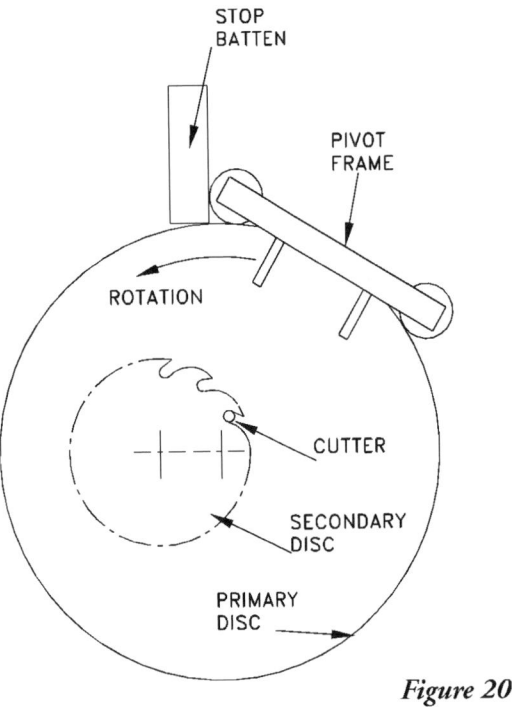

Figure 20

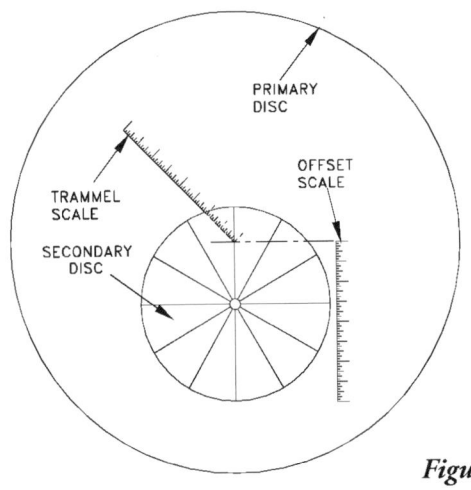

Figure 21

The two settings shown in Fig.15 are materially assisted by the provision of a pair of hand-drawn scales on the primary disc, imperial or metric, as preferred (Fig.21). The cutter radius is served by means of a scale drawn on a convenient radius of the primary disc, from the dead centre. The offset scale is drawn parallel to the slot in the primary disc, such that it almost touches the secondary disc. It is therefore only useful for one size of secondary disc; for other sizes, other scales need to be drawn, or a ruler used instead. If the number of holes in any given secondary disc is divisible by 4 (eg. 24,20 etc.), there will always be a hole 90° away from that engaged with the stop, which can be used for alignment against the scale. This hole will of course be related to the secondary disc centre. With the primary/secondary disc system described, the Pivot Frame has the ability to carry out repeat operations to a high order of accuracy, thus enabling sets of identical objects to be made. A

particular advantage of the Pivot Frame is that it can be removed from the primary disc and replaced at will, with no loss of accuracy. It is suggested that for any given 'repeat' project a prototype is made to assess its appearance, suitability etc. At the prototype stage, all the settings involved in its making are noted and subsequently used for repeat work.

A primary disc of annular form enables the capability of the Pivot Frame to be extended in a number of ways The most obvious perhaps is the accommodation of workpieces of greater thickness than would be permitted by the flat disc (Fig.22). By this means, the maximum ride height permitted by the jig itself may be extended. Note that this attribute is not to be confused with the maximum available depth of cut which will of course always be limited by the length of the router cutter. The effective offset of the secondary disc may also be increased, as shown in Fig.23. This arrangement

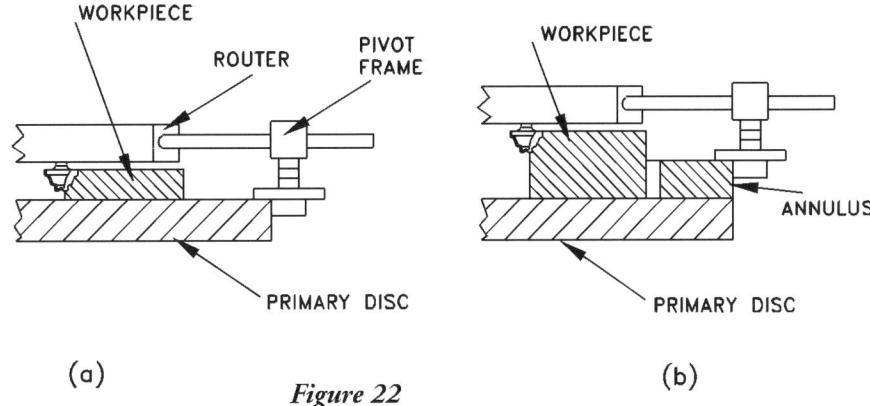

Figure 22

(a)   (b)

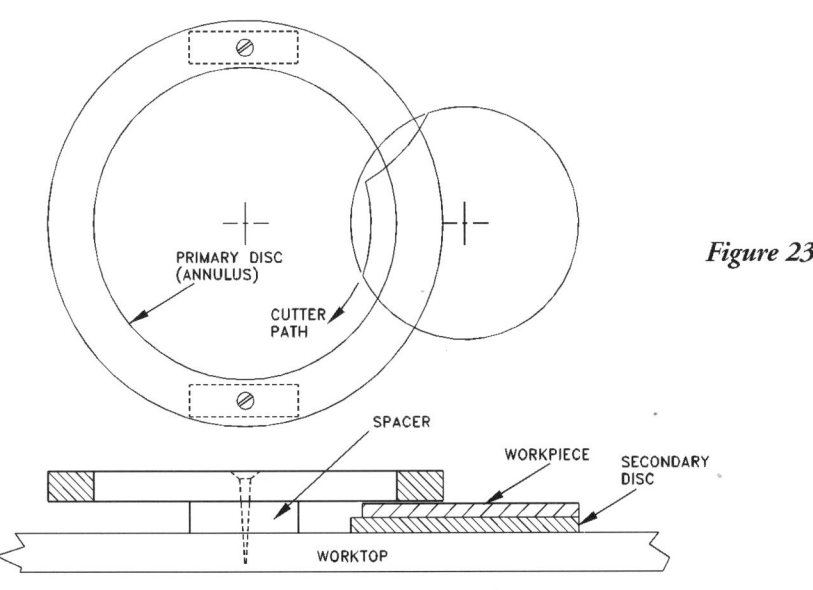

Figure 23

does however, require the primary disc to be mounted on the worktop with a number of spacers interposed, and it is recommended that the method is only used where absolutely necessary, since the annular nature of the disc renders it rather weak and, since it is clearly not possible to place a spacer in the area occupied by the workpiece, there is inevitably some overhang of the annulus.

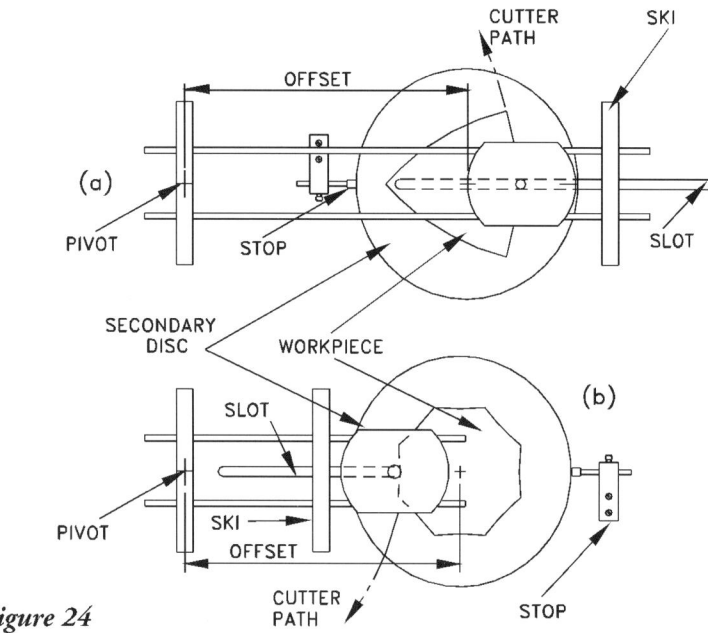

Figure 24

Large secondary disc offsets are usually best managed in a standard beam trammel configuration (Fig.24). The restriction here, as discussed earlier, is simply one of minimum available radius of the cutter path. This is rarely a problem where scalloped work is involved, since too *small* a radius can result in rather pronounced and unacceptably sharp points (Fig.25(b)).The simplest beam trammel set-up has already been discussed in relation to the making of primary discs. Two other modes are possible, both of which use only one pivot bar, complete with shoes, as a ski. In the first arrangement (Fig.24(a)), the pivot is mounted on a spacer block to allow the router to ride above the workpiece. The spacers on the outer pivot bar are adjusted such that the router base is level. This arrangement will cater for most indexed designs where the workpiece is not unduly large. A further set-up allows the router to overhang the ski pivot bar (Fig.24(b)). This arrangement can be used for large work. The overhang of the router can however

lead to tipping (Fig.26(a)), unless the pivot is held down in some way. This is very easily implemented by means of a nut and washer on the underside of the pivot bolt (b). Even with this precaution, a large overhang will make the router rather 'springy' on the rods, and appropriate care must be exercised.

Mention was made earlier of the difficulties encountered with a beam trammel set-up requiring the pivot point to be in direct contact with the workpiece. No such difficulty is encountered in the modes illustrated in Fig.24, since the pivot point is always *off* the workpiece. Moreover, except in the case of enclosed channels, the depth of cut can usually be set off the workpiece also. Thus, the plain beam trammel may be used for a wide range of decorative work, the only difference between this and the Pivot Frame being one of available machining radius.

There is however, one application of the Pivot Frame which cannot easily be matched by other methods. This involves the machining of small diameters where no contact other than the cutter may be permitted between the jig and the workpiece. Many of the projects feature this facility, and it is therefore extensively illustrated and described but, for the moment, Fig.27 shows one application, and also demonstrates a 'crossed hands' technique which allows a full 360° sweep to be made without walking round the

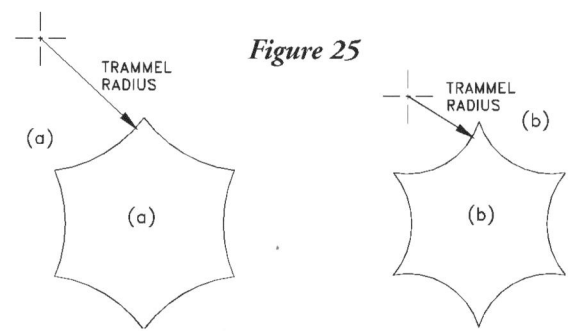

Figure 25

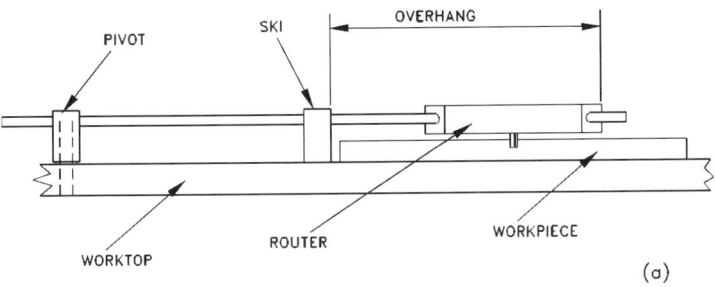

PIVOT   SKI   OVERHANG

WORKTOP   ROUTER   WORKPIECE

(a)

Figure 26

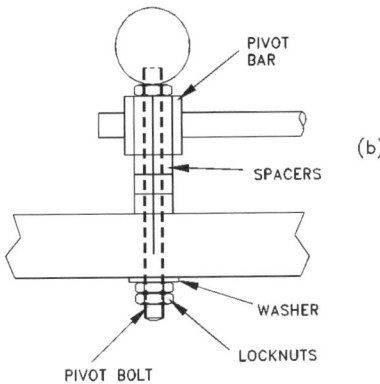

PIVOT BAR

(b)

SPACERS

WASHER

LOCKNUTS

PIVOT BOLT

Figure 27

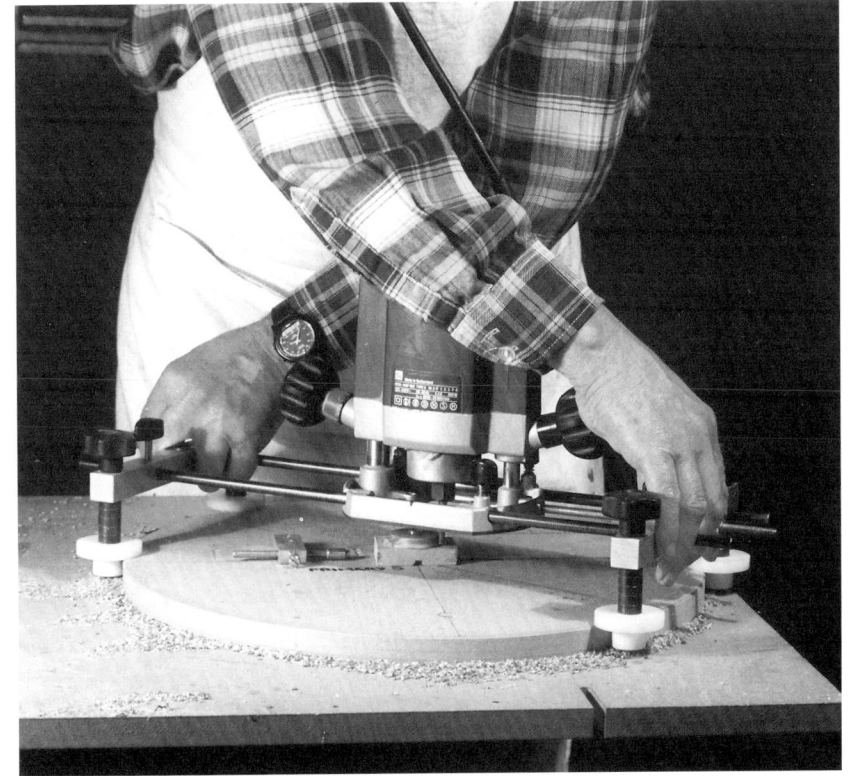

worktop.

To conclude this chapter, the remaining illustrations provide an overview of some of the work which may be undertaken. An obvious application is the machining of small discs and rings, as illustrated in Fig.28. These do not perhaps have a great deal of value as 'stand alone' items, but as inlays in larger work they have a number of applications, particularly when interlinked. The inherent accuracy of the Pivot Frame allows the rings and their mating recesses to be machined to a very high order of accuracy, thus providing hairline joints. A further application of this principle is encountered in a number

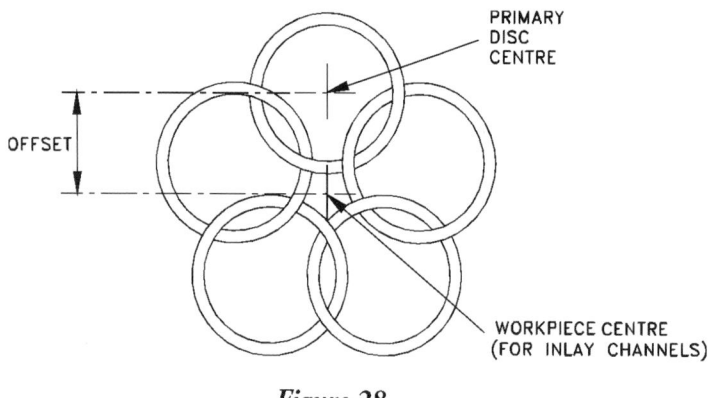

Figure 28

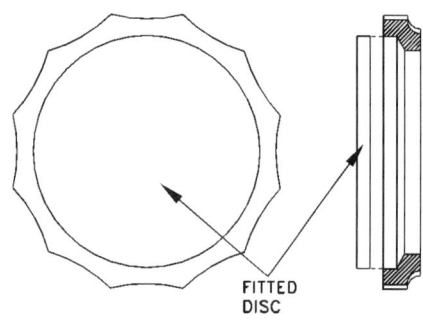

Figure 29

of other projects, where mirror-backs are required to be fitted, again to a high degree of accuracy (Fig.29). It is also possible to make segmented work where the segments are curved, rather than straight (Fig.30), although this work can also be undertaken in most cases by the beam trammel. Finally, the provision of small 'eyes' in segmented work can add to the decorative value (Fig.31). The applications are mentioned only briefly here since they are either featured in one way or another in the projects, or may be very easily adapted by the reader.

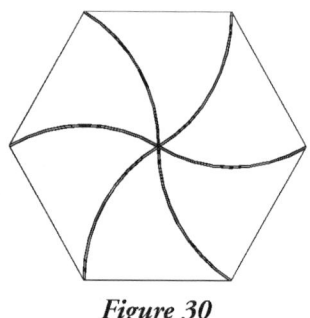

Figure 30

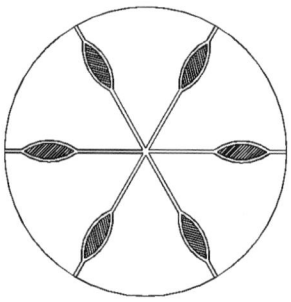

Figure 31

PIVOT FRAME

FURTHER APPLICATIONS

The decorative capabilities of the Pivot Frame are by no means confined to the essentially circular work described thus far. The jig may be regarded very much as a 'maid of all work'. The remaining modes are now briefly covered. All of them are highly useful, but not all are appropriate to the content of this book. Those that are, will be dealt with extensively in the Project section. It is true that most of them are within the capabilities of a ski system. The Pivot Frame does however, combine all functions covered here and elsewhere in the book in a single package.

The device may be arranged to operate in a linear mode, by means of a pair of straightedge side battens on a flat worktop. This set-up has a number of uses, perhaps the simplest being the planing of 'non-prepared' timber (Fig.32). Even the owners of planer/thicknesser machines will occasionally be faced with the problem of timber which is just a little too wide for the machine, or is maybe a little warped in one way or another. Perhaps the worst problem of the latter kind is that of 'winding', since this can be very difficult to deal with on conventional machines. All of these problems can be handled with the Pivot Frame and, moreover, in such a way that the maximum thickness can be extracted from the stock. The essential requirements for the set-up are that the worktop is dead flat, and one edge at least, of each side batten, is dead straight. The workpiece is held down to the worktop by dabs of hot-melt glue, applied from a gun, preferably at the ends. Twisted timber may be fixed by fitting suitable packing beneath the high spots, before applying the glue (Fig.33(a)); timber which is simply bowed either lengthwise or crosswise is fixed to the worktop concave side down (b). Planing is a simple matter of fitting a suitable flat-bottomed cutter in the router and passing it over the work in a succession of lengthwise sweeps.

Figure 32

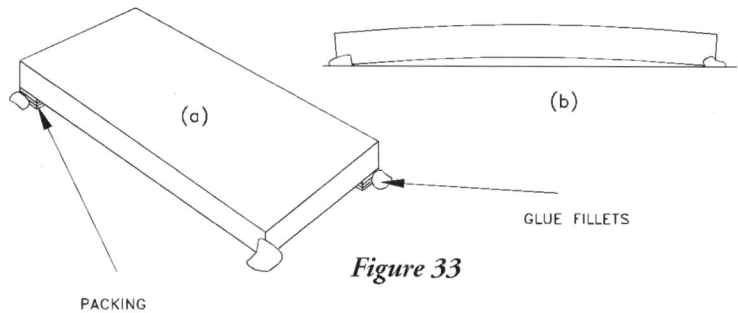

(a)   (b)

GLUE FILLETS

Figure 33

PACKING

Here, a few small technical tips may be of help. The highest spot of the work is first found by simply using the plunge facility to make contact between the cutter and the work at its highest point, with the machine switched off. The depth of cut may then be set at about $1/16$" below this setting, thus eliminating the risk of cutting too deeply anywhere. Succeeding cuts are taken with similar depth increments; light cutting is to be preferred in most applications, but particularly in this one. For rapid working, a large diameter cutter is suitable. Surprisingly perhaps, a better finish can often be

Figure 34

FEED

achieved with a smaller diameter cutter, at the expense of rather more passes over the work. The reason for this is bound up with the essential 'tolerances' to be found in any piece of working equipment. Normally, the tolerances to which manufacturers are obliged to work are so small as to render them unnoticeable to the user. In this case however, the possibility that the guide rods are not perfectly straight, for example, can lead to a slight tilting of the cutter with respect to the skis. This will produce a series of tiny ridges along the work which will require sanding; a rotary 'scouring' appearance may also be apparent. A smaller cutter will of course produce the same effect, but to a much reduced degree. Where the workpiece is wide, and therefore the length of guide rod between the pivot bars is fairly long, some vertical 'springing' of the router over the workpiece will occur as a result of hand pressure on the plunge knobs. This is avoided simply by setting the depth of cut and starting the router clear of the workpiece, and then handling the assembly by the pivot bars only. The router may be left free to slide on the rods (provided the fit is not sloppy – and it shouldn't be) and simply nudged across with the thumb for each successive pass. Alternatively, for small work, the side battens may be dispensed with, and the jig used freehand. Fig.34 illustrates this method, and also indicates the advised feed direction of the router. This is somewhat at odds with the normal 'safety' advice given but, in this case, the tendency of the cutter will be to move away from the cutting line rather than pulling itself further into the work. For a full explanation of this effect see Chapter 7. Thicknessing is of course, simply a matter of turning the work over and repeating the exercise – a much easier task, once a flat mounting surface has been established.

Batches of segments can be brought to a common thickness by grouping them together and passing the jig over them collectively, as illustrated in Fig.35. This system also has an advantage over the machine planer, since very small workpieces can be 'flatted' and thicknessed with no handling difficulty or danger. This is actually one of my favourite party pieces, since it is an excellent means of demonstrating that the router really is an inherently safe machine. Much the same argument applies to very thin work although, in this case, some means of holding the entire workpiece dead flat against the worktop (eg. a vacuum system) is necessary, more from the viewpoint of workpiece safety than that of the operator. Note from the illustrations that the guide rod length between the pivot bars is kept as short as possible, consistent with cutter access to the full width of the work, in order to avoid the 'springing' effect mentioned earlier. Note also that in freehand mode the shoes are reversed on the pivot bars, to provide a smoother ride over the worktop. This particular set-up can also be used where templates are necessary, or where the workpiece itself becomes a template for further profiling in elevation with cove or ovolo cutters for example. The templates can be either 'lower', against a ballrace at the end of the cutter, or 'upper', against either a ballrace on the cutter shank or a guide bush fitted to the router. Fig.36

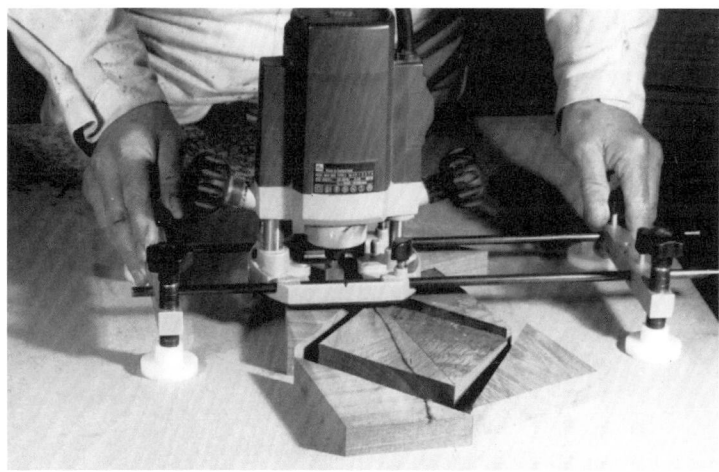

Figure 35

shows a template prepared by disc sanding, and the workpiece to which it is applied. Fig.37 shows the assembled set-up for use with a guide bush on the router.

Whilst on the topic of templates and guides, it is sometimes difficult to use a full ski system, due to the shape of the workpiece. Fig.38, although not a project

Figure 36 & 37

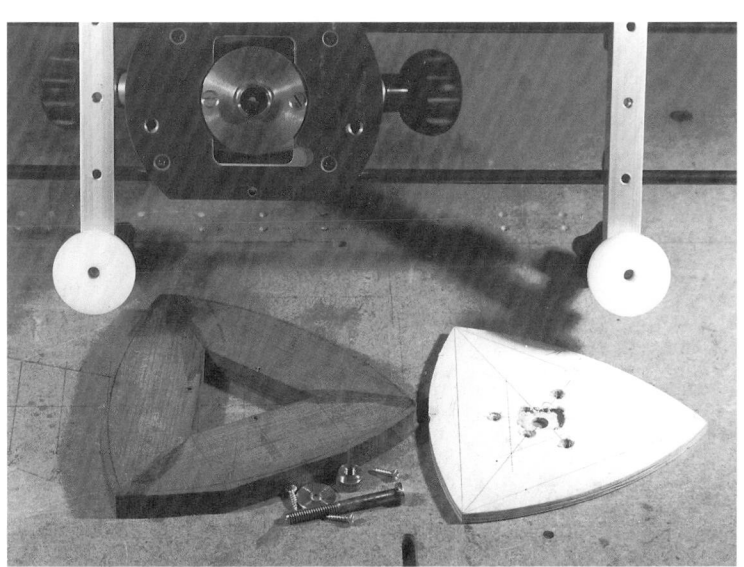

in this book, provides a useful example. It would be possible to machine the groove with a full ski system by moving the router such that the skis remained more or less parallel to the long sides of the workpiece at all times. This would actually require rather longer guide rods than those shown, to allow cutter access to the full width of the work. Far worse however, is that the necessarily awkward router handling caused by such an arrangement would present a very real risk of the guide bush momentarily leaving the template, particularly at the ends, and thus overcutting the outer flank of the groove. It is far better that the router is moved around the work, keeping the guide bush pressed firmly against the template at all times. A one-legged ski system will solve many problems of this nature but does of course require that the workpiece is flat and is machined on a flat worktop. To ensure that the base of the router is dead flat against the top face of the workpiece or template, it may be necessary to fine tune the height of the pivot bar with one or two thin washers, in addition to

the normal spacers. These, if not available from the 'odds and ends' box, may be made on the spot in more or less any material, eg. cardboard.

Perhaps the most valuable attribute of the guided planing mode, using the side battens, is the facility it offers for providing parallelism in the *width* of the work. This is achieved simply by setting the router to the appropriate positions on the guide rods and applying preferential pressure to *one* batten only, in effect treating it as a single fence. The arrangement can be a dis-tinct improvement over the normal side fence supplied as standard with the router, since the router rides above the work, rather than on it, from which it follows that the workpiece itself need not be dead flat. An obvious application is the provision of parallel grooved housings for the sides of a box, for example. For my own part, I find also that the machining of accurate dovetail slides in man-made materials (eg. Tufnol) a very valuable attribute when making jigs. This particular activity will be covered in far more detail in Chapter 6 but, for the

Figure 38

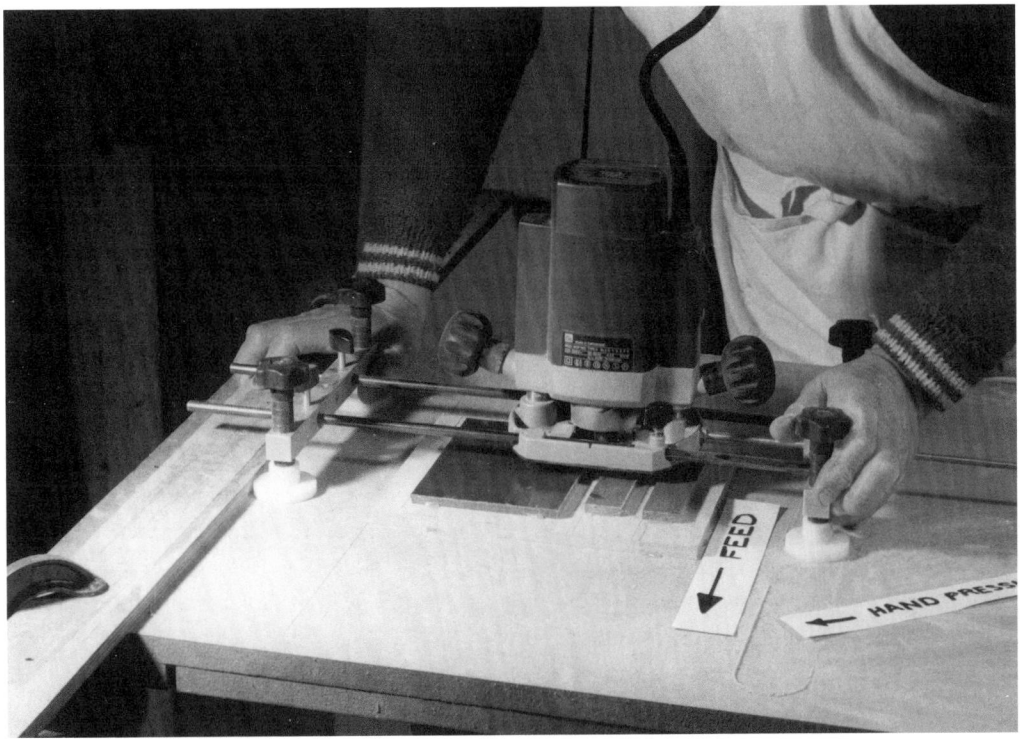

Figure 39

moment, Fig.39 shows the set-up being used to machine dovetail flanks on a group of Tufnol pieces. It is very important to note that the narrower workpiece is being machined in this illustration. The feed direction indicated is thus in a direction normally described as 'against the rotation' of the cutter. Feeding in the opposite direction, for the identical operation illustrated, is referred to elsewhere in the book as 'climb-milling', particularly in Chapter 7. This has a number of useful applications but, for relatively hard material such as Tufnol, is positively *not* recommended; the snatching tendency is far too severe. Also, the fence technique illustrated is not one which I would normally recommend, since there is a possibility of the ski leaving the fence and overcutting the work. It is used here on the smaller pieces for convenience. It is highly necessary on the larger (slider) piece however, since both flanks of this piece must be dovetailed parallel. The easiest way of managing this is to machine them at the same set-up, against the same fence. Note the strong pressure against the fence with the left hand, and the further assistance provided by nipping the pivot bar and the batten together with the right hand. Fig.40 shows another application, that of machining parallel sets of slots, in this case on an acrylic disc. The cross battens cramped fore and aft provide end stops to ensure that all slots are of the required fixed length.

It is also possible to combine the linear and circular

Figure 40

modes of the Pivot Frame. There is no 'official' title for this mode of operation but, for what it's worth, I call it the 'step and repeat' mode. The set-up is illustrated diagrammatically in Figs 41 and 42. It is in fact a special case of the 'raised annular disc' technique, illustrated in Chapter 1, Fig.23. In this case, the workpiece is slid between two parallel battens beneath a small annular disc, allowing a repeated pattern of circles or arcs to be machined at regular intervals along its length. The bolts which hold the disc to the battens also provide clamping for the workpiece. The arrangement is useful for providing 'carved' linear decoration to strips of timber which may then be added to cabinet work. In view of the fact that this book covers only small work, no projects are offered. Figs 43 and 44 do however, illustrate the process.

Finally, a brief mention is made of the capacity of the Pivot Frame (with a few significant home-made additions) to cut ellipses in very small sizes. I consider this to be a very powerful addition to the armoury. For this reason full coverage is given in Chapter 3 the device also features in a number of projects.

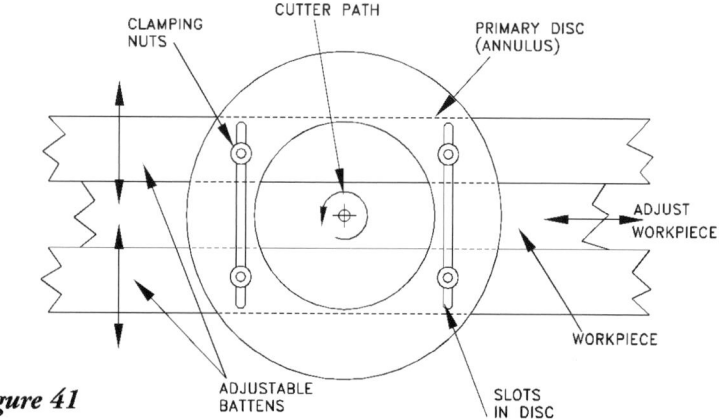

Figure 41

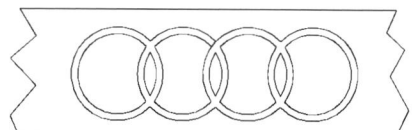

Figure 42

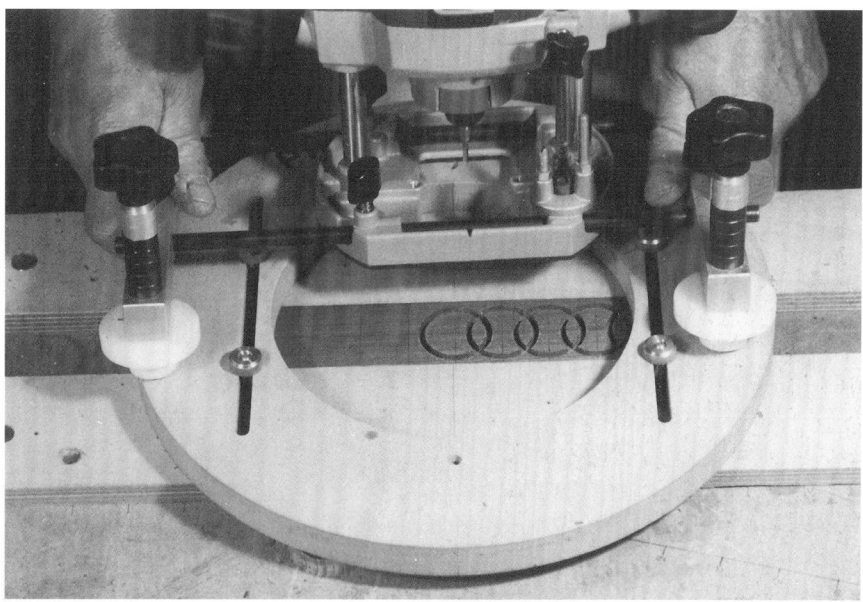

Figure 43

Figure 44

3

ELLIPSE JIGS

This chapter offers three basic methods of producing ellipses with a router. The choice of method will depend partly upon available equipment and partly upon size and aspect ratio of the required ellipse. Chapter 8 describes the geometric principles underlying each. Only the practical usage of the methods is covered here.

It is possible to cut ellipses without special equipment. The method involves making templates from pencil drawings, using any of the geometric construction methods given in Chapter 8. These may be drawn either directly on to the template material or on paper which is subsequently stuck to the material. Occasionally, it is possible to dispense with the template, and operate directly on the workpiece. The latter method involves some risk in that a mistake will spoil the job itself; it is always less painful to discard a template made from inexpensive material. A highly effective if somewhat expensive method of sticking paper in place is with double-sided adhesive tape. This has the particular advantage of avoiding paper distortion which might arise from the use of any 'wet adhesive' method. Another method involves the use of 'glue film'. This is a hot-melt adhesive, sold in sheet form on a paper backing. Its primary use is for veneering. The method of application on veneer is simply to use a domestic clothes iron (on a fairly low heat setting) to lay the film on to the back of the veneer. The backing paper is then peeled off, the prepared veneer transferred to the workpiece and ironed

in place. The same method may be used quite successfully with paper. If the paper design is in the form of a photocopy (I use photocopies a great deal where repeat designs are required), it is wise to remember that photocopy ink is heat-sensitive. For this reason, the backing paper is re-used over the drawing when ironing in place, to avoid smearing the design. The nature of the backing paper makes the ink reluctant to adhere to it.

The template is sawn slightly oversize, and the final profiling carried out with a disc sander (Fig.45). This operation is performed as carefully and accurately as possible, since the remainder of the work depends upon it. Even so, a 'perfect' elliptical template will not generate a perfectly elliptical workpiece, due to the finite diameter of any cutter used. There is but one exception, this being where the cutter and the guide bearing are of the same diameter, thus producing an exact replica of the template in the workpiece (Fig.46). Normally, errors of this nature are quite minor and unimportant, but readers requiring precision in this respect are advised to read Chapter 8 before proceeding further.

'External' templates are easy to make and use. The finishing of 'internal' templates can be difficult, and there is often a strong temptation to use external templates for internal work. This method, although not impossible, is fraught with problems, most of them of a nature likely to damage the workpiece. Rather, I would advise the use of the following method, employing a combined internal and external template of annular form.

The method involves the making of two external templates, the second being of a size which allows the generation of the internal profile on the first, after making due allowance for guide bush and cutter diameters. Note that this method does not permit the use of bearing-guided cutters, other than to remove small 'nibs'. Since both templates must be accurately aligned together, the major and minor axes are drawn on each. The templates are held together and to the worktop by at least two woodscrews to retain alignment and prevent rotation under cutting load. A channel is now machined in the lower template to within about $^1/_{16}$" of full depth as illustrated in Fig.48(a). The guide bush must be kept in firm contact with the top template at all times, otherwise the overcutting error illustrated in Fig.47 may occur. The screws and upper template are now removed and the inner waste on the lower template sawn away, leaving a tiny protrusion to allow for final profiling.

Figures 45 & 46

Figure 47

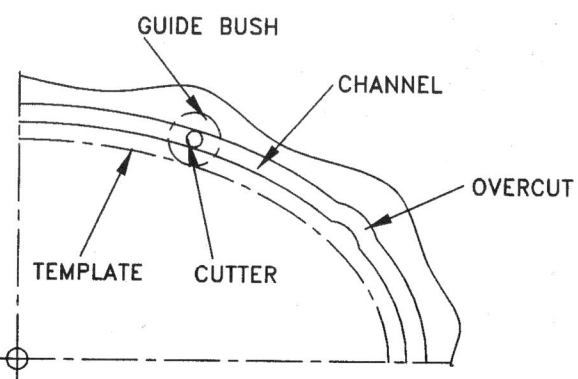

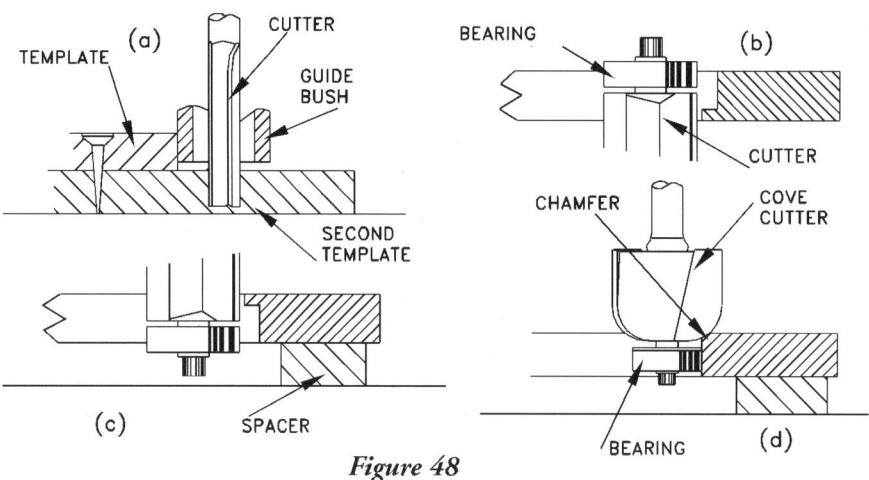

Figure 48

This is removed with a 1:1 bearing-guided cutter, either on a spindle moulder (Fig.48(b)), or with a ski system (c). If a 1:1 cutter is not available, an equivalent result is obtained by machining a small chamfer with a bearing-guided cove cutter (d). In ski mode, it will be necessary to raise the work on spacers to provide clearance for the bearing attachment fixture. The resultant combined template may be used directly on the workpiece for inner and outer profiling, with no risk of overcutting. If little waste material is available on the final workpiece, the template is held down with double-sided adhesive tape. If waste is available, hot-melt glue may be used in stages as shown in Fig.49, first on one flank and then the other. Note that, for the second operation, the original glue fillets are removed, to avoid clogging the cutter. Note also that guide bushes are not shown in Fig.49, for clarity. Fig.50 shows a typical operation, on an elliptical mirror frame.

Given reasonable care, the finish and accuracy of line on the second template will match that of the template used to generate it. If the finish is poor, or where the inner profile is generated directly from a drawing, a

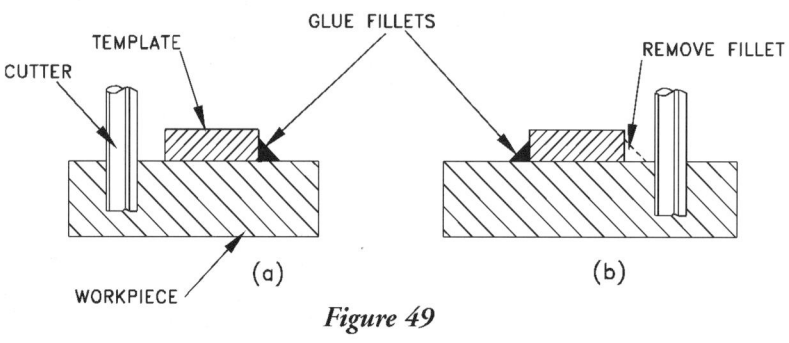

Figure 49

drum sander will be required to complete the piece. Two points need to be observed here: the diameter of the drum must not be greater than the minimum radius of curvature of the ellipse at the ends of the major axis. If made too small however, there is some risk of indentation of the workpiece as sanding proceeds. Fortunately, it is very easy to 'custom make' a selection of drums from plywood or MDF, using the Pivot Frame. These may be arranged to fit a common arbor, which may be home-made or purchased. Strips of abrasive are stuck to the periphery of the drum with double-sided tape; these may be removed as desired for replacement or grade change. In the absence of a pillar drill, a lash-up may be arranged with a portable power drill (Fig.51). Drill speed should be at the lowest setting to avoid overcutting and snatching.

The home worker may face restrictions on rebate-machining technique arising essentially from lack of suitable cutters. Square or circular work can usually be accommodated by means of suitable fences or trammels; ellipses are less easily managed. For this reason, the initial choice of template dimensions is made only after careful consideration of *all* subsequent machining operations. In most cases, the inner and outer profiles of the final workpiece are machined first; the inner profile of the workpiece is then used as a template for rebating. This process ideally requires the use of bearing-guided cutters, where the cutter diameter is greater than that of

Figure 50

Figure 51

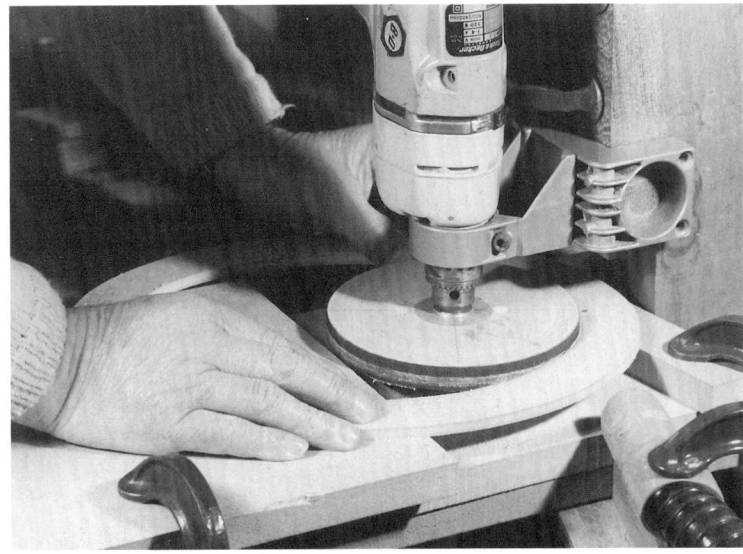

the bearing, a typical cutter being shown in Fig.52. Available cutters may not permit a rebate of sufficient width, in which case a slotting cutter may be used in the same way. This will require several passes over the work, increasing the depth of cut by increments. This may in turn require more than one bearing (of the same diameter) on the arbor, as shown in Fig.52. A machining operation of this type is illustrated in Fig.53; the machining direction must be clockwise, as viewed from the

Figure 52

Figure 53

top. Where necessary (and where dimensions permit) a second template may be generated from the original by similar means, either internally, or externally as shown in Fig.54. Note that the feed direction is anticlockwise in this case.

Figure 54

It is not a particularly good idea to use a guide bush with a cutter of larger diameter than the bush (see Chapter 7). Where only a guide bush arrangement is available, it is better to design the template to machine the rebate rather than the inner profile and then use the rebate itself as a template. It is also possible to use this technique for making a second template, as illustrated in Fig.55.

The word 'trammel' embraces a variety of geometric principles. Many of them have been mechanised to allow the direct machining of geometric forms; the reader will already be aware of the beam trammel, used for cutting circular arcs. The first device to be described here is also a trammel but, in this case its function is the direct machining of elliptical profiles. The device is manufactured and marketed in two sizes by the Trend Company. The larger size is suitable for table tops and work of similar dimensions; the smaller version, featured here, is better suited to mirror frames and similar pieces.

The component parts of the jig are illustrated in Fig.56 and comprise a circular base, with two slider bars running in a pair of machined channels set at right angles to each other. This part of the jig is attached to the workpiece, usually with woodscrews but, where defacement of the centre of the workpiece is not permissible, by adhesive methods. The router arm is also fitted with two sliders, which are slipped over the two dowels protruding from the base sliders These are adjusted to determine the ellipse major and minor axes, and then locked in position. The router is bolted to the circular platform at one end of the arm. The kit also includes a pen, which may be fitted in place of the router – a very useful tool when planning and designing a layout.

It is necessary for the device to work on a flat surface which must also be large enough to accommodate the entire router platform. This requirement arises from the necessity to avoid fouling by the workpiece of the step on the underside of the platform (visible in Fig.56). It is

Figure 55

Figure 56

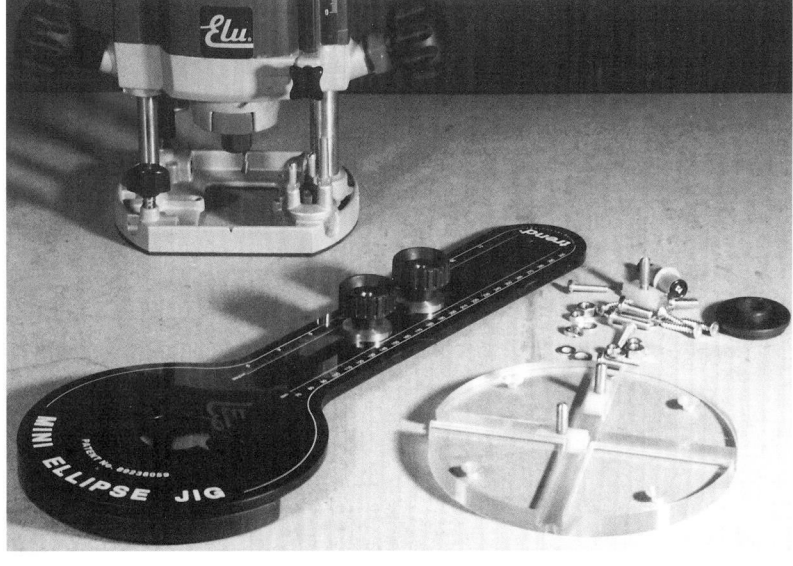

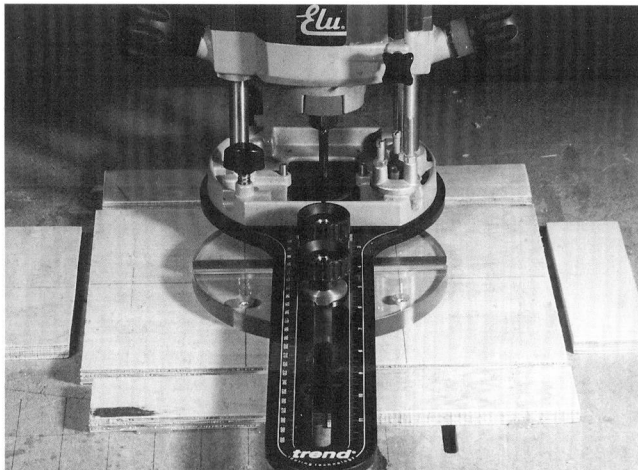

Figure 57

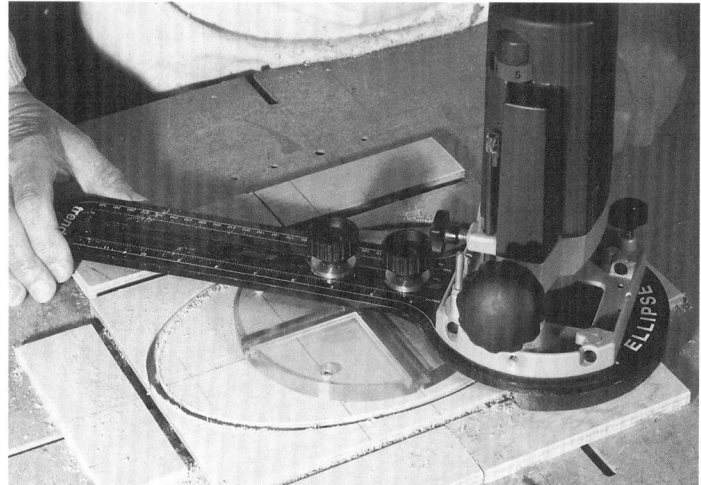

Figure 58

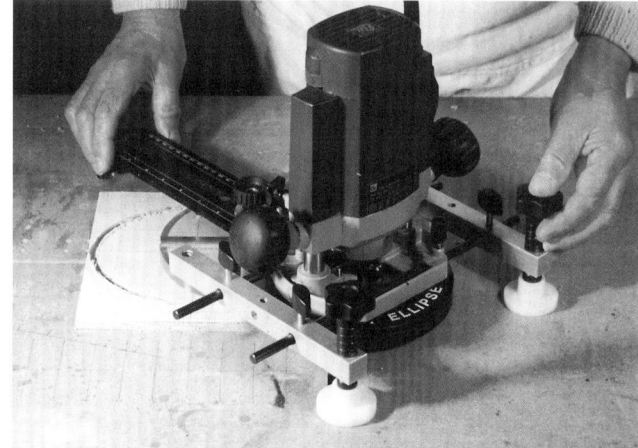

Figure 59

by no means necessary to use a piece of material much larger than the required ellipse. Figs 57 and 58 illustrate the use of scraps of material, which must be of the same thickness as that of the workpiece, to provide the necessary support. A much more convenient arrangement involves the use of a one-legged ski system, as shown in Fig.59. In this particular illustration, the ubiquitous Pivot Frame is used, requiring only moments to set up. This is very much an unplanned use of the Pivot Frame, but it works beautifully! The jig is an excellent device for directly machining ellipses to a very high order of accuracy. Moreover, by suitable adjustment of the sliders on the router arm, it will cut elliptical rebates and other elevation profiles without the need for templates and their attendant guided cutters. A detailed description of the geometry of the device is given in Chapter 8.

For smaller work and, in particular, where a wide range of aspect ratios is required, a jig working on a rather different principle may be used. Currently, the jig, although based on the Pivot Frame, is not commercially available, but can be home-made with the aid of a little metalwork. Although the device will cut (or draw) ellipses of any aspect ratio down to a theoretical minimum of zero, there is a maximum size limitation, determined by the size of primary disc used. Obviously, the larger the primary disc, the more versatile the device. Therefore, the design offered here is based upon the longer (500 mm, or $19^{11}/_{16}$") pair of guide rods supplied with the Elu MOF 96(E) router. This allows the use of a primary disc of $19\frac{1}{2}$" diameter. It is not possible to be precise about the maximum ellipse dimensions available from the system. The operation of the device is somewhat complex and maximum dimensions are closely linked with aspect ratios. As a guide, a reasonable practical maximum is of the order of 9" by 5".

The jig is shown in outline form in Fig.60. The primary disc is fitted with a dovetail slide system, running through the centre of the disc. The central slider carries a worktable, to which the actual workpiece may

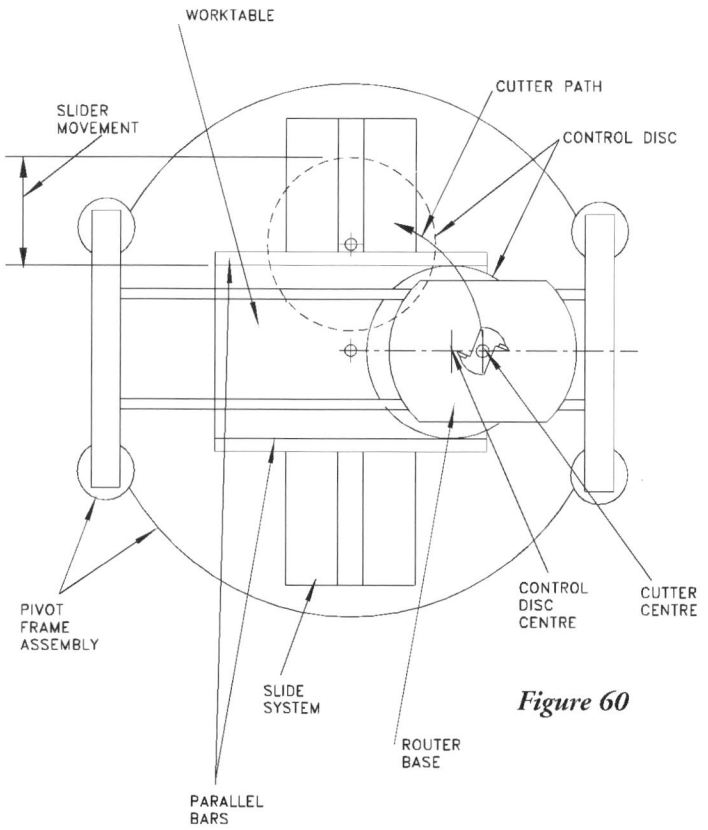

SLIDER MOVEMENT

WORKTABLE

CUTTER PATH

CONTROL DISC

CONTROL DISC CENTRE

CUTTER CENTRE

PIVOT FRAME ASSEMBLY

SLIDE SYSTEM

ROUTER BASE

PARALLEL BARS

Figure 60

Figure 61

be fitted, usually by adhesive methods. The worktable also carries a pair of raised parallel bars. The router base is fitted with a 'control disc', which may be adjusted laterally along the axis of the guide rods, such that the centre of the disc may be offset from that of the cutter by any chosen amount. Adjustment is by means of a micro-adjuster fitted to the disc.

In use, the Pivot Frame is placed upon the primary disc in the normal way, but also with the control disc sliding between the two parallel bars on the worktable. The jig is shown set up for use in Fig.61. It will be seen from this illustration, and also from Fig.62, that the primary disc is itself in two parts, comprising the main disc, surmounted by an annular ring of the same

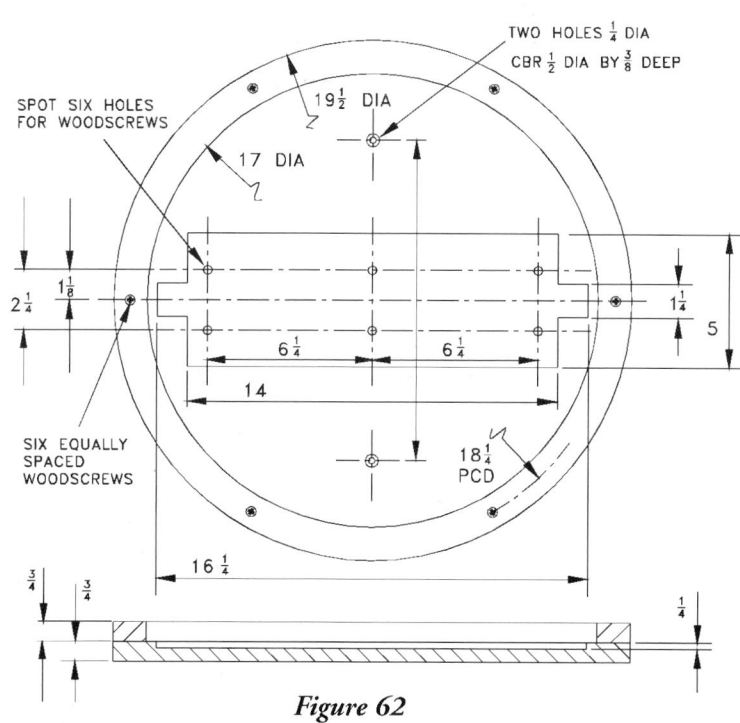

TWO HOLES $\frac{1}{4}$ DIA
CBR $\frac{1}{2}$ DIA BY $\frac{3}{8}$ DEEP

SPOT SIX HOLES FOR WOODSCREWS

19$\frac{1}{2}$ DIA

17 DIA

2$\frac{1}{4}$

1$\frac{1}{8}$

6$\frac{1}{4}$

6$\frac{1}{4}$

14

1$\frac{1}{4}$

5

SIX EQUALLY SPACED WOODSCREWS

18$\frac{1}{4}$ PCD

$\frac{3}{4}$

$\frac{3}{4}$

16$\frac{1}{4}$

$\frac{1}{4}$

Figure 62

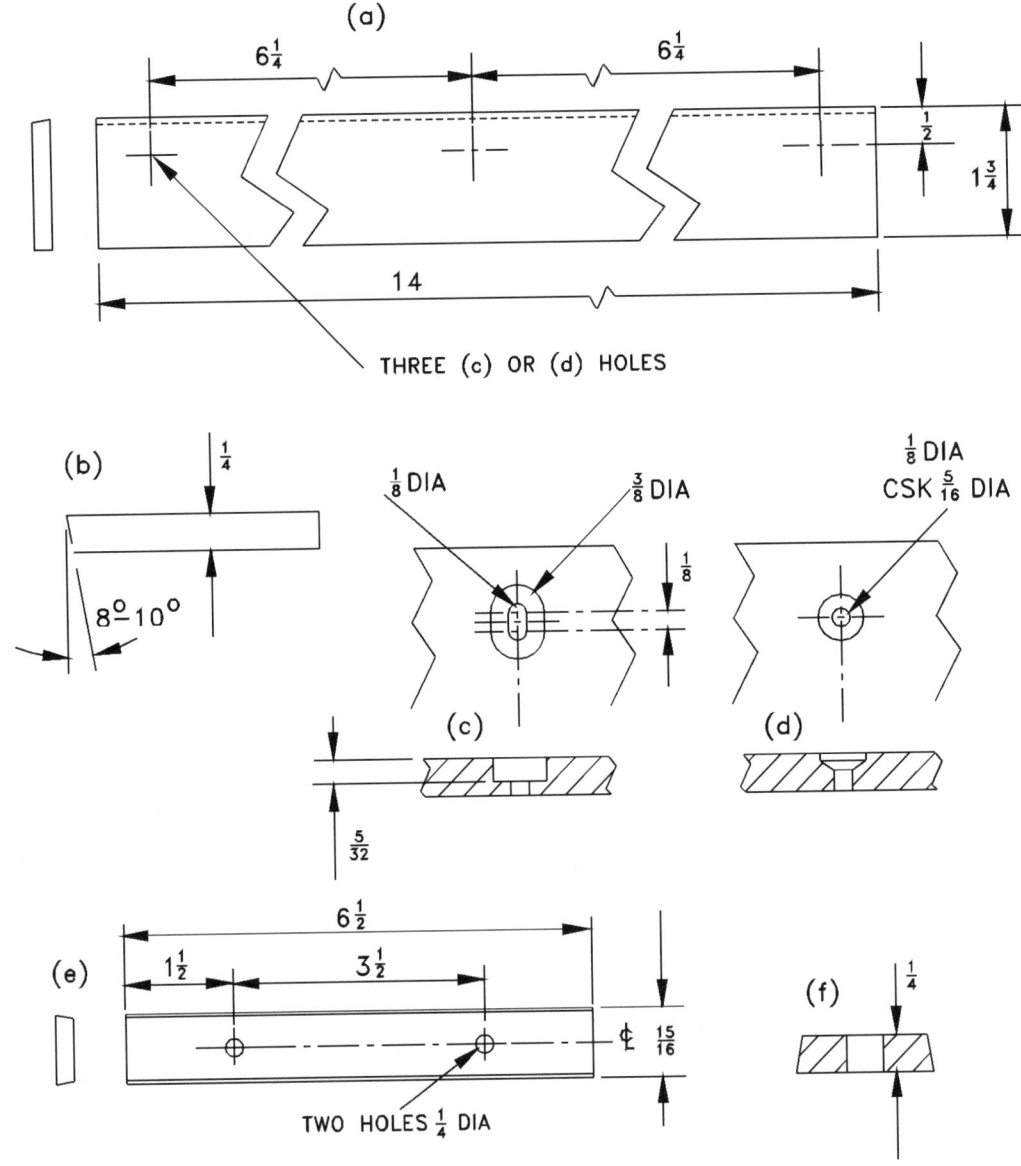

(a)

6¼   6¼

½   1¾

14

THREE (c) OR (d) HOLES

(b)   ¼

8°–10°

⅛ DIA   ⅜ DIA

⅛ DIA
CSK 5⁄16 DIA

(c)   (d)

5⁄32

(e)   6½

1½   3½

⊄ 15⁄16

TWO HOLES ¼ DIA

(f)   ¼

Figure 63

external diameter. The purpose of the ring is simply to restore router 'ride height' lost by the thickness of the worktable.

The primary disc slide system is very easily homemade. The material chosen is Tufnol, mainly on account of its dimensional stability (although it is rather hard on cutters). Dimensions are given in Fig.63. It is important that the slides are machined accurately; in particular, the flanks of the short central slider (e) and (f) must not only be dead straight; they must also be parallel. The longer outer slides (a)–(d) merely need to be straight on their dovetailed edges. A suitable router cutter is a plain dovetail of 8°–10° flank angle. The router is used in ski mode against a straight fence on a flat worktop. Any accurate ski system which allows fine lateral adjustment, and also incorporates a means of placing the router above the work (rather than on it) will serve. The three workpieces comprising the slide system are sawn slightly oversize, and glued to the worktop such that their long edges are parallel to the fence and have a working gap between them to allow lateral adjustment of the router cutter. The arrange-

ment is shown (for a different jig) in Chapter 2 Fig.39. Machining is simply a matter of positioning the router on the guide rods to machine each dovetail in turn. Obviously, the cutter must be set to full depth; nothing else is permissible for dovetails. It is still possible however, to take as many cuts as necessary, including a fine finishing cut, by moving the router laterally. If necessary, the non-dovetail flanks of the longer pieces are machined with a straight cutter at the same time. Given a sharp cutter and a regular even feed, no further work on the slides should be required. If cutter marks do occur, they may be eased out with fine wet and dry abrasive, used wet, wrapped around a strip of wood or metal. Holes and slots may then be machined. Note that only one of the longer pieces is fitted with adjustment slots as illustrated in Fig.63(c). The two holes in the centre slide are drilled or routed as accurately as possible, in terms of both diameter and spacing, since these must take two metal dowels which form an integral part of the sliding worktable.

The main primary disc is recessed to house the slide system. This too may be carried out with a simple ski

Figure 64

and fence arrangement. It is important that the top faces of the outer slides are flush with that of the primary disc to ensure that, when the sliding worktable is fitted, it is supported by the primary disc. To guarantee this, the housing is machined just a trifle over depth. Final height adjustment may then be made by inserting strips of paper or even thin plastic adhesive tape beneath the outer slide members (the centre slide will eventually take care of itself). When fitting up the slide system, one outer member may be screwed permanently in place. The other is adjusted, with the aid of the machined screw slots, such that the centre slide moves freely but without undue play. This operation can be carried out without fitting the worktable (Fig.64).

The worktable base is made from acrylic sheet, $\frac{1}{4}$" thick, to the dimensions given in Fig.65. The shape is arranged to maximise the amount of lateral movement of the table within the primary disc, hence the cutaway corners. The two dowels must fit the central slider easily, but with no sloppiness, thus enabling the worktable to be easily fitted and removed. At this point it can be seen that the presence of the worktable has no effect upon the tightness or otherwise of the actual slide system, since it simply drops into place and is supported

Figure 65

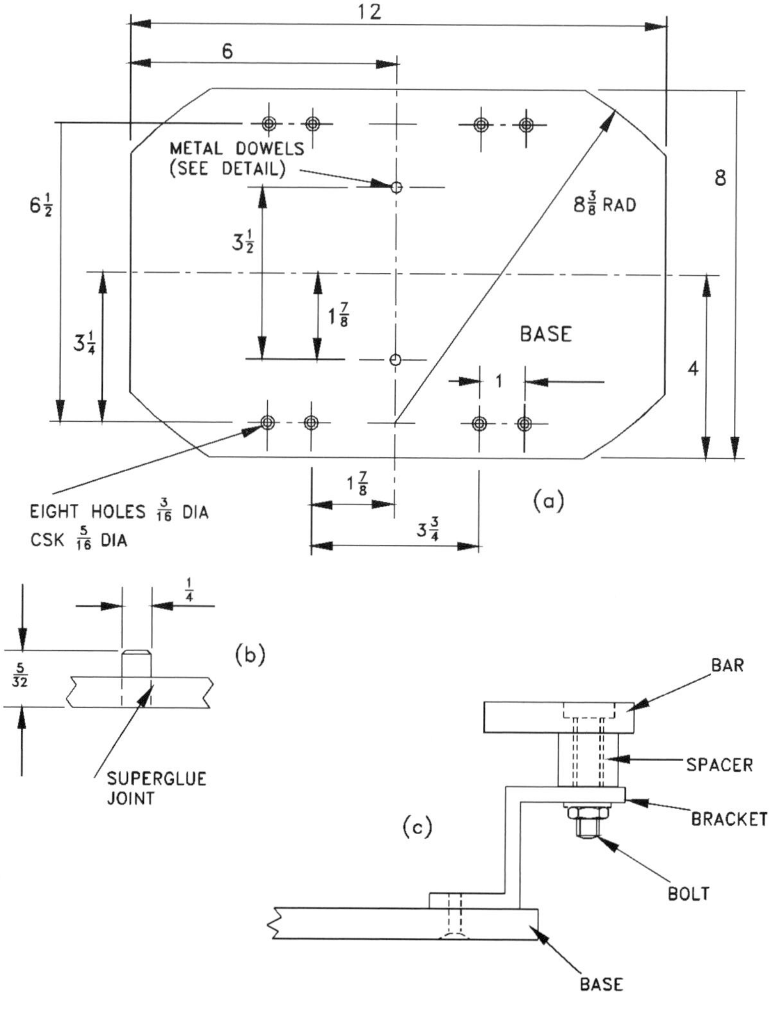

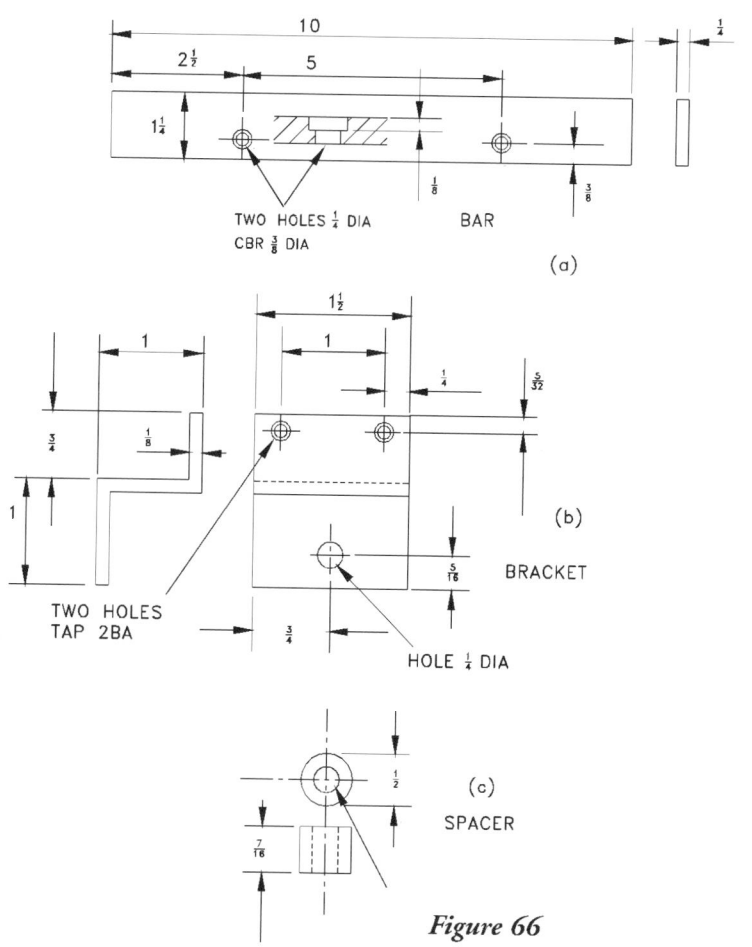

Figure 66

by the top face of the primary disc. My original design allowed for the worktable base to be screwed to the slider also, but I found this totally unnecessary in practice and no longer use it.

The two parallel bars (Fig.66(a)) which also form part of the worktable are designed to engage with the control disc on the router, and their height above the worktable base is arranged with this in mind. The cranked design of the support system (Fig.65(c)) maximises the lateral working range, and it is therefore worthwhile to undertake the extra work involved in making the design shown (it is quite possible to purchase brass angle of this form). The bars represent plain machining and may be made in acrylic or Tufnol sheet, again using the router with a side fence in much the same way as for the slides. One of the bars may be in a fixed position, but the other may require provision for a little adjustment. This is not actually shown in any of the drawings, but may be added in a similar manner to Fig.63(c) if found necessary. Remaining worktable components are shown in Fig. 66(b) and (c). It will be found convenient to arrange for the mounting of further sacrificial platforms on the worktable, either by adhesive methods or fixing screws. The worktable assembly is shown fitted to its slide system in Fig.67.

The control disc is free to slide laterally on the router base via a slide system, under the control of a micro-adjuster. The disc is shown in Fig.68(a), and is a very easy router task. The micro-adjuster comprises the parts shown in (b)–(e); these must be made in metal, prefer-ably brass. The two outer sections of the slide system, which are also fitted to the disc, are shown in Fig.69(b)–(d). Note that these are made as a right and left-handed pair. Ideally, the slide system would be dovetailed, as for the primary disc slides but, for ease of making, the simpler rebate plate arrangement is used instead, and actually works rather well. The plates are riveted to the slides as shown in (d).

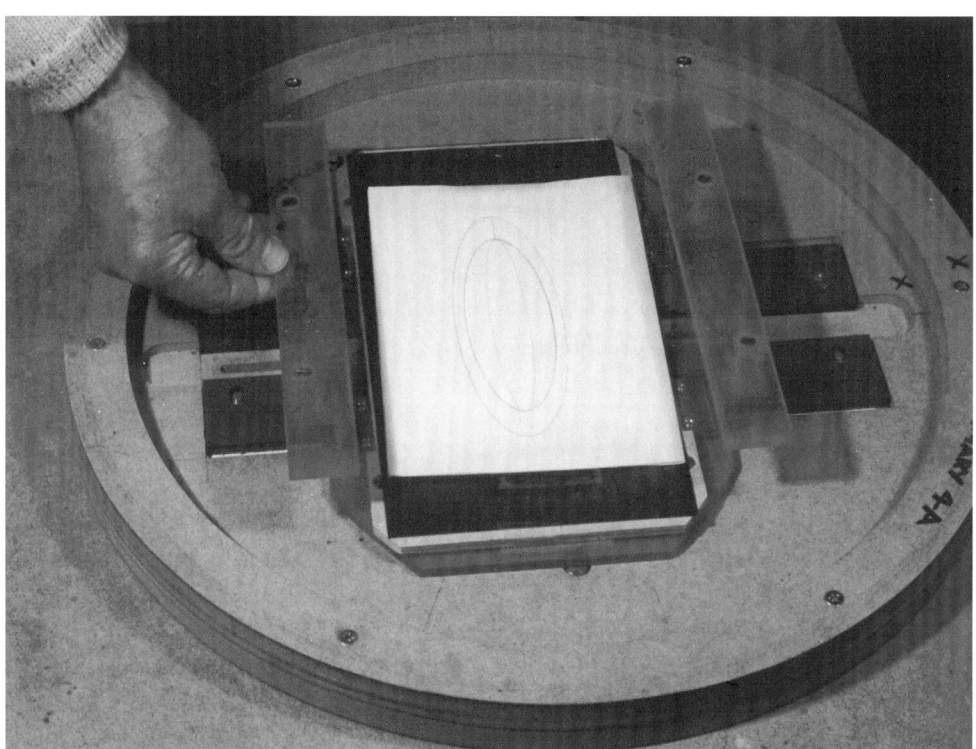

Figure 67

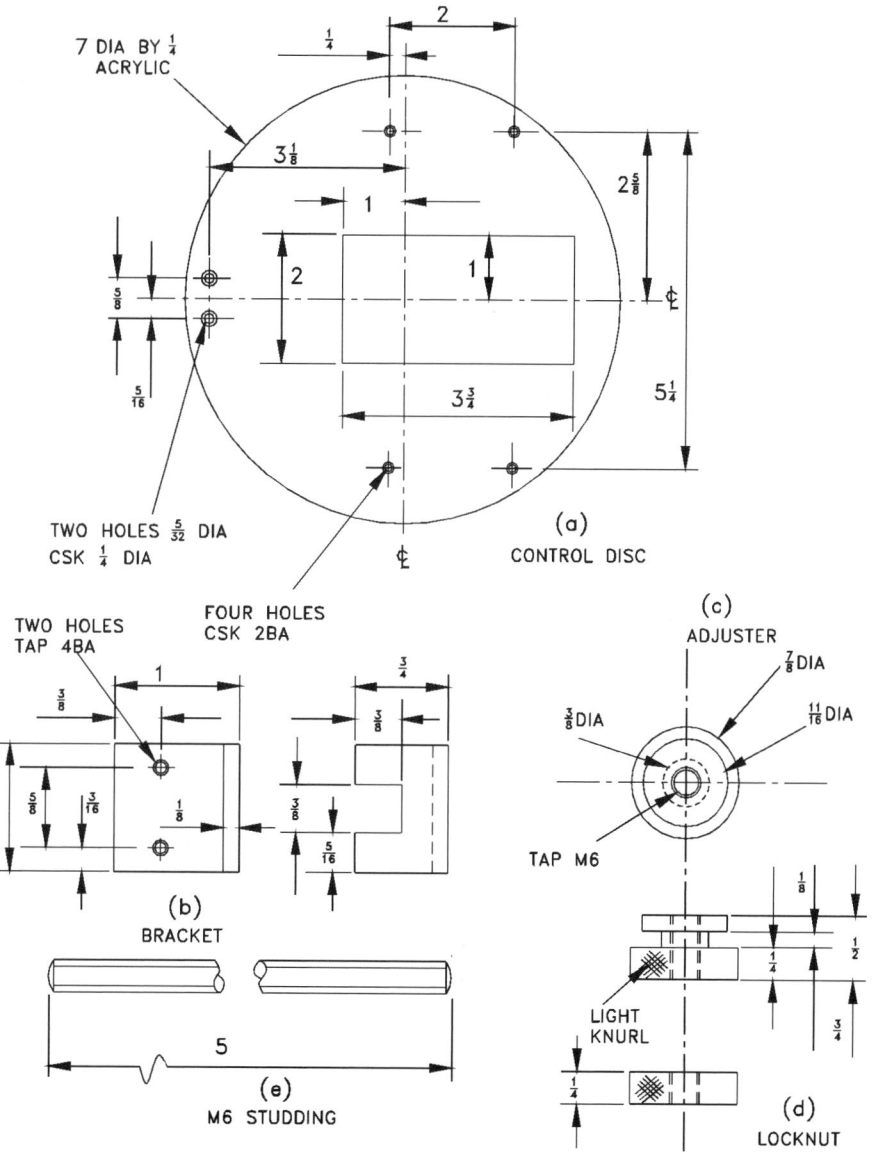

7 DIA BY ¼ ACRYLIC

TWO HOLES 5/32 DIA CSK ¼ DIA

FOUR HOLES CSK 2BA

(a) CONTROL DISC

(c) ADJUSTER

7/8 DIA
3/16 DIA
11/16 DIA
TAP M6

TWO HOLES TAP 4BA

(b) BRACKET

LIGHT KNURL

(d) LOCKNUT

(e) M6 STUDDING

Figure 68

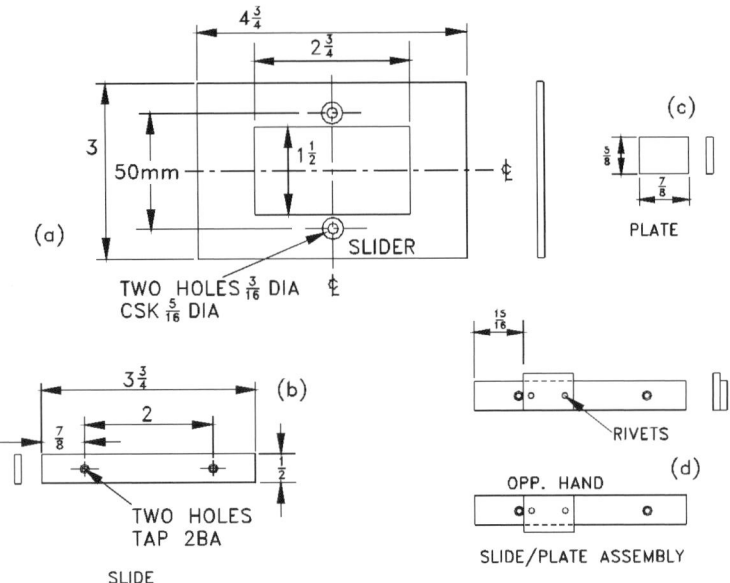

SLIDER

4¾

2¾

3

50mm

1½

(a)

(c)

⅝

⅞

PLATE

TWO HOLES 3/16 DIA
CSK 5/16 DIA

3¾

(b)

2

⅞

½

TWO HOLES
TAP 2BA

SLIDE

15/16

RIVETS

OPP. HAND

(d)

SLIDE/PLATE ASSEMBLY

ALL PARTS FROM ⅛ THICK BRASS

Figure 69

The slider plate (a) is fixed to the router base via the two tapped holes which normally carry guide bushes. All parts are illustrated in Fig.70, and the complete assembly in Fig.71. No form of lateral adjustment for fit is shown, although slots could be provided in one of the outer slides if necessary. Since the movement is fairly small a good sliding fit can be obtained quite easily with a little hand filing and polishing.

The Pivot Frame is fitted with its own fine adjuster which accurately determines the length of the major axis of the ellipse. The position of the control disc, which is set by the fine adjuster attached to it, determines the length of the minor axis with equal accuracy. The system is capable of work of very high precision and, subject to certain size limitations, there is virtually no limit to the type of ellipse which may be produced, since

Figure 71

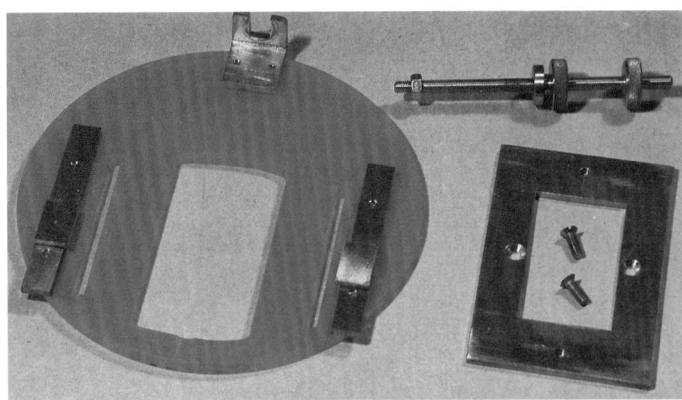

Figure 70

the control of aspect ratio is continuous.

So what are the limitations? Obviously, maximum size is one of them. This is determined by the size of the primary disc, which in turn is determined by the length of the guide rods. Since these are generally made from standard stock rod and are fairly readily available, it is perfectly feasible for the user to make them of any required practical length, and to machine a primary disc to suit them. Thus, the upper size limit may be determined entirely by the user. There is a second limitation which is a little more subtle (and which is also rather difficult to explain satisfactorily in words). The sliding movement of the worktable across the primary disc becomes greater as the minor axis dimension is reduced (regardless of the length of the major axis). This movement is of course ultimately limited by contact between the worktable and the annular disc. In practical terms, this means that narrow ellipses are obliged to be shorter than wider ones. Thus it is not particularly easy to define the limitations of the device for a given primary disc size, since much will depend upon the type of ellipse required.

Use of the device is very simple and straightforward. The workpiece is attached to the sliding worktable by any suitable means. I have even used a vacuum chuck, although this is not featured in the design offered, for simplicity's sake. The major and minor axes are set by means of the adjusters, and the Pivot Frame simply swung around the primary disc in the usual way; the jig takes care of the rest. One or two small practical hints may be in order here: it can be very helpful to use the jig to draw ellipses on a sheet of paper taped to the worktable. This materially assists original design work, and can also be very helpful in allowing precise cutter settings to be made against the drawing whilst it is still on the worktable. Clearly it is not possible to simply stick a pencil into the router collet, but a stylus comprising a length of pencil lead fitted in a hole in a length of metal rod can be very helpful. I have actually gone overboard a little in this respect, since my pencil is fitted with a tiny collet, and is also spring-loaded. I also have a device which allows a Rotring pen to be used. Despite the fact that both devices are tremendously useful, I have chosen not to include details, since they require rather precise metal-turning.

It is only fair to describe one fault with the jig (albeit a minor one). Devices which comprise many parts will invariably suffer from machining and assembly tolerances, particularly when home-made. In this particular instance, for complete accuracy, the control disc must slide with its centre precisely on the centre line of the Pivot Frame assembly. The chances are that, in practice, it won't. The result will be a tendency for the axes of successive ellipses drawn or machined on the same centre to rotate slightly as they are made smaller. The fault is unlikely to cause major problems, but it is as well to be aware of it.

I am acutely conscious of the fact that the metalworking content of the device may pose some difficulty. Nevertheless, if the reader can manage this (or persuade somebody else to), the resultant piece of equipment will be found a very valuable tool, since it has complete control of both major and minor axis dimensions (and hence aspect ratio). To the best of my knowledge, no other device currently available, short of NC machining, can manage this. Moreover the jig is very easy to use, as will be seen from the projects involving it.

4

VACUUM CHUCKS

Any work involving the use of the router in overhead manual mode will require the work to be held down to a worktop in some way. A number of methods are available; many of them are included in this book. This chapter is concerned with the most convenient, and certainly the least messy, that of vacuum chucking.

Let it be said at once that the 'all singing, all dancing' vacuum solution does require some financial outlay on a motorised pump. This is an essential requirement where lengthy tasks are involved, and/or where the vacuum seal at the workpiece is imperfect; in both cases a reliable, continuous refreshment of the vacuum is necessary. An inexpensive manually operated pump is described later in this chapter, as a starter kit which will at least introduce the reader to the concept and which will serve quite well for small tasks.

Either method will require a vacuum chuck to hold the workpiece. This can be home-made quite easily since most of it can be constructed in acrylic plastic. A small amount of light metalworking is necessary, but this too will be found generally within the capacity of the home workshop. The vacuum system can be a very powerful 'hold down' device. Most commercial pumps can be relied upon to provide at least 12 pounds per square inch (psi), given a good gas seal throughout the system; the manual system has been checked at only marginally less (11 psi). For a sealed perimeter of say, two inches square, this equates to about 48 lb. holding

pressure. A fourteen inch square seal will provide an equivalent pressure of just over a ton!

To digress momentarily: when describing the advantages of vacuum chucking, I have been asked on more than one occasion: 'If the pressure is a ton, why doesn't the worktable buckle under the weight?'. Readers familiar with the laws of physics may well smile at such a naive question; they might then like to try the mental experiment of explaining matters in lay terms; it isn't that easy to do so convincingly. As an attempt, I would merely offer the following: Air pressure exists all around us. In Fig.72(a), which depicts a worktop and a workpiece, air pressure exists both above and below them, and even in the minuscule gap between them. Remove the air from this junction, and the air pressure goes with it, leaving only that above and below the assembly, which may now be considered as a single unit (b). Thus, the 'ton of pressure' exists only around them, and is not transferred to the legs of the worktable, the floor or anywhere else.

One of the easiest ways of providing a simple vacuum chuck is to cut a plain enclosed channel in a flat smooth surface and fill it with a gasket made from material which is both compressible and itself impervious to air (Fig.73). Compressibility is very important, not only to furnish an effective seal, but also to ensure that the workpiece eventually contacts the chuck itself, thus maintaining level and rigidity. Within the enclosed area, some means is provided for extraction of air, such

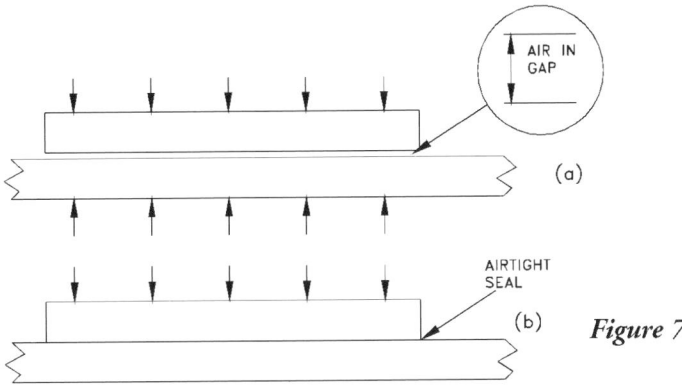

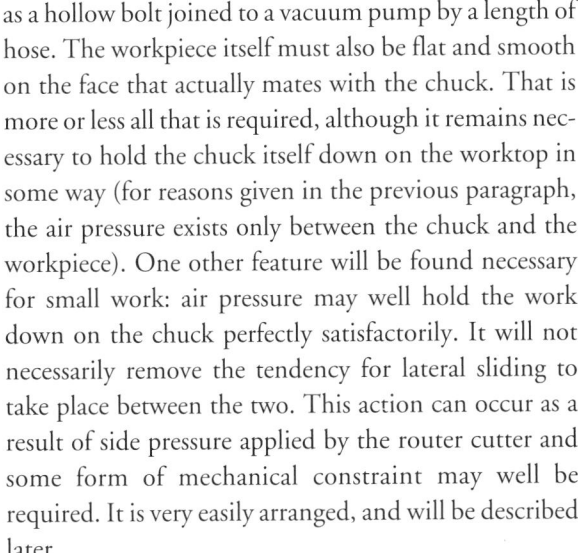

Figure 72

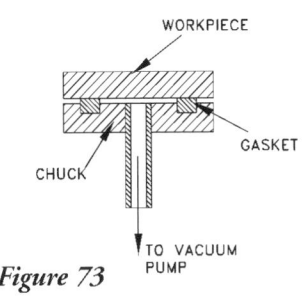

Figure 73

as a hollow bolt joined to a vacuum pump by a length of hose. The workpiece itself must also be flat and smooth on the face that actually mates with the chuck. That is more or less all that is required, although it remains necessary to hold the chuck itself down on the worktop in some way (for reasons given in the previous paragraph, the air pressure exists only between the chuck and the workpiece). One other feature will be found necessary for small work: air pressure may well hold the work down on the chuck perfectly satisfactorily. It will not necessarily remove the tendency for lateral sliding to take place between the two. This action can occur as a result of side pressure applied by the router cutter and some form of mechanical constraint may well be required. It is very easily arranged, and will be described later.

Some idea of the usefulness of vacuum chucking for small work may be gained from Fig.74, which illustrates an experiment performed to check the efficiency of the home-made manual pump described later. In this case, the vacuum is drawn between two acrylic discs. The larger disc is held to the worktop by the hollow bolt supplying the vacuum. The upper disc is cemented to the block attached to the spring balance. The outer diameter of the gasket is a little under $1\frac{1}{2}$" diameter, and the reading on the balance is 19 lb. It would be unwise however, to take the foregoing entirely at face value. The gas seal between two pieces of acrylic is far

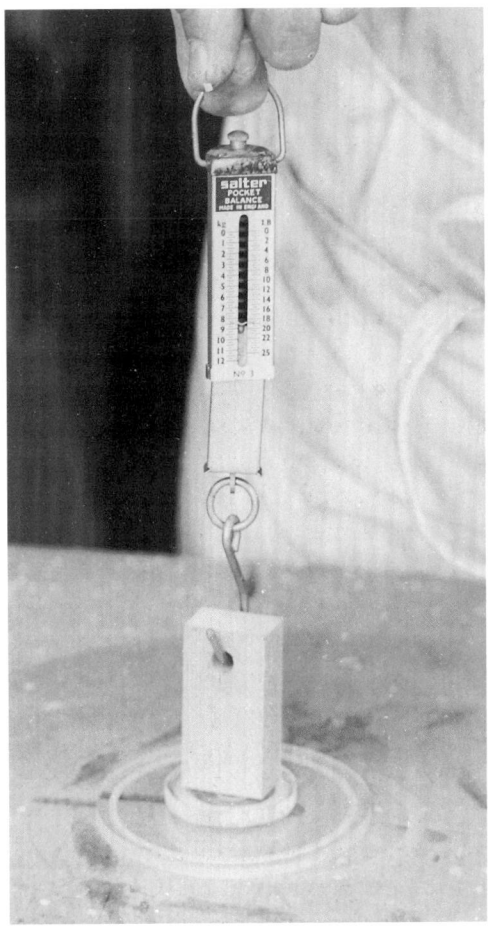

Figure 74

better than that between acrylic and wood, however well-finished is the latter.

For Pivot Frame and other trammel work, it is convenient to combine the vacuum chuck with the secondary disc and angular indexing system described in Chapter 1. The only real difference lies in the choice of material for the device. For a really efficient air seal, acrylic sheet is difficult to beat. Tufnol comes a close second, provided that the original shiny pressed surface is retained at the chuck/workpiece interface. Both materials are acceptably flat, smooth and dimensionally stable. Both can be machined with the router, although Tufnol is rather severe on cutters, and the machining 'swarf' is in the form of a fine dust, requiring particular attention to face-masking and dust extraction. Acrylic

can be machined with normal router cutters, but better results are obtained with cutters specially ground for this material, the essential difference here being a much greater clearance behind the cutting edge, to reduce friction and thus the risk of heat-softening the material slightly. The biggest nuisance with acrylic lies with the swarf. This does not pose a severe health risk but is produced in the form of fine flakes which, due to electrostatic charge, stick to just about anything and are very difficult to clear up.

A design which has worked particularly well for me is shown in Fig.75. With any form of routing, there is always some risk of inadvertently machining the jig or the worktop surface (we all do it). For this reason, the secondary disc, which carries all the indexing features and therefore represents a good deal of work, is used as a carrier for a further series of discs (which I will call the vacuum discs). These, whilst not exactly to be regarded as 'expendable' due to general wear and tear, are at least sufficiently easily made to be considered as replaceable items. They can also be customised in terms of gasket profile, to suit individual tasks. Machining of both the secondary disc and the vacuum discs may be carried out with the router. Due to the relatively small diameter of the vacuum disc and its matching recess in the secondary disc, a Pivot Frame will be found of particular assistance. There is nothing particularly sacrosanct about the dimensions given; like much of my jig work, dimensions were chosen to suit available offcuts of material.

The secondary disc actually comprises two blank discs of $\frac{1}{4}$" thick acrylic sheet, cemented together with superglue (Fig.76(a)). The lower component is a plain disc, with a $\frac{1}{4}$" diameter hole at the centre. It also requires to be marked out for indexing before any machining is undertaken, but this procedure is described later. The upper component is an annulus. Both discs are sawn slightly oversize, with the centre also sawn away in the case of the annulus. The plain disc requires the central hole to be bored prior to sawing, to a diameter which

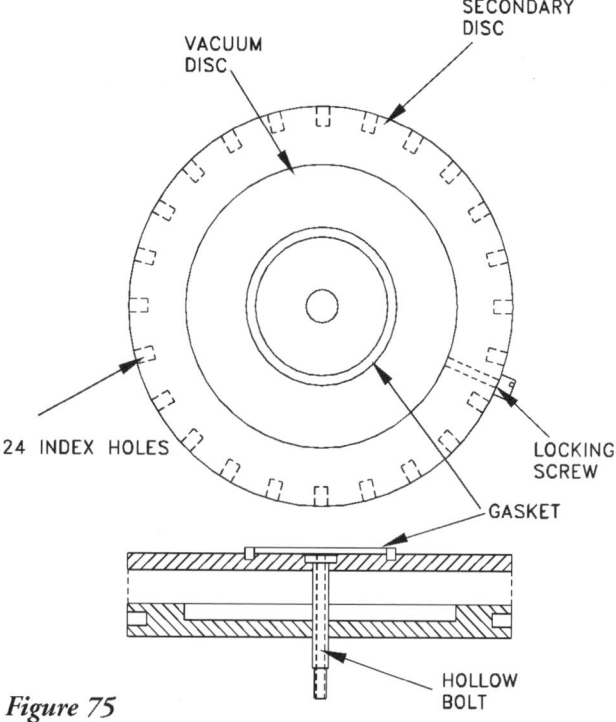

Figure 75

allows a hollow central bolt (to be described) to be inserted and withdrawn without undue free play. After cementing together, the pair may be machined on the Pivot Frame. The assembly is held via the central hole, with a suitable bolt through the centre of the Pivot Frame primary disc. This ensures concentricity of the machining with the central hole. To prevent unwanted rotation under machining load, a small piece of double-sided adhesive tape may be placed on the underside of the workpiece. Final profiling of the inner diameter of the annulus is carried out at the same setting. Machining should be carried out to the full depth of the annulus. If this entails slight machining of the base of the lower disc, so be it; operation will not be impaired, and it is essential that the inner flank is completely square to the base, allowing the vacuum discs, when fitted, to lie flat in the housing, and dead flush with the upper face of the secondary disc.

Before any machining is carried out on either disc, the lower disc must be marked out to encompass the necessary angular divisions. It is a great help if the marks are made on the *underside* of the disc. The material is transparent, and it is often useful to use these marks against registration marks on the primary disc (or worktop). I have found that an excellent way of producing them is with the aid of an accurate full-circle draughtsman's protractor, taped to the disc such that its centre lies precisely over the centre of the disc. For best accuracy, the protractor should be as large as conveniently possible, and the sawn acrylic disc should be (at least initially) slightly larger than the protractor. In this way, the necessary marks may be made on the disc with a scriber, against the divisions at the edge of the protractor. Since this operation requires careful setting up, one might as well make full use of it by scribing lines at 5° intervals, even though the indexing holes will be drilled at 15° intervals (for a 24-station indexing system); subsequent usefulness will justify the extra effort. The marks are then used to scribe full diametrical lines across the face of the disc, which may now have its centre hole bored, and remaining work carried out as previously described. An 'optional extra' piece of marking-out

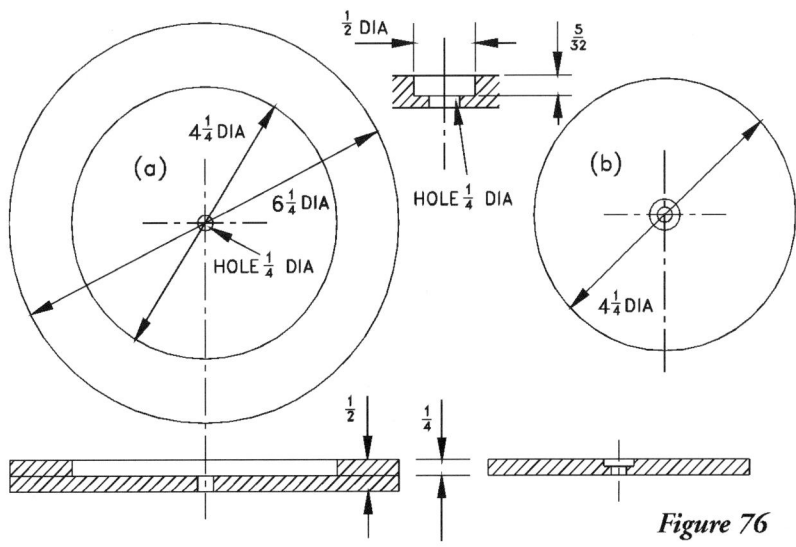

Figure 76

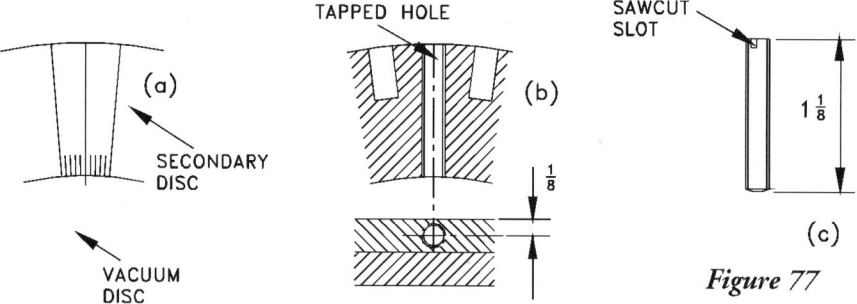

Figure 77

which I have found rather useful, is to make a series of 1° marks as shown in Fig.77(a) on a small section of the *top* face of the disc. These may be aligned against a single scribed line on each vacuum disc, thus allowing slight registration errors to be corrected (and recorded where necessary), by minor adjustment of the vacuum disc against the secondary disc. Unfortunately, due to parallax errors, it is not at all easy to line up these marks with those on the underside, simply by viewing from the top. At the expense of a little extra effort however, I can offer a method which works rather well: after assembly of the two discs, a very light machining of the outer diameter of the pair is made on the Pivot Frame. This should not be taken to the final required diameter, but should be sufficient only to provide a smooth machined rim, such that scriber marks can be seen easily on it. In this way, three adjacent diametrical lines may be transferred from the underside to the top, by scribing around the edge

with the aid of a trysquare. Individual 1° marks may then be interpolated between them. It is difficult to find a really accurate means of doing this by hand; in my case it was a matter of trial and error. When all marks have been made satisfactorily the full machining process may be carried out.

After machining, the disc is transferred to the jig described in Chapter 6, to have its peripheral holes bored. Whilst on the same jig, an extra hole is bored in the rim, completely through the width of the annulus. The hole is then tapped 2BA or M5 (Fig.77(b)), to suit a matching bolt or length of studding, preferably of brass (c). This bolt is used to lock the vacuum disc in position when fitted.

It is sensible to make a number of vacuum disc blanks at a single session. These are prepared initially by sawing slightly oversize discs from $\frac{1}{4}$" thick acrylic sheet, each with a counterbored hole at the centre (Fig.76(b)). The

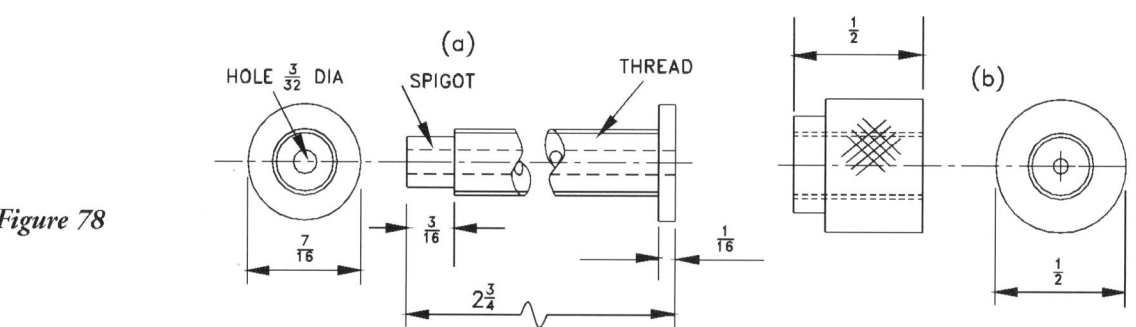

Figure 78

outer diameter may then be machined directly on the Pivot Frame. For the first disc, the diameter should be gradually reduced, no more than a few 'thou' at a time, until it fits the machined recess in the secondary disc with no sloppiness whatever. The Pivot Frame is locked at this setting and the remaining discs machined to the same diameter.

Further work on the vacuum discs depends upon the use to be made of them, since they can now be customised to suit a number of tasks; moreover, the router can be used for this purpose also. Before describing this work however, it is necessary to make a hollow bolt to apply the vacuum to the chuck. The bolt must be long enough to go through the vacuum/secondary disc assembly, and then through any worktop, including a Pivot Frame primary disc where necessary, and still leave sufficient to fit a nut on the underside, and a spigot to receive the vacuum hose. It must also have a flat shouldered top to fit in the counterbore of the vacuum disc. Such a task will be easy meat for the owner of a metalworking lathe and Fig.78(a) is offered for this reason, together with a suitable nut (b). The job will be rather less easy for others, but an alternative is given in Fig.79 (note however, that a pillar drill is a minimum requirement, even for this version). The base material is brass studding, threaded to choice, but generally in the region of $\frac{1}{4}$" Whitworth or BSF, or M6 for those who prefer metric; this material is quite readily obtainable. A length of about $2\frac{3}{4}$" is needed. The hard part is the drilling of a $^3/_{32}$" diameter hole right through the studding. Finding the centre of threaded rod is not possible by inspection, since the true centre will not be where it appears by viewing the end (Fig.80), so the idea of a quick 'centre pop' is out. A better solution, and one which also grips the studding for drilling is shown as a simple jig in Fig.81. A suitable offcut of timber, preferably not less than $1\frac{1}{2}$" thick is required. Exact dimensions are unimportant but, for best accuracy, the bottom face at least should be dead flat. A hole exactly the

diameter of the studding is drilled through the jig with a pillar drill, and a sawcut then made through the hole, thus providing a simple cramp which may be tightened by application of a woodscrew. The studding is cramped in the hole, sitting about $\frac{1}{2}$" below the top surface. Its end may then be spotted with the same drill, after which, the $^3/_{32}$" drill is used to make the required hole to about half the length of the studding. The studding is then reversed in the jig, and the entire procedure repeated, the operation being shown also in Figs 82 & 83.

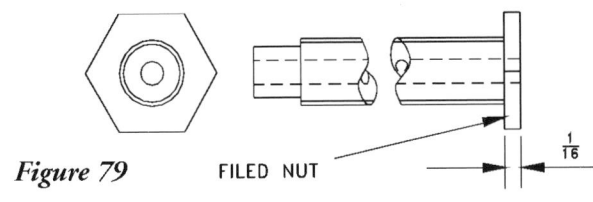

Figure 79   FILED NUT $\frac{1}{16}$

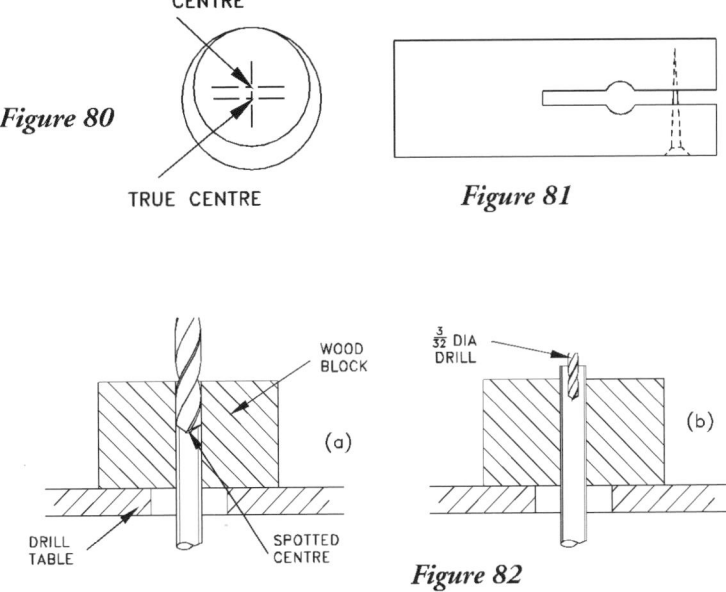

Figure 80   APPARENT CENTRE   TRUE CENTRE

Figure 81

Figure 82   WOOD BLOCK   DRILL TABLE   SPOTTED CENTRE   (a) $\frac{3}{32}$ DIA DRILL   (b)

Figure 83

The next task is to provide a spigot at one end, to suit the bore of a length of small-diameter hose or plastic tubing. This is carried out on a trial basis, to suit available hose, by fitting the studding in a power drill and filing the end whilst the drill is running. Finally, a brass nut is fitted to the other end, locked in place with superglue, and filed down to a suitable thickness in a vice (Fig.79). A matter of safety, peculiar to drilling in brass, must be mentioned here, Normal engineering twist drills as purchased, are ground to cut steel (and metals with similar machining characteristics). In this condition, they have a distinct angle of attack or 'rake', as shown in Fig.84(a). When drilling certain types of brass, the drill will snatch at the metal, an action which can take the operator by surprise and which can be quite dangerous. The problem may be avoided with a few strokes of a slipstone on each lip of the drill as shown in (b), leaving a bright 'witness' mark (c). This reduces the rake to approximately zero, and the drill will now cut brass quite freely and safely, although it won't be much use for steel and aluminium without regrinding.

The vacuum discs may now be completed to choice. All that is required essentially, is a machined channel in the top surface to suit the work in hand. A simple circular channel, as shown in Fig.75, is described for convenience. The gasket may be made from neoprene, available in sheet or strip form. This is a compressible material having many of the characteristics of very soft rubber, and may be purchased with a self-adhesive layer on one face, protected by a paper backing, which is peeled off immediately prior to application. It may be cut quite easily with scissors or knife and may, in strip form, be guided around the contours of a suitable channel (Fig.85(a)). This activity will of course deform

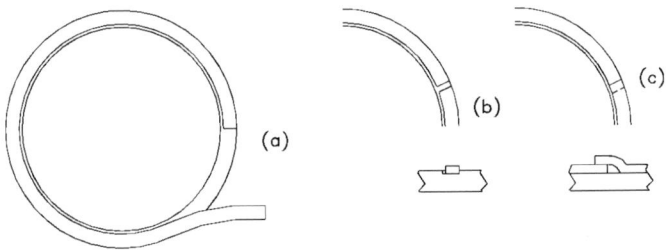

Figure 85

the material slightly; since it has a 'memory' it will try to creep back slowly to its original shape. The only problem which requires watching in this connection is the eventual appearance of a gap in the seal (b); this is best dealt with by providing a degree of overlap in the first place (c). The thickness of the material must first be determined, and the machined channel in the disc must be made to a depth which will allow the neoprene to sit about $1/32$" proud of the surface when fitted. My own

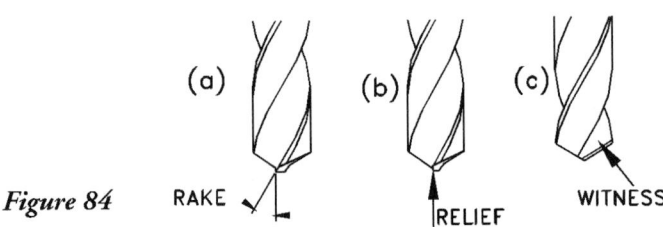

Figure 84   RAKE   RELIEF   WITNESS

supply of neoprene is $^1/_{16}$" thick, and the channel machined in the acrylic is therefore $^1/_{32}$" deep. The channel width is $\frac{1}{4}$", machined on the Pivot Frame with a straight cutter of this diameter. The neoprene is cut into strips just a little under $\frac{1}{4}$" wide and, after removing the backing paper, fed around the channel, making a slightly overlapped joint of the form shown in Fig.85. The neoprene is made slightly under width merely to make fitting easy; there is no need to allow room for sideways spread of the material, since it will compress easily without necessarily expanding elsewhere. There is no need to worry about the overlap either, since this too will compress sufficiently. It is also necessary to make a gasket to fit between the bolt head and the vacuum disc, in the form of a small washer (Fig.86). This *can* be cut with scissors and small craft knife, but the central hole is not easy. It is far better to make a small steel punch for the centre hole at least. This can be done fairly easily (in the absence of 'proper' metalworking machinery) with a jig of the type illustrated in Fig.81. In this case, a short length of steel rod $\frac{1}{4}$" diameter is fitted into the jig, and spotted and drilled with a $\frac{1}{4}$" centre drill (Fig.87). These drills are obtainable in all standard sizes, this particular size bearing the reference 'BS3'. The hole is drilled to the point where the maximum diameter of the drill just touches the end of the rod, thus producing a sharp circular rim. The operation requires a light feed and plenty of lubrication; even so, a little light dressing with a slipstone may be required afterwards. For best

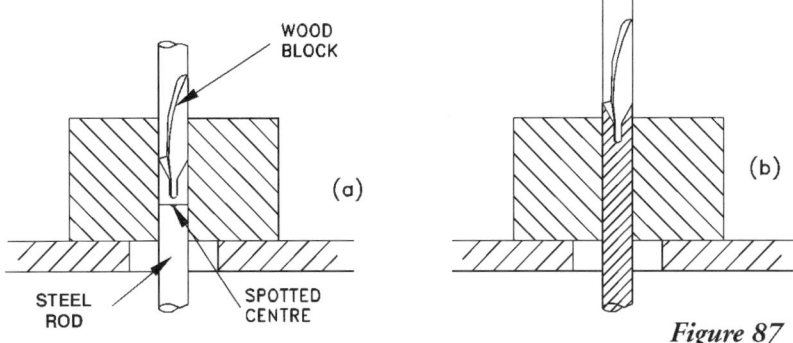

Figure 87

results, the steel should be of a type which may be hardened, but this is not essential for the rather light task required of it. In use, the neoprene is placed on a block of softwood and the hole punched with the aid of a small hammer. The outer diameter of the washer may be cut accurately enough with scissors. After removing the backing, the washer is fitted into the counterbore of the vacuum disc and becomes a permanent part of it. This just about completes the vacuum chuck, apart from fitting a length of tubing between the spigot of the bolt and the vacuum source. Fig.88 shows my own kit,

Figure 88

Figure 86

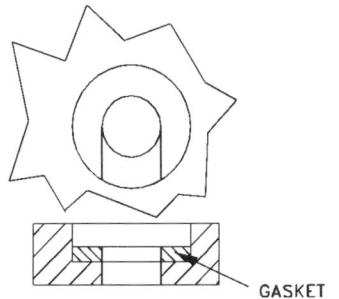

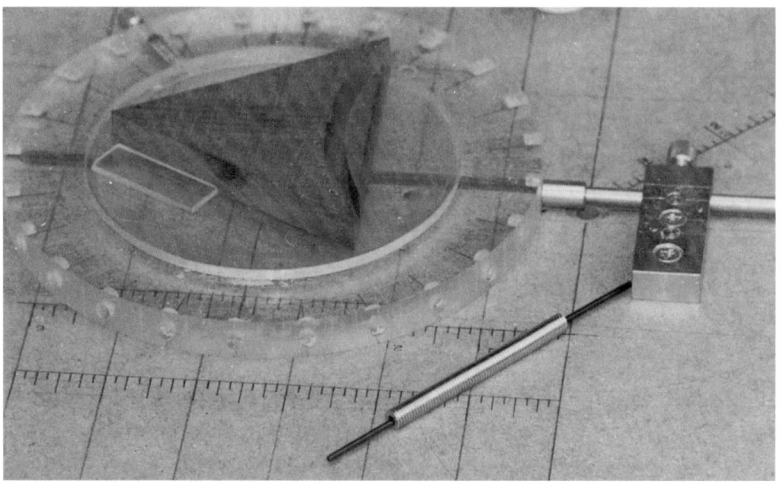

Figure 89

simply comprises a minimum of two side fences, which may be cut (and shaped if necessary) in acrylic sheet. These may be stuck down to the vacuum disc with superglue or double-sided adhesive tape. With the latter material, they may be prised off and replaced with others where necessary. In some cases, in order to maximise vacuum area, it may be necessary to offset the centre of the gasket channel from that of the vacuum disc, as shown in Fig.90(c).

For some work, particularly that of appreciable depth, and dependent also upon placement of the fences, the arrangement described may not be sufficient to prevent slight sideways slippage under cutter load. An extra

comprising a vacuum pump with foot switch, and a length of hose ending at one of my many vacuum discs. Fig.89 shows a chuck mounted in the secondary disc; note in the foreground, the length of threaded brass rod, drilled clean through by the pillar drill method described.

The workpiece to be machined should be smooth and flat on the underside. For small work, this is easily achieved with a disc sander. In use, the work is simply placed on the chuck and the vacuum applied. Note that the vacuum exists only between the workpiece and the vacuum disc, which can be rotated within the secondary disc as required and then locked in position with the locking screw.

For 'repeat work' in particular, such as machining a number of matching coasters, or a set of identical curved segments for a platter, the system has no equal. It is quick and easy to apply and remove the workpiece, particularly if the vacuum motor is fitted with a foot switch, and it could scarcely be cleaner. One or two additions will however, make the system even better. It helps a good deal on repeat work if the workpiece can be located on the chuck in a known position. This is readily achieved by the simple system shown in Fig.90, which

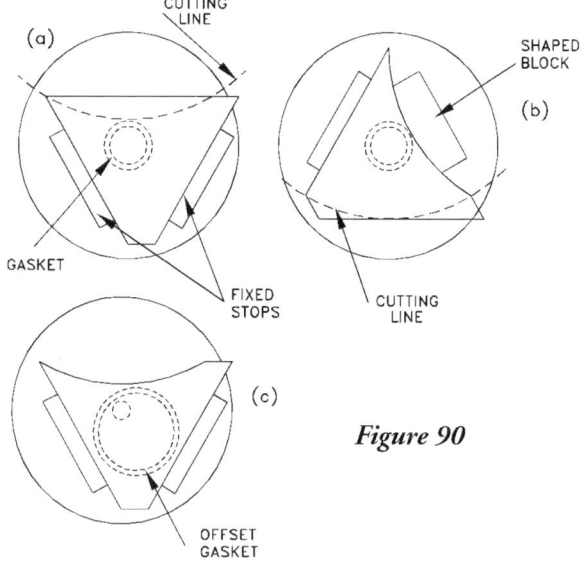

Figure 90

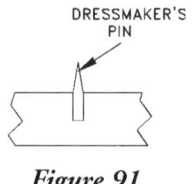

Figure 91

feature, which I have personally found completely satisfactory in all situations currently known to me, is illustrated in Fig.91, and comprises a couple of small protruding points which enter the base of the workpiece. It does unfortunately require the use of a very tiny drill of about .030' diameter. The problem here is not so much the actual use of the drill – this can easily be managed in a normal pillar drill without risk of breakage (I have even used such drills in a hand-brace) – rather it is that the drill will almost certainly be too small to be gripped in the average drill chuck, and may therefore require a small extra chuck, known as a 'pin-chuck' which itself is fitted into the larger chuck. The pins themselves may be made from hardened steel dressmakers' pins clipped to length; for some reason, these always seem to be .026" diameter, wherever they are purchased. A couple of holes are drilled part-way into the top face of the vacuum disc in more or less any convenient position and the pins inserted and held with superglue. The pins should not protrude more than about $^1/_{32}$". Any excess superglue on the surface must be scraped or chiselled away afterwards to maintain the flatness of the disc. The pins are sufficiently small and sharply pointed to leave no blemish in the workpiece after removal. There is one snag with the arrangement: the pins are very sharp, and careless handling of the chuck can be painful. An alternative method involves the use of strips of thin plastic adhesive tape stretched over the workpiece and the flanks of the jig. This will actually add to the hold-down power (although it would be risky to use it alone), but its real purpose is the prevention of lateral slippage. The disadvantage is that it requires a fresh piece of tape for every workpiece, thus tending to reduce the convenience of the vacuum chucking method.

It has been pointed out that vacuum chucking is very useful for repeat work. Sometimes it is possible to dispense with the secondary disc system and use a custom made chuck, fixed directly to the worktop. This type of chuck is very useful for repeat work which requires a particular chuck shape, and which also re-quires multiple operations on each piece, with the chuck remaining in a fixed position throughout. This is typi-cally illustrated by Fig.92, which has been borrowed from one of the projects. In this case, the operations involve thicknessing, scalloping the outer flank and cutting biscuit housings on either side of the segment.

This arrangement is extensively used in the projects, and will be encountered a number of times.

It cannot be denied that the router is a moderately noisy beast. Normally, I do not find this a problem but router noise can completely mask that made by the vacuum pump. It pays therefore to give a little tug to the workpiece, to ensure that it is firmly held, before rout-ing. Failure to do so can lead to the result illustrated in Fig.93. I would have liked to photograph the workpiece also, but I couldn't find it after the accident.

Figures 92 & 93

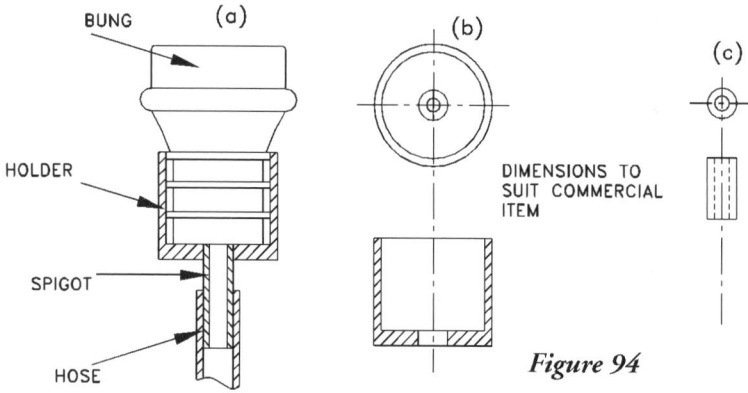

Figure 94

A major drawback to the whole idea of vacuum chucking is the undoubted expense of the pump. For extended periods of work, such a pump is essential. It is possible however, to lash up a suitable manual system, which involves a little work and time, but very little financial outlay. The prime mover in this instance is a small plastic hand-operated pump, sold in most supermarkets for the purpose of drawing a vacuum in partly-consumed bottles of wine. The kit is sold complete with a couple of rubber bungs which have a slit in the centre, which allows the vacuum to be drawn, and also serves as a non-return valve (Fig.94(a)). Squeezing the bung releases the vacuum. A holder is required for the bung (the equivalent of a bottle neck); this is shown in (b) and (c). No dimensions are given here, since it is better to make the components to suit the commercial item. The holder may however, be machined in a block of acrylic, which may be built up from a few scraps of $\frac{1}{4}$" sheet with superglue. It is also necessary to make a small 'vacuum reservoir' (Fig.95) to cope with any leakage between chuck and workpiece. The reservoir is absolutely essential since, without it, the workpiece cannot be held long enough to perform any useful operation. It comprises a length of acrylic tube, with a machined disc at each end. Each disc is fitted with a hollow brass

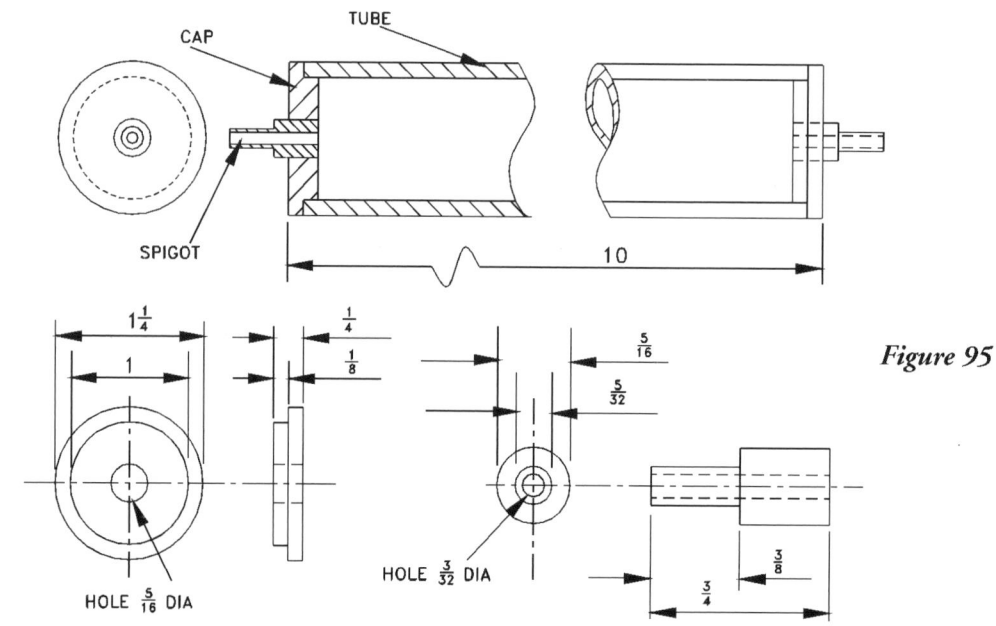

Figure 95

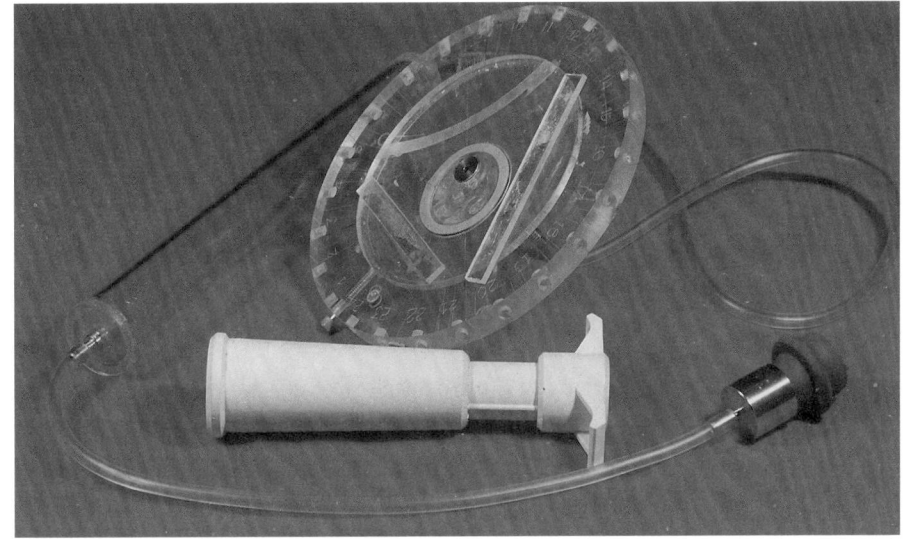

Figure 96

Figure 97

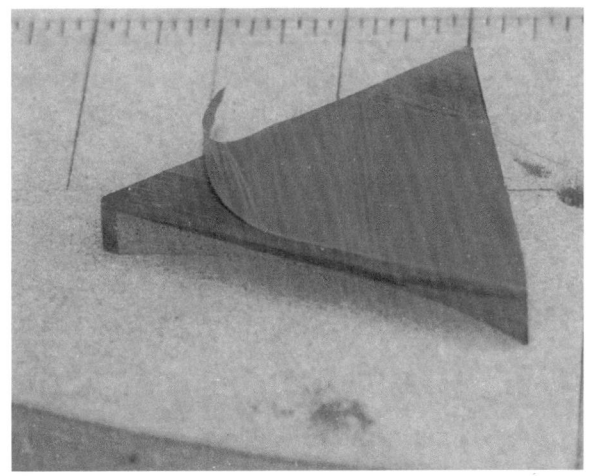

spigot, drilled on a jig as previously described (see Fig.82), the entire assembly being held in place with superglue. Connection between the individual items is made with suitable plastic tubing. It is possible to draw a vacuum giving about 12 PSI pressure with the system. The one snag is that air leakage at the chuck/workpiece interface requires the reservoir to be refreshed from time to time with a few strokes of the pump. The system does work remarkably well however, and at the very least, provides an inexpensive entry into the technique of vacuum chucking. However it cannot, by any stretch of the imagination, be regarded as a substitute for a motorised pump. My complete home-made system is illustrated in Fig.96.

Finally, it must be noted that wood is to some extent porous, and will itself give rise to leakage, particularly if fairly thin. In difficult cases, this may be dealt with by thin plastic adhesive tape, of the kind used for wrapping parcels etc. fitted to the underside of the work. It is easily peeled off after use (Fig.97).

5

EMBELLISHMENT

The production of a piece of routed decorative woodware doesn't normally stop when the router stops; some form of finishing is usually called for. In addition it may be desirable to enhance the appearance of the piece by applying veneer in one or two areas. This chapter is concerned with both activities, but is not intended in any way to be a basic treatise on either, since there are very many books on both topics readily available. Rather it is to be regarded as a collection of small tips and jigs, all of which have a strong bias towards the project content of this book.

To begin with veneering, perhaps one or two basic definitions may be of help: For the purposes of discussion, veneering might be broadly divided into two types. The first involves relatively large areas of timber, covered with sheets or 'leaves' of veneer which may or may not be laid in relatively straightforward patterns of halves, quarters etc., to exploit the

decorative possibilities of the veneer. The second type, which is of more direct interest in the present context, is the use of small pieces of veneer, invariably involving a variety of timber types to form a picture or pattern of some kind. Again it is necessary to make a distinction: The making of pictures is termed 'marquetry'; the generation of designs or patterns, geometric or otherwise, is called 'parquetry', and it is this last technique which forms the basis of the following notes. The lid decoration of one of the projects, which is quite a comprehensive exercise, is used to illustrate the techniques involved, the result being shown in Fig.98. The tools required are very simple, comprising a craft knife, a steel straightedge, a hot-plate, and a home-made trammel, plus one or two other odds and ends which will be dealt with as they are required. It might be worth adding at this point that the processes to be described can provide a great deal of pleasure in

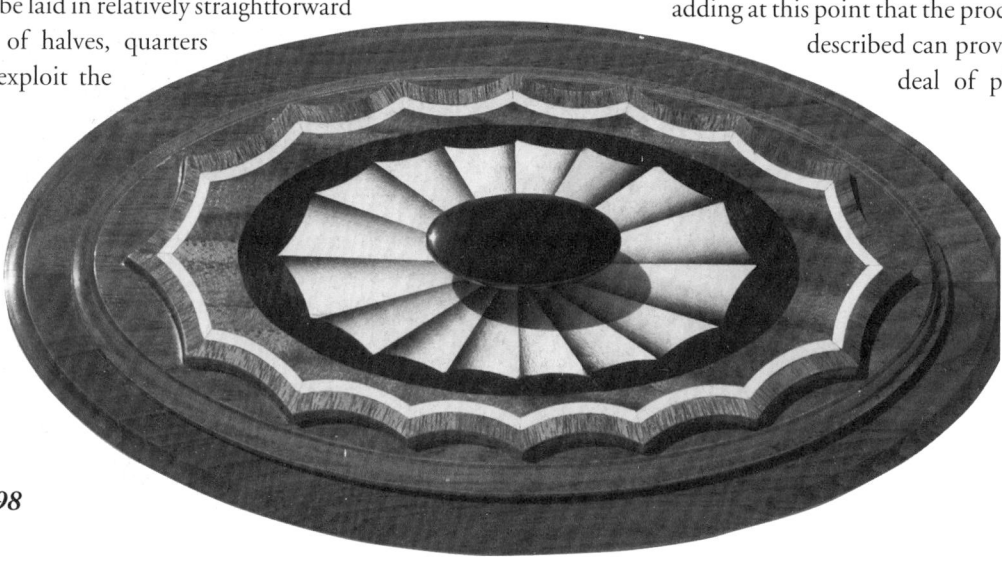

Figure 98

(a)   (b)

Figure 99

their own right, and the reader will, I am sure, find the entire exercise enormously satisfying.

Craft knife blades come in various shapes and sizes, two typical profiles being shown in Fig.99. My personal preference is for (a) since the acute angle formed by the back and the cutting edge allows the blade to negotiate tight curves without ploughing up the veneer on either side, or allowing itself to be pulled off line. This is an important attribute where tight curves are required. A very helpful device in this respect is known as a 'beam trammel', comprising a rod with a point at one end and a stylus of some kind at the other – in this case a knife. It is easily lashed up from a length of dowel and a couple of wood blocks. That shown in Fig.100 is rather more elaborate, due to the fact that I do a good deal of work of this kind. Regardless of how the device is made, a couple of points require a little thought: Although not immediately obvious, the device is required to possess four significant attributes, as illustrated in Fig.101. The

first is that the tip of the knife must be at the same distance from the beam as the point of the pivot. This ensures that the beam is parallel to the work face, which in turn ensures that the knife blade is at right angles to it (a). The second point is that the cutting edge of the blade must be at about 70° to the work-face (b). If the setting is too steep, the point of the knife will simply scratch the work rather than cut it; if too shallow, then too much of the edge will be in contact with the work. When cutting tight curves, this will tend to plough the veneer up on either side of the cutting line. Thirdly, the vertical alignment must put the tip of the blade in line with the pivot point under normal conditions of usage (b). This is actually to ensure that the cutting edge is always tangential to the circumference of the circle being cut (c). If the blade leads or lags the pivot, it will tend to pull inwards or outwards and drift away from the intended cutting line; it will also tend to plough the veneer at the sides. Finally, the tendency for the veneer itself to pull the blade off-line must be dealt with. Craft knife blades are necessarily thin, to ensure clean cutting, but this attribute also makes them a little flexible. Hard veneers are perfectly capable of pulling them in the wrong direction. The tendency can be controlled if the

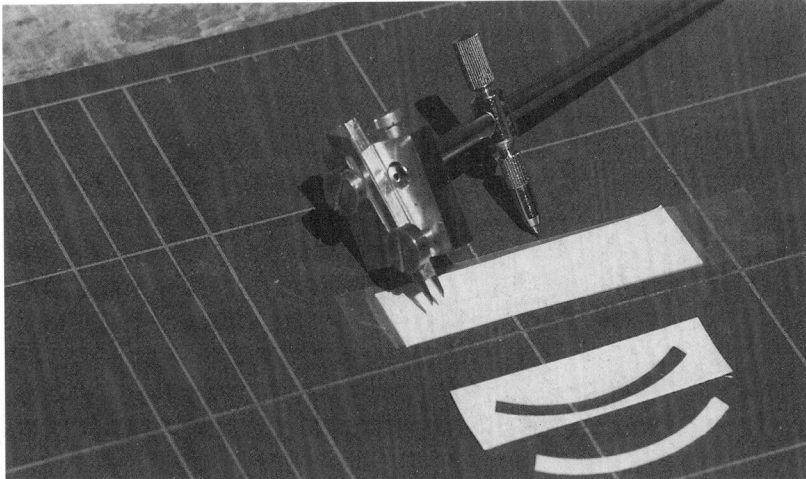

Figure 100

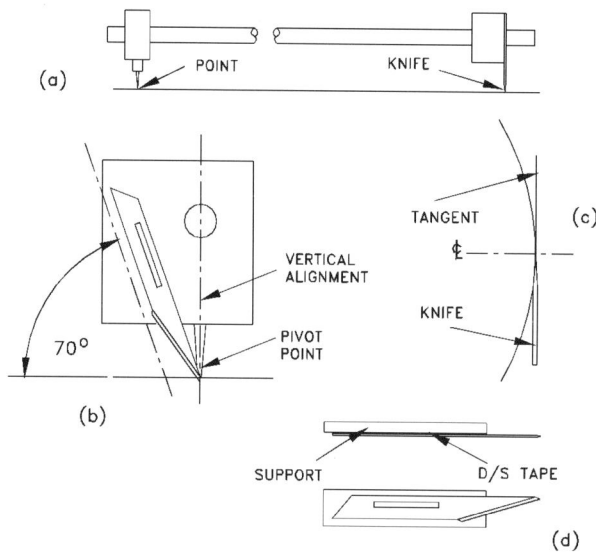

Figure 101

knife is being used by hand alone (it's part of the skill) but, under the constraint of a trammel, there is little opportunity to apply corrective action. The only practical solution is to endeavour to restrain the blade mechanically. Since the blade will be required to penetrate, at most, only two layers of veneer, it is quite in order to fix a metal support to it as shown in (d). This can be done with superglue but, in the interests of rapid blade changing, double-sided adhesive tape is to be preferred. A double bladed version of the trammel can be used as illustrated in Fig.100, to cut curved strips of veneer of a constant known width. In this case, two blades are stuck to either side of a metal support of the required thickness. A further point to note from the photographs is that the tape holding the veneer is transparent, allowing inspection of the cut as it is made. Using tape of any kind also prevents lifting and breakout of short grain.

One small word of warning about veneers might be in order at this point. Many 'exotics' are very difficult to handle. They can be hard, brittle, inclined to split, and tend to take the knife where they want it to go. Macassar ebony, in particular, has caused more spoilt work and displays of bad temper in my own workshop than all the others put together. Strongly coloured timbers (with ebony and blackwood as major culprits) can throw up another problem The colour in these is often in the form of a natural dye, which is soluble in many finishing materials and which can therefore leach or 'bleed' into adjacent veneers to produce a rather muddy effect. To the best of my knowledge there is no perfect solution to this problem but it can, in some circumstances, be alleviated by an application of cellulose or shellac sanding sealer prior to the final finish. The reader is warned however, that this doesn't always work. It is also advisable, if this procedure is adopted, to ensure that the sealer used is compatible with the final finish. A little prior experimentation is time well spent. As far as black (or even various shades of brown) veneer is concerned, there is one method which does not give rise to colour leaching. The method involves burning the timber to some degree, which leads neatly to the topic of sand shading.

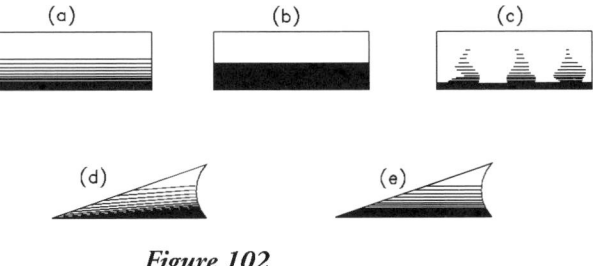

Figure 102

A popular form of decoration, particularly on veneered clock cases, is the shaded elliptical 'fan' illustrated in Fig.98. These may be purchased from veneer suppliers, built up on adhesive paper tape, and are intended to be let in to the main veneer panel. They are glued to the groundwork with the paper tape outermost; the tape is then sanded away when the glue has set. Assemblies of this type are intended to suggest a three-dimensional effect, produced mainly by the shading but enhanced somewhat by the scalloped outer edges. In order to support this illusion it is important that the shading on each individual segment is a smooth transition from dark to light (Fig.102(a)), with no hard edges (b). It is (in my view at least) equally important that the width of the shading is proportional to that of the segment at all points; in other words, the shading pattern must itself be of triangular form (d), rather than that shown in (e). To aid both shading and cutting, the grain of the veneer should be parallel to the longer edge of the blank.

The desired effect is achieved by a careful arrangement of a heat source and a sand tray. The tray, needs to be nothing more than a discarded tin of (preferably) rectangular form, about 1" deep, filled to about two thirds of its depth with clean silver sand. The preferred heat source is a thermostatically controlled hot-plate which, together with the sand tray, must be allowed to stabilise its temperature (determined initially by experiment) before serious work is undertaken, because it is necessary to establish a steady temperature gradient in the sand, ie. hot at the bottom, and less so at the top.

This will produce a corresponding 'blackening gradient' in the piece being shaded. On no account should the sand be raked over or disturbed once the gradient is established, since this will even-out the sand temperature and produce a solid block of black with a hard edge. Readers should be aware that hot sand (and even the veneer being treated) can give rise to painful burns on accidental contact. For this reason, the equipment should be placed in an area where the risk of such contact is limited, and the veneer handled with tweezers or pliers.

Choice of veneer is important. Generally speaking, the lighter the timber, the better the shading effect will be. I have a personal preference for sycamore since it is usually of a creamy white colour which can provide a smooth, attractive transition to a dense black if properly handled. It is also a very 'docile' veneer when being cut. The veneer should be selected to be as bland as possible, and the rippled 'fiddleback' configuration avoided, since the shading is inclined to travel unevenly up the ripples and spoil the three-dimensional effect (Fig.102(c)). Once the temperature gradient has been established, the degree of shading is controlled by the immersion time of the veneer in the sand which, for convenience and control, should be arranged to be about ten to fifteen seconds. The reader is advised that a high temperature and a very short immersion time may well produce a satisfactory result on the surface, but the veneer may not be fully blackened throughout its thickness, leading to disappointment after final assembly and treatment with abrasives. The result is best judged by dipping the veneer into water after shading, and then quickly blotting it on absorbent paper. This procedure will restore moisture lost during heating and will also give a very good idea how the veneer will appear after finishing (which will be appreciably darker than in the dry natural state).

It is of course possible to overdo things. Heating timber in the absence of air is a traditional way of making charcoal. Undue heating will produce carbonisation of the timber at the lower edge, leading to crumbling of the veneer. It is by no means necessary to reach this stage in order to produce a good dense black throughout the veneer thickness. Crumbling is an obvious sign of over-heating, but this is by no means the final criterion. Final checks must be made by cutting thin slivers along the black edge with the craft knife, the object being to produce blanks which may be satisfactorily cut into segments and assembled without damage. However, it is an inescapable fact that some weakening of the timber will occur as a result of partial carbonisation, and it must be expected that the blackened portions will always be rather more fragile than the untreated areas.

It will be seen from Fig.98 that a black ellipse surrounds the basic fan assembly. This is made from sycamore segments. The heat treatment is given by laying the blanks dead flat on a smooth metal plate which itself sits on the hot-plate. A degree of temperature control may be achieved by choosing an appropriate thickness of plate. From Fig.103 it can be seen that the veneer is held down on the metal plate by two

Figure 103

metal rods which are actually rubbed over it during the process. One of the rods is provided with a sharp point, which is used to flip the veneer over once or twice, and also to dip it into water on completion (Fig.104). Note also that the rods are fairly long; they need to be, since the radiated heat can become very uncomfortable.

With the basic materials to hand, the design may now be cut and assembled. This follows established parquetry practice, and requires little elaboration here other than perhaps to suggest that the blackened edges of each fan segment are dealt with first, since the first cut will be of a fairly arbitrary nature, and the second cut to final size will be on the rather less fragile white edge. Knife work is best made directly over a drawn plan. In this way, the segments may be cut precisely to size and shape at the possible expense of a few photocopies. Rather than work all round the design, ending up with a single segment which will require very careful trimming to fit, it is preferable to make the assembly in two identical halves which then only require a straight line to be cut on one or both to obtain a good fit.

The complete assembly is then taped to a photocopy of the master drawing (a photocopy is very necessary here, since it will be destroyed during the following process). Despite the fact that the assembly will hide most of the drawing, it may still be aligned accurately by means of the major and minor axes on the drawing and the corresponding joint lines on the workpiece. The trammel is set to the required radius, and its pivot point placed on each of the marked centres on the drawing in turn to cut the scallops. Each individual scallop is taped to the drawing at its outer edge. The trammel knife thus cuts through the tape and the veneer in a single stroke, thus preventing lifting and breakout of the veneer (Fig.105). The tape may be removed at each stage to inspect progress, but fresh tape must be added at intervals, to maintain registration with the drawing.

The set of fully blackened segments are now used to form the elliptical surround for the fan. These are

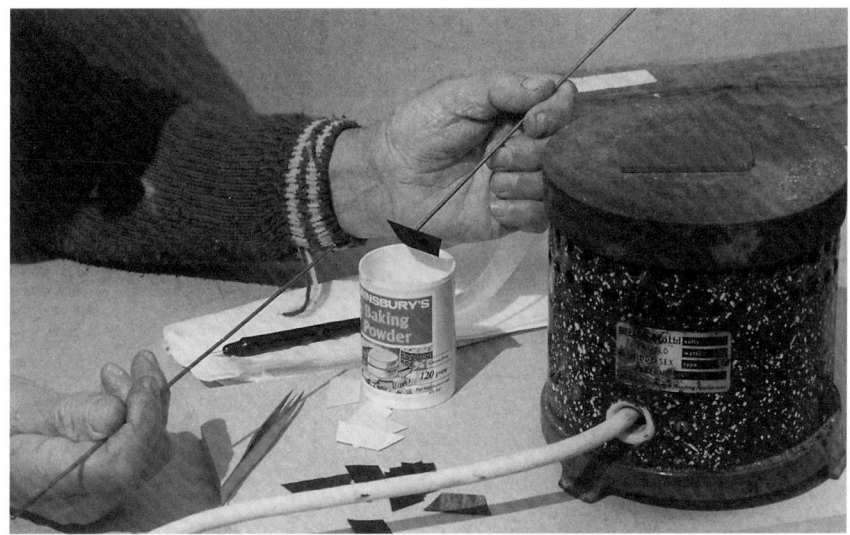

Figure 104

prepared initially by taping them individually to the cutting mat and forming the necessary radius on the shorter of the two long edges, with the trammel setting unaltered. Each segment in turn is now fitted and taped to one of the scallops on the fan, and its straight flanks trimmed against a straightedge, using the joint lines on the fan as a guide. As the fitting of each piece is completed it is attached to the fan on the underside with thin plastic tape. The outer edges are roughly trimmed to a slightly oversize ellipse as work proceeds.

The following operation is perhaps that which requires the most care, as it involves cutting through two leaves of veneer at once, to provide a clean elliptical joint line between the completed assembly and the veneer sheet base into which it is fitted. The base veneer should be sufficiently large to cover the final 'groundwork' of the box lid, with a generous spare allowance all round. The assembly is first taped reasonably centrally to the base veneer, and then a drawing of the required elliptical joint line is taped to the assembly. Note from Fig.106 that the drawing includes major and minor axis lines, and that the centre of the drawing is cut away. This

Figure 105

Figure 106

ference being that the bandings are cut using a double-bladed trammel knife as illustrated in Fig.100. The parts are fitted to the main assembly with thin plastic tape on the underside, as before. Finally, the entire top surface is divested of all traces of clear plastic tape and examined very carefully to ensure that no small pieces have been missed. It is then re-taped all over with gummed paper tape, as marketed by veneer suppliers for this specific purpose. The plastic tape on the underside is then removed, at which point the assembly is ready for fitting to the groundwork.

This particular operation may be carried out with cold setting 'white' glue (PVA). I personally coat only the groundwork, since I find a 'one side' coating adequate. It can be quite tricky to evenly coat the veneer assembly in any case, since there is plenty of opportunity to cause damage. A wide spreader or a brush with short stiff bristles is to be preferred, to ensure all-over even coating. The glue is allowed to become tacky before the veneer is presented to the groundwork; this reduces risk of movement under cramping.

It is very important to have everything prepared for this final stage. In particular, registration marks must be made on both the veneer assembly and the groundwork to ensure swift accurate location (the tackiness of the glue will rarely allow a successful second attempt without risk of damage to the veneer assembly). It is also sensible to have a fairly stout, flat baseboard of approximately the same size as the groundwork, to ensure that plenty of cramps may be applied all round the work. Finally, the top cramping plate may be a sheet of clear acrylic, about $\frac{1}{4}$" thick. This can be supplemented by as many local wood cramping blocks as necessary, to spread the load and avoid marking the acrylic unduly. The primary purpose of the acrylic is only to allow inspection of the work as initial cramping proceeds; it may be more or less fully covered by cramping blocks as more are added.

With regard to finishing more or less any type of

allows accurate registration of the ellipse with the fan. Note also from this illustration that, although the knife is angled with the veneer in the direction of travel, it is at right angles to it in the crosswise plane, thus producing a vertical cut between both pieces. Some workers angle the knife such that the fit between the pieces is slightly wedge-shaped in cross section. Whilst I regard this technique as useful if pairs of veneers are sawn (it tends to remove the gap left by the saw kerf), I do not see it as necessary for knifed work. This is of course a purely personal view. When cutting is judged to be complete, the entire assembly is turned over and inspected to make sure. Any uncut parts of the lower section may tear away on separation and spoil the work. The central portion of the base veneer is placed in the offcut box (never waste anything), and the fan assembly fitted inside the base veneer and securely taped on the underside all round, again using very thin plastic tape. The scalloped banding may now be added, using exactly the same techniques as previously described, the only significant dif-

woodware, my own preference is for a high-gloss effect. I appreciate that this is not to everybody's taste, and the following notes are included only for the reason that a finish of this type will reveal the slightest blemish or unevenness in the groundwork, and is therefore arguably the most demanding in terms of timber preparation. Regardless of type of finish, the basic task is that of bringing the bare wood to a state where it is actually worth putting a finish on it. I suspect that more work, of otherwise excellent quality, is spoilt by lack of attention to this process than from any other cause. Master cabinet-makers will achieve this on their work directly from a well-honed (and cunningly used) plane or scraper. This is rarely possible with routed work; it will require further attention with abrasive paper or cloth, my own preference being for an aluminium oxide abrasive, resin-mounted on a flexible cloth backing. Even the best abrasives can become clogged, particularly if used with resinous timbers (many 'exotics' have this characteristic). Apart from its general nuisance value, the clogging can accumulate into hard spots, which can then scour the work and thoroughly upset the finishing process. It is wasteful to simply discard the abrasive when it becomes clogged; far better is the use of a proprietary cleaning block made from a rubbery compound. This is at its most efficient when applied to a revolving sanding disc for example, since the motor does all the hard work. It is very effective however, when applied manually. Fig.107 shows a shaped sanding block being cleaned by this means. Although something of a chore, it should be done regularly.

I very rarely use abrasive coarser than 240 grit for bare wood preparation. I can think of only two exceptions offhand, both being concerned essentially with the removal of wood rather than finishing. The example illustrated in Fig.108 is the use of a power drill to form a dome on a small knob, in the absence of a lathe. The second example deals with a rough finish left by the router cutter. This may usually be ascribed to the type of

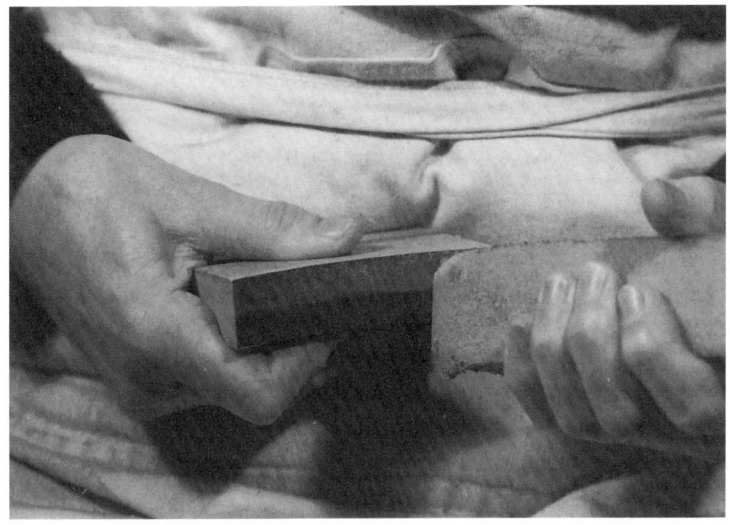

Figure 107

Figure 108

is involved, finishing of the internal sharp corners in particular can pose a few problems. It is sometimes possible to avoid these altogether by designing the project in such a way that the individual parts can be assembled after finishing. In the particular case illustrated

Figure 109

timber being worked, rather than careless use of the router. A typical example is illustrated in Fig.109, which depicts a 'before and after' situation. The timber in this case was particularly loose in the grain, resulting in the characteristic lifting and triangular tearing exhibited by the sample on the left. The sample on the right, which started life in much the same state, shows the result of the application of 120 grit abrasive. Because the amount of wood removal in such cases is significant, a shaped sanding block is an essential requirement to avoid losing the intended profile of the piece. There is in any case, a strong argument for using shaped blocks for the true finishing operations. They help to avoid dubbing over on edges (Fig.110) and are a great help in dealing with sharp internal angles (Fig.111).

To some extent, wood finishing begins with the initial design of the piece. Where segmented work, built up from a number of parts of the type shown in Fig.110

Figure 110

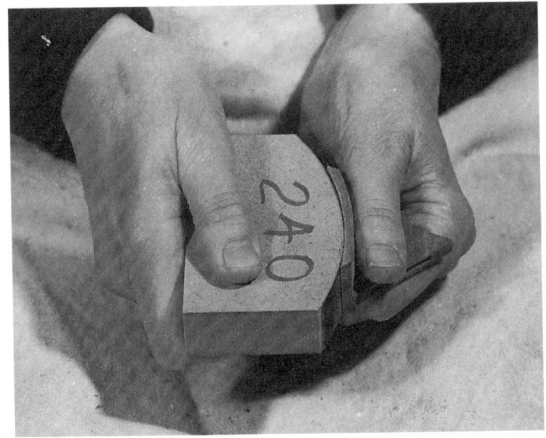

Figure 111

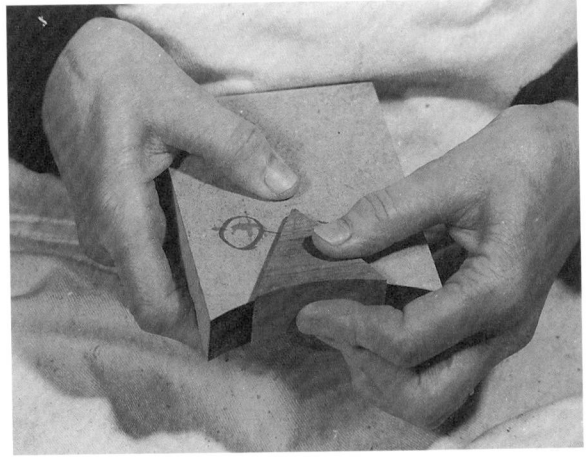

in Fig.112, it was possible to polish the base as a completely flat object and insert the pre-finished scalloped sides afterwards. Although the preferred solution in this case, techniques of this kind can often succeed only in transferring problems from finishing to assembly.

Regardless of the type of abrasive work in progress ie. bare wood or finish coats, local over or under-sanding must be avoided, particularly where glossy finishes are required. A widely used method of dealing with the internal corners of a box or tray is the use of a wood block with abrasive sheet stuck to it. The hardness of the block can lead to one or two difficulties however: Perhaps the worst is the generation of radial ripples (Fig.113(a)). These are insidious faults. On bare wood, they can go completely unnoticed. Only when the finish builds up to a transparent gloss do they decide to reveal themselves, and it's too late then. Although the intention is always to keep the block dead flat, this cannot be guaranteed and is thus one cause of the problem; another is simply that of staying in one area too long. A hard block also tends to cause loss of abrasive grains at the edges and the corners (b) and can also encourage clogging and hard spots in the abrasive. Blocks of the type illustrated in Fig.114 go a very long way towards solving the problems. They are easily custom-made in any shape or size from scrap materials. Acrylic sheet is suitable for building up the blocks, since this accepts superglue readily. The blocks are faced with hard rubber sheet, also with superglue. In the absence of more suitable material, a discarded car or motor cycle tyre will serve, provided the block is not sufficiently large for the compound curvature of the rubber to become a problem. After assembly, the entire sandwich is profiled on a disc sander. Finally, a piece of abrasive sheet is fixed to the rubber with double-sided adhesive tape, and trimmed with a knife (which will require re-sharpening afterwards). Blocks of this type are particularly valuable when rubbing down hard finishes with 'wet-and-dry' abrasives, as they don't mind getting wet.

Figure 112

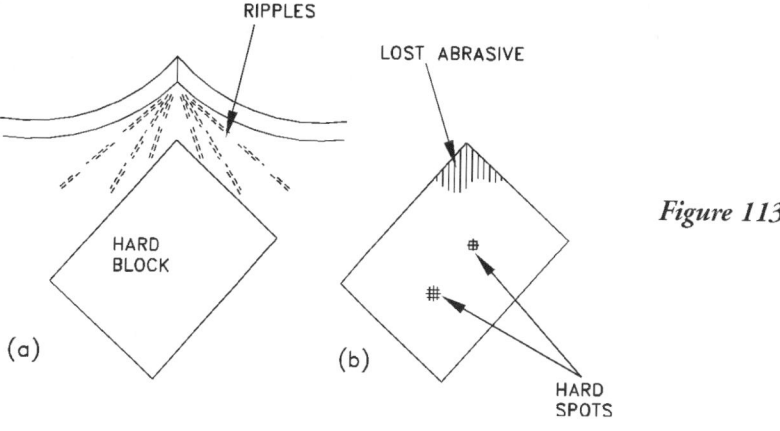

Figure 113

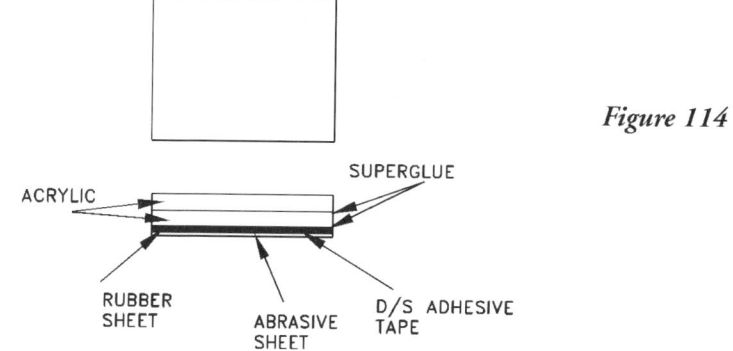

Figure 114

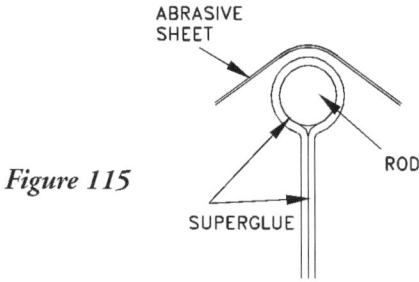

ABRASIVE
SHEET

ROD

SUPERGLUE

Figure 115

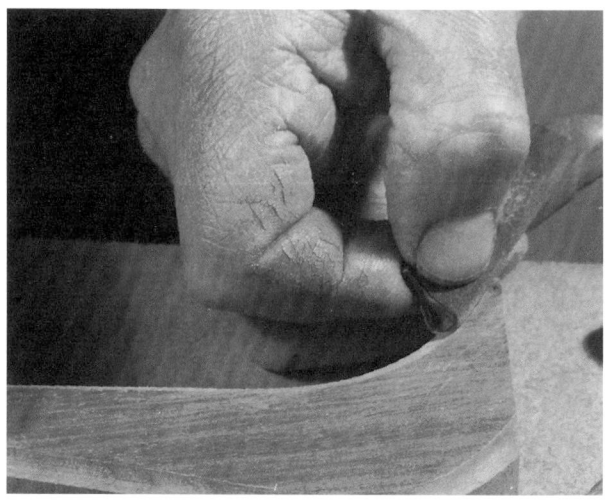

The principle may be extended to deal with cove profiles. These can be a problem where the plan-form of the workpiece is also curved, since the resultant cove presents a compound curve to the abrasive. In this case, a small piece of rubber sheet is coated with superglue, wrapped round a short length of metal dowel of any desired diameter, and quickly popped into a vice, to provide a former of the type shown in Fig.115. The abrasive is simply wrapped over the former, rather than being stuck down, since the abrasive needs to be changed fairly frequently due to the small area of contact with the work. It is shown in use for wood preparation in Fig.116, and for rubbing down in Fig.117.

Sanding the bore of small items such as napkin rings is difficult enough at the best of times. If the surface of the bore is at all rough, it becomes virtually impossible by hand methods. A simple drum sander mounted in a power drill, as shown in Fig.118 is very effective. For best results, the diameter of the drum should match the bore of the workpiece fairly closely, but then requires some care in use (and a low drill speed), since it is inclined to snatch. The process can also generate a surprising amount of dust, and an extraction system is very desirable.

Whilst on the subject of small items, the actual application of liquid finish can present a problem or two. The first is the obvious one of holding the work. Small cylindrical plastic containers, as supplied with 35mm. film cassettes can be put to good use if they are cut up and

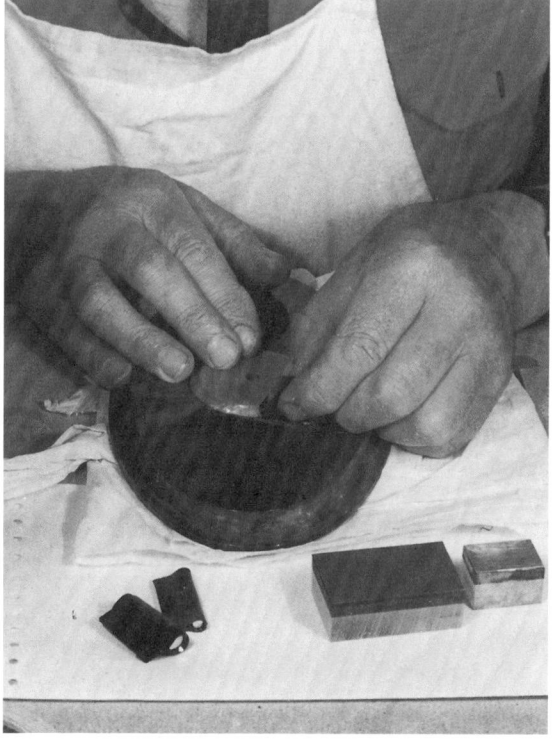

Figures 116 & 117

Figure 118

Figure 119

inserted into a mandrel as shown in Figs 119 and 120. The plastic is sufficiently springy to hold the bore quite firmly whilst applying finish to the outer surface. Note the use of a wheel-brace to rotate the work; this is a great help, not only when applying the finish, but also for a short time afterwards, to ensure that the finish doesn't run to the lowest point and cause a build-up.

Figure 120

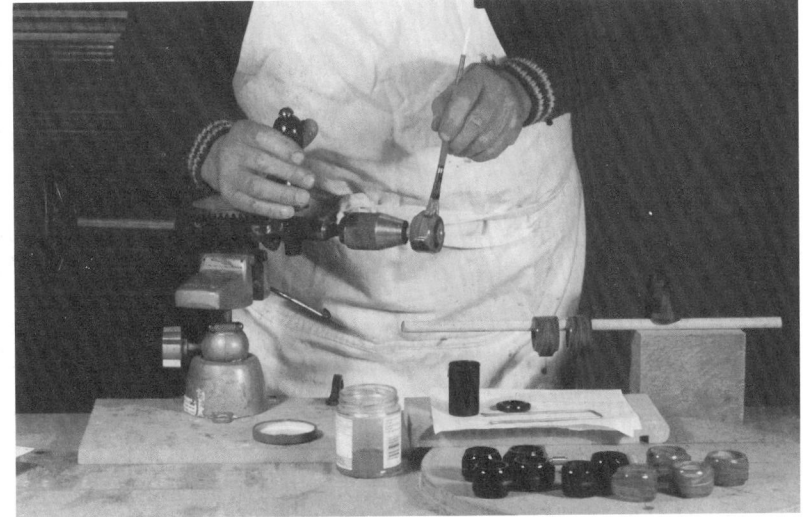

6

OTHER JIGS

The jigs in this chapter were originally developed in support of the projects later described but they have since found uses beyond these and may therefore be considered as general purpose jigs. The first to be described is one of my personal favourites due to its versatility, despite the fact that it was originally intended only to cut the indexing holes in Pivot Frame secondary discs. In the form illustrated and described, it is designed for use with the Elu MOF96 router series, although it could be modified to suit other router types without undue difficulty. Basically, it is a device for boring the edges of flat workpieces. It comprises a flat horizontal panel for mounting the router, fixed to a vertical panel, which is actually the work-surface. The two are joined very accurately at right angles and well-braced, such that they cannot move or flex in use. The router cutter is intended to overhang the vertical workface by some predetermined amount. In its most elementary form, the router is simply cramped or screwed to the top panel in a fixed position, and indeed this is the way I used it originally for indexing secondary discs (Fig.121). If the top panel is fitted with a slider, which may be set and locked in position, as shown in Fig.122, other tasks are possible. The router is fixed to the central moveable slide, using the tapped holes in the router base normally used for fixing guide bushes. In the ELU MOF 96 series routers, these holes are tapped M5, but readers are advised that the imperial 2BA screw will also serve. The fixed slide members are slotted, to allow an initial setting-up of the jig such that the centre line of the router cutter is aligned with the centre line of the vertical panel. This panel is bored with one or two ˇ" diameter holes on its vertical centre line. These allow secondary discs to be fitted and rotated as necessary, to bore the indexing holes in the rim. It may be found necessary at a later stage, dependent upon the type of work undertaken, to add one or two 'random' holes in the vertical panel for the purpose of attaching a simple home-made clamp, as shown in Fig.123. The arrangement is very useful for boring holes in segmented work, particularly where the timber grain is likely to cause a normal drill to wander off line. A num-ber of horizontal lines are also drawn across the vertical face and used for the alignment of flat-edged workpieces requiring dowel holes to be bored in their edges. The lines are also used for the alignment of horizontal straight-edged battens, which can be used as fixed supports for edge-boring on repetition work, or supports for work which is required to be moved laterally for successive boring operations. The depth of hole is of course set by means of the plunge stop on the router itself.

The basic panel assembly as illustrated in Fig.124 is very easily constructed from MDF or comparable material. The only point to watch is that the two panels are very firmly fixed and are dead square to one another. The real 'meat' of the job lies in the sliders (Fig.125).

Figure 121

Figure 122

Figure 123

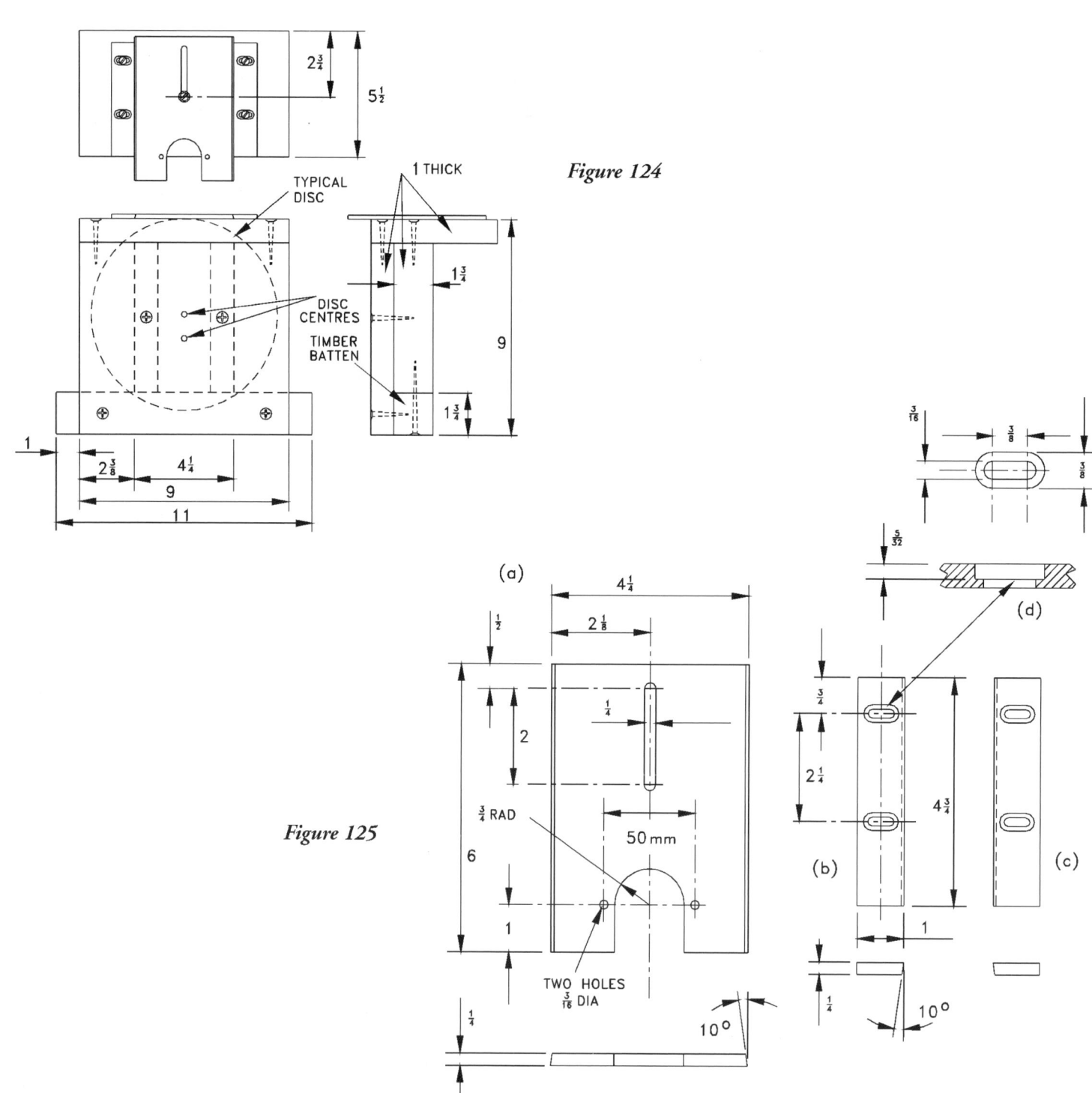

Figure 124

Figure 125

The slide material chosen here is Tufnol, mainly on account of its dimensional stability. It is most important that the dovetail slides are machined accurately. In particular, the flanks of the central slider must not only be straight; they must also be dead parallel. The outer slides merely need to be straight on their dovetailed edges, since a degree of adjustment may be made when they are finally fitted in place. A suitable cutter is a plain dovetail cutter, of about 10° flank angle; this should be of tungsten carbide, due to the abrasive nature of Tufnol. The router is used in ski mode (any accurate ski system incorporating the router guide rods will serve) against a dead straight fence, on a flat worktop. The three workpieces comprising the slide system are sawn to the required overall dimensions and attached to the worktop such that they are parallel to the fence, and have a working gap between them to allow plenty of lateral adjustment on the cutter. The reader is referred to Fig 39 and its associated description in Chapter 2 for this task, with particular reference to feed direction. The remaining holes and slots in the slides may then be routed, using a similar fence system to machine the counterbored slots.

Tufnol is not a particularly easy material to work with. Feed direction is of the utmost importance, since even a light cut will snatch if fed in the wrong direction whilst constrained by a fence. When machining short slots, it is also very easy to allow the router to drift off line as Fig.126 bears witness. In this particular case, since the device is ultimately a workshop jig, the loss of appearance is merely annoying, rather than disastrous.

The second jig will machine strips of veneer, or even thin bandsawn timber to a predetermined thickness. There is an initial amount of trial and error in setting up, involving the router depth stop, either by means of a calibrated screw adjustment (if present), or with feeler gauges used in conjunction with the simpler rod and anvil stop. Once set, the thickness of the strip will show little more than .001" variation, wherever it is meas-

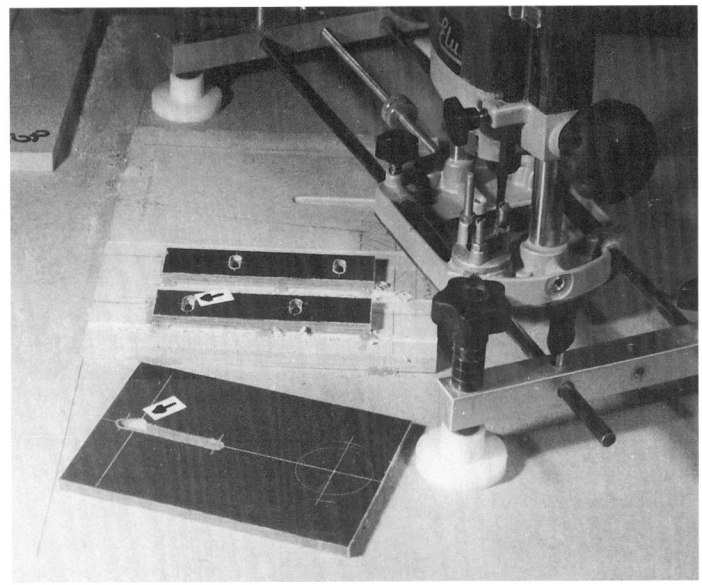

Figure 126

ured. Moreover, this accuracy will be maintained over as many strips as required. Most of the credit must go to the router itself, since the jig is little more than a flat plate screwed to its base.

Although useful in a wide variety of applications, the jig is in fact specialised in that it serves only the purpose stated earlier (I haven't been able to think of any others as yet). It will therefore only be of use to readers intending to carry out inlay work, typically as described in some of the projects. It has the advantage of being very easy to make. In my own case, the transition from initial idea to the full working model illustrated in Fig.127, 128 and accompanying photographs, took little more than half a day's work. On the other hand, the jig does require a vacuum pump, since it is very difficult to hold veneer down for this type of machining by other means. Unfortunately, the simple manual pump described in Chapter 4 cannot be used. As will be

Figure 127

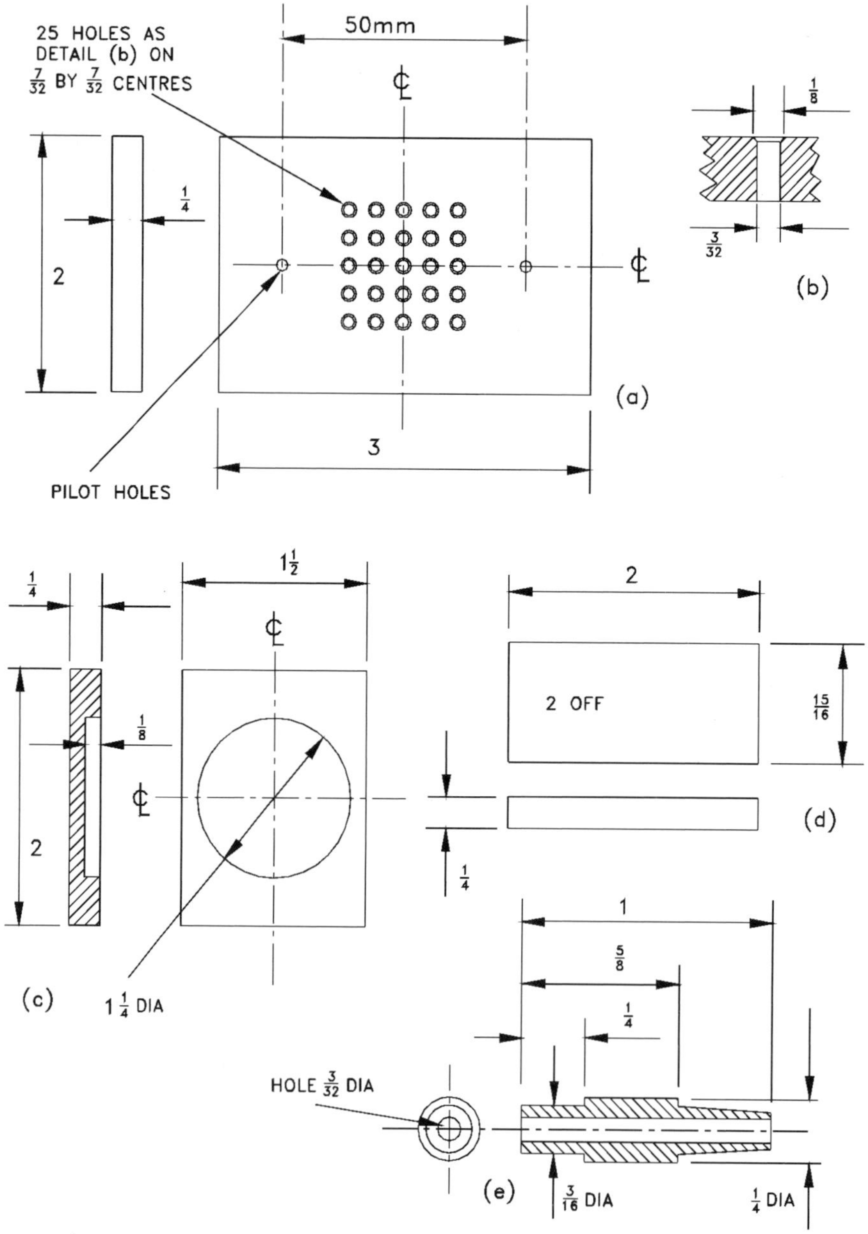

25 HOLES AS
DETAIL (b) ON
$\frac{7}{32}$ BY $\frac{7}{32}$ CENTRES

50mm

$\frac{1}{4}$

2

3

PILOT HOLES

$\frac{1}{8}$

$\frac{3}{32}$

(b)

(a)

$\frac{1}{4}$

$1\frac{1}{2}$

2

$\frac{1}{8}$

2 OFF

$\frac{15}{16}$

2

$\frac{1}{4}$

(d)

(c)

$1\frac{1}{4}$ DIA

1

$\frac{5}{8}$

$\frac{1}{4}$

HOLE $\frac{3}{32}$ DIA

(e) $\frac{3}{16}$ DIA $\frac{1}{4}$ DIA

seen, the veneer is drawn through the jig as it is machined; this implies a degree of air leakage, which cannot be maintained by the manual pump.

It might be sensible to outline the problem to begin with: router cutters come in fixed sizes, and will therefore machine grooves of fixed dimensions when used in a single pass. They are remarkably accurate in terms of diameter, and can therefore be relied upon to deliver the goods as specified. One or two surprises may be thrown up by the timber itself. Wood is compressible, to a degree which varies from one species to another. This is not normally a problem but, when working to very tight tolerances as demanded by inlay work, the resultant variation in channel width, although tiny, may make all the difference between a good fit and a bad one. It is of course always possible to vary the width of cut simply by adjusting the router a little on its fence or trammel. I do not care for this method, and only use it in cases of dire necessity for the following reasons. A slight over-cut on channel width may ruin the job beyond recovery. Even if a successful result is obtained, it can only be guaranteed for the actual work in progress, and must be re-done if repeat jobs to the same design are required at a later date. Finally, it is by no means unheard-of for a given design to be repeated in another timber type; in this case, further adjustment may be necessary for the reason given earlier. It is far safer (from the viewpoint of the main workpiece) to deal with the inlay material instead. The accuracy of the jig allows very precise thickness settings to be achieved and, even if mistakes are made, the material (and effort) wasted is fairly trivial. All this may sound just a little 'over the top'. I can only invite the reader to make a joint with a 'five thou' gap in it, and see how obviously poor it is. Cabinetmakers, who do not normally talk in dimensional terms at this level, nevertheless work to them, often by hand, and would not tolerate a 'five thou' joint. On the other side of the coin, an inlay which is too thick by much the same amount, wouldn't fit, wood compressibility notwithstanding.

Some idea of the capabilities of the jig may be gauged from Fig.129. This segment is actually a 'waster' from one of the projects, and is used here only as a demonstration piece. Both inlay channels were machined with a $1/16"$ diameter cutter. The width of the channels was measured at .062". The stock sycamore veneer thickness was measured at .023", and was reduced to .020" for the three-layer inlay, and to .012" for the five-layer inlay.

Jig parts are made in $\frac{1}{4}"$ thick acrylic sheet, apart from the vacuum spigot, which is (preferably) in brass. Acrylic provides the smooth impervious surface essential to vacuum work and is very easily 'gas-tight' jointed with superglue. It is also easily worked by hand if necessary. Figs 127 and 128 are, I think, self-explanatory in terms of making and assembling the jig, but Figs 130 and 131 will help also. Note however, that both the spigot and the fixing holes are drilled after assembly.

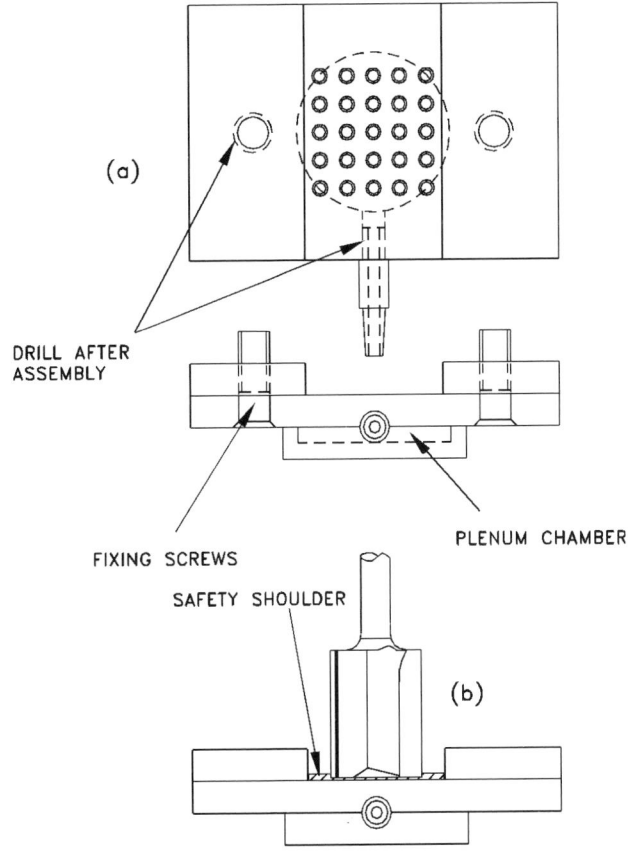

Figure 128

Figure 129

Figure 130

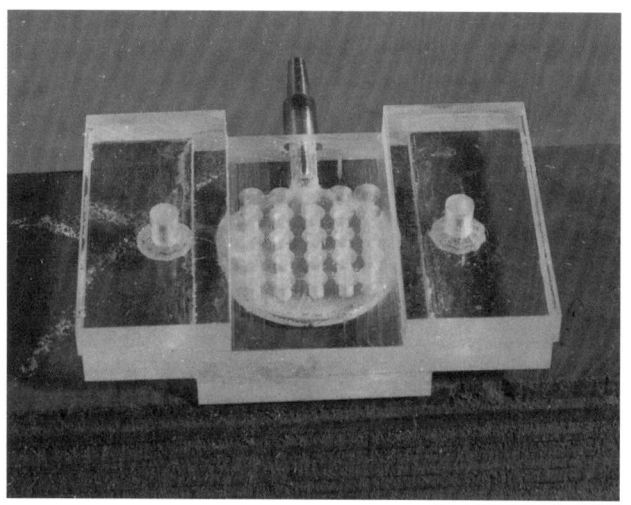

Figure 131

The veneer, which is initially knifed into strips 1" wide, is drawn across the platen, guided by the two acrylic side cheeks. The vacuum holds the veneer dead flat to the platen, thus allowing the veneer thickness to be determined with reference to the surface of the platen. The reason for the light countersinking of the twenty-five small holes is to increase air pressure at the interface with the veneer, without unduly weakening the structure. Since the jig is bolted dead flat to the router base, there is no question of 'spring' when plunging the router; this is where the accuracy comes from. It is very important that the cutter is not allowed to approach the edges or the ends of the strip. The cutter diameter must be chosen to leave a slight shoulder at the sides, as shown in Fig.128(b). If the cutter contacts either edge, it will lift the veneer, even against the vacuum. This does not present a hazard to either the jig or the operator, but the veneer will be torn to pieces.

Similarly, the process must be started and finished leaving a short un-machined section at each end, in order to ensure that the platen holes are not uncovered whilst the cutter is rotating. The veneer is conveniently controlled by attaching a strip of plastic adhesive tape to one end, and using this to pull the veneer through the jig.

In use, the veneer is laid on the platen, the vacuum applied, and the cutter brought down to lightly touch the veneer surface, and the plunge knob locked. Extra depth as required is now set on the depth stop, which is then locked at this setting. The plunge knob is released, the motor started, and the cutter plunged to the preset depth and locked. The veneer is then simply pulled through the jig (Fig.132). The plunge is released and the router and vacuum pump switched off. After trimming away uncut waste, the veneer is ready for use. The reader is advised that .010" is about the minimum thickness limit. There is no reason in principle why the jig itself could not do better than this, but timber porosity in relation to available vacuum becomes a problem and, in any case, it would be difficult to envisage a practical application for the resultant veneer.

The next item, although a jig of sorts, is really a 'universal' worktop which allows Pivot Frame and beam trammel applications to be set up rapidly. It is basically nothing more than a large sheet of MDF bearing a number of holes and slots. Many of the photographs in the book show the worktop in use in one way or another. It is intended to be used with a 'Workmate', since this allows underside access to the fixing bolts, both at the edges and at the centre. A minor snag in this configuration is that the worktop tends to determine its own flatness. This is not a problem when primary discs are fitted to it, but where it is used alone, as in planing or beam trammel work, it should be checked for flatness and either it or the workpiece adjusted with packing if necessary. A better arrangement, if space permits, is to provide it with its own stand.

The entire worktop, set up with two Pivot Frame

Figure 132

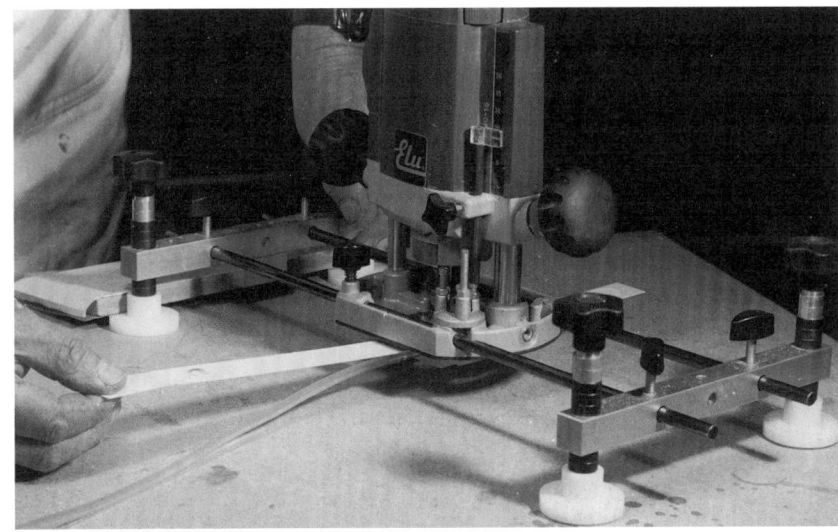

Figure 133

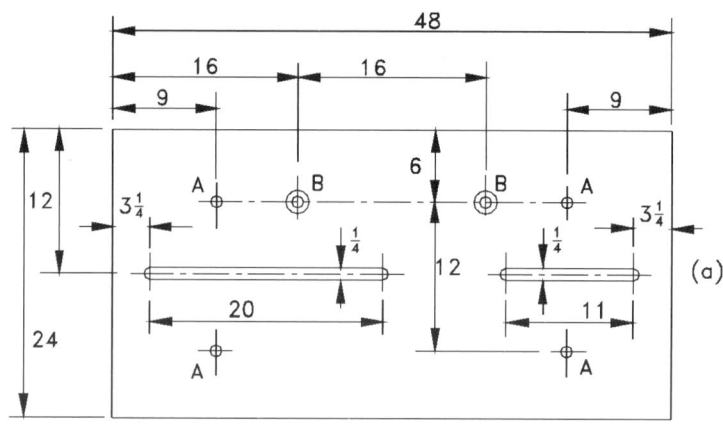

(a)

HOLES

A $\frac{1}{4}$ DIA

B $\frac{1}{4}$ DIA CBR $\frac{5}{8}$ DIA
     BY $\frac{1}{4}$ DEEP

C $\frac{1}{16}$ DIA PILOT FOR
     NO.8 WOODSCREW

NOTE: HOLES AND SLOTS
          NOT DRAWN TO SCALE

Figure 134

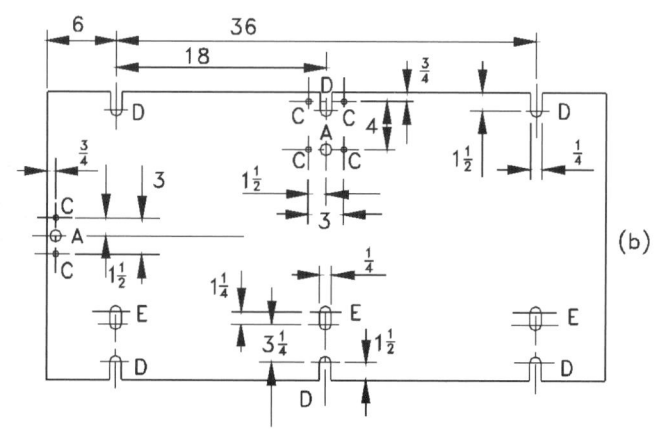

(b)

applications is shown in Fig.133, and the layout in Fig.134. The two views in the drawing each show some of the holes and slots required, in the interests of clarity; the complete worktop does of course require all of them. The two counterbored 'B' holes are used to attach the worktop to a Workmate, using existing holes in the latter. It is as well to check the hole spacing on the Workmate to begin with, as this can vary in different editions of the device. The four 'A' holes accommodate primary discs, one at each end. Although the user may have only one Pivot Frame, it is likely that more than one primary disc will be available, and it is often convenient to transfer from one to another. The two slots permit secondary discs to be used, since they sit immediately beneath the slots in the primary disc, allowing clamping bolts to pass right through. The longer slot is also used where a secondary disc is used directly with a beam trammel. The left-hand group of 'A' and 'C' holes provides a station for a pivot block, which may be made from a scrap of hardwood (Fig.135). This may be clearly seen in Fig.136, which also shows the router overhanging its ski, as required for large radii. Two further stations for the same block are provided: at the top centre of Fig.134(b) is a set of 'A' and 'C' holes; these allow a full 180° swing of a beam trammel. The pair of 'C' holes immediately above, in conjunction with the central 'D'

Figure 136

slot, serve a similar purpose but, in this case, allow a small increase in available radius at the expense of a reduction in arc length. A typical set-up is illustrated in Fig.137, but no projects are offered for this configuration.

The six 'D' slots are intended to be used in conjunction with a pair of straightedge guide battens, made from $\frac{1}{2}$" thick plywood, as drawn in Fig.138. The slots

Figure 137

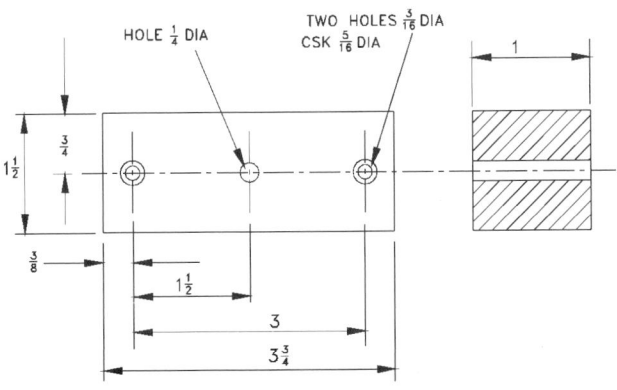

Figure 135

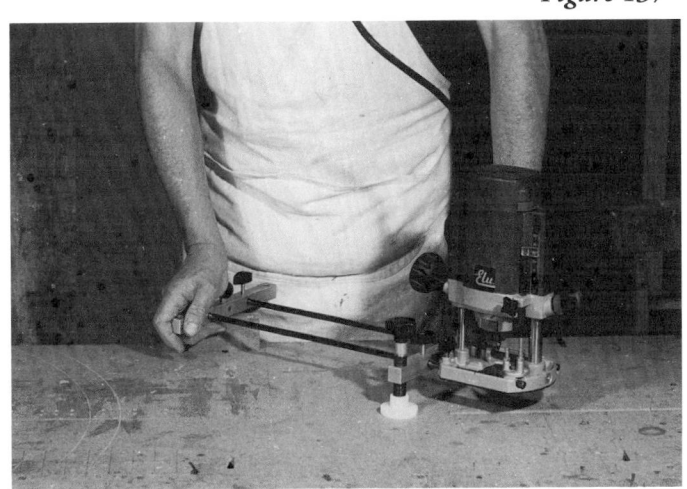

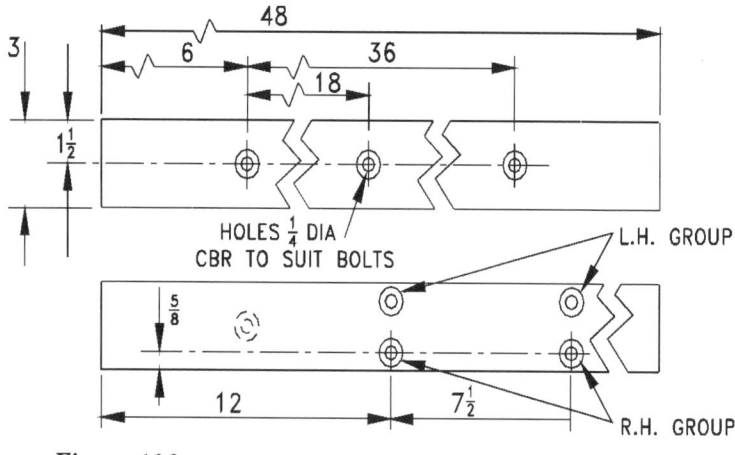

Figure 138

permit adjustment of the batten positions, to ensure that they are parallel in planing mode. They can also be used for slotting applications in conjunction with temporary end stops, as illustrated in Fig.40, Chapter 2. Finally, the top batten may be transferred to the 'E' slots, to provide a narrow channel for step and repeat work (see Fig.41, Chapter 2).

The remaining items in this chapter deal essentially with primary disc details. Whilst discs will generally be made in accordance with user requirements, one or two observations may be in order. A slot intended for use with a secondary disc must lie on a radius with the pivot point as centre; any lateral offset error is bound to impair machining accuracy. The length of the slot is somewhat arbitrary. I find it convenient to terminate the slot about 2" from the edge of the disc (Fig.139(a)),

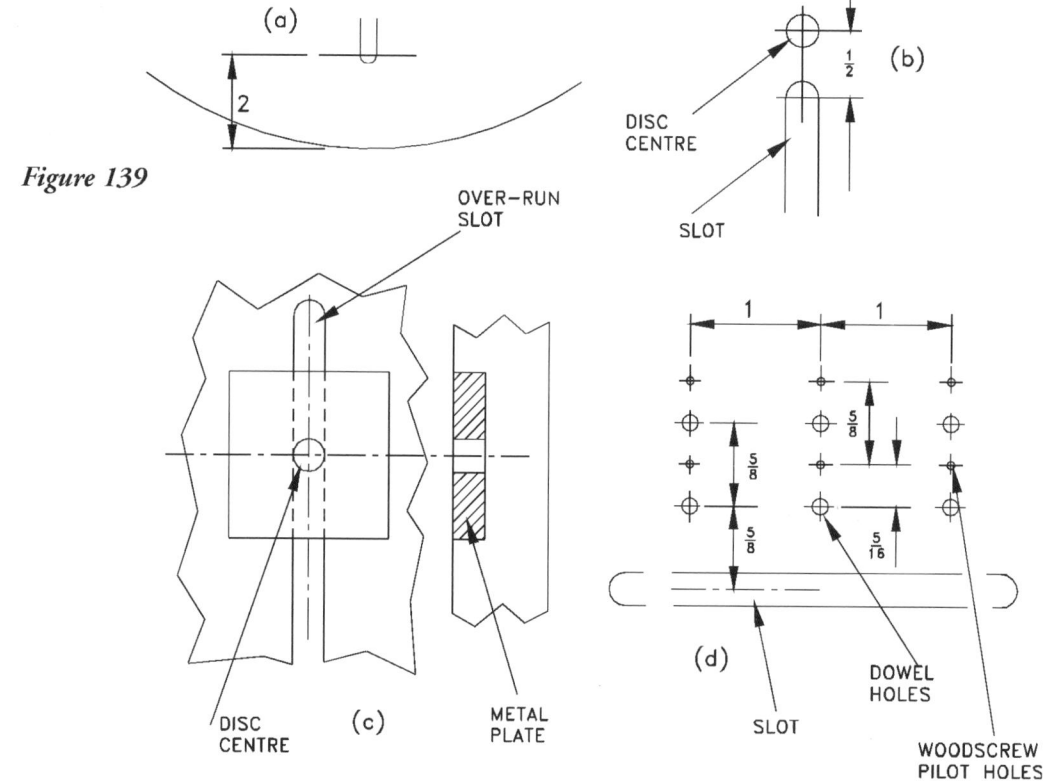

Figure 139

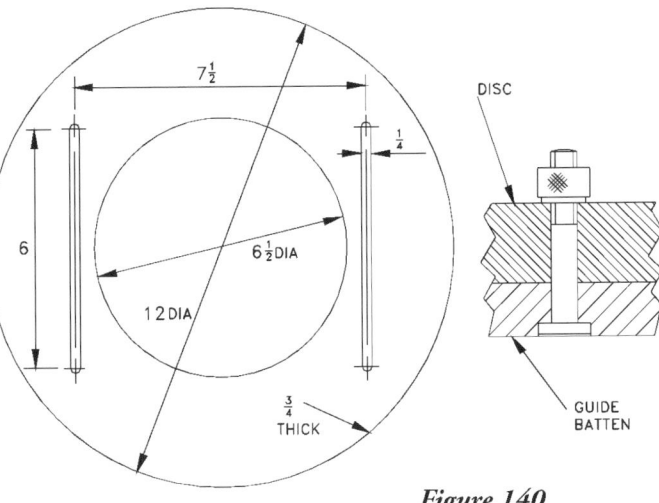

Figure 140

regardless of disc diameter. Two options are open at the centre of the disc which, for maximum convenience, should retain its centre in the form of a $\frac{1}{4}$" diameter hole. The first is simply to stop the slot short of the hole (b). The second option (rather better to my mind) is to mount a removable metal plate in a recess, to maintain the centre, but at the same time allowing the slot to overrun the centre (c). This feature will be found useful on occasion, since the arrangement shown in (b) will not permit a minimum offset capability.

It will be found convenient on both primary discs and the universal worktop to provide a series of identical hole patterns at convenient intervals (d) to accommodate a number of positions for the stop blocks illustrated in Fig.17, Chapter 1. The holes must be arranged such that the axis of the metal rod lies precisely on the centre line of the slot.

A primary disc suitable for step and repeat work, using the short router rods is illustrated in Fig.140. This should be studied in conjunction with the guide battens (Fig.138). Note that the disc counterbores are on the opposite face of the battens from those intended for

fixing to the worktop, and that they also cause the battens to be right-and left-handed. In use, the general idea is that the workpiece is slid a step at a time along the channel between the battens and is arranged to stand very slightly proud of them. The nuts holding the disc down, when screwed finger tight, will thus clamp the disc to the workpiece. The slots in the disc allow it to be adjusted laterally with respect to the workpiece. To this end, the disc may be marked with suitable registration lines on its inner edge; these can then be aligned with similar marks made on the workpiece itself. It is important that the slots in the disc are machined parallel and at right angles to the axis of the guides (and hence the workpiece). It is equally important that the holes in the battens are accurately placed; any error which causes the slots to incline with respect to the workpiece axis will make registration impossible. Finally, the bolts holding the disc to the battens must be as short as possible to avoid fouling the base of the router, and their heads must be a reasonably tight fit in their counterbores to allow the nuts to be tightened without rotating the bolts. Figs 43 and 44, Chapter 2 give some idea of the capabilities of the set-up.

One of the major attractions of the Pivot Frame jig is that it constantly presents new possibilities. The following jig, which is in the form of a minor addition, is very much a recent thought and I have yet to explore its

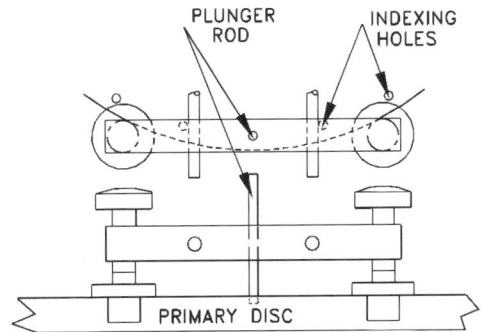

Figure 141

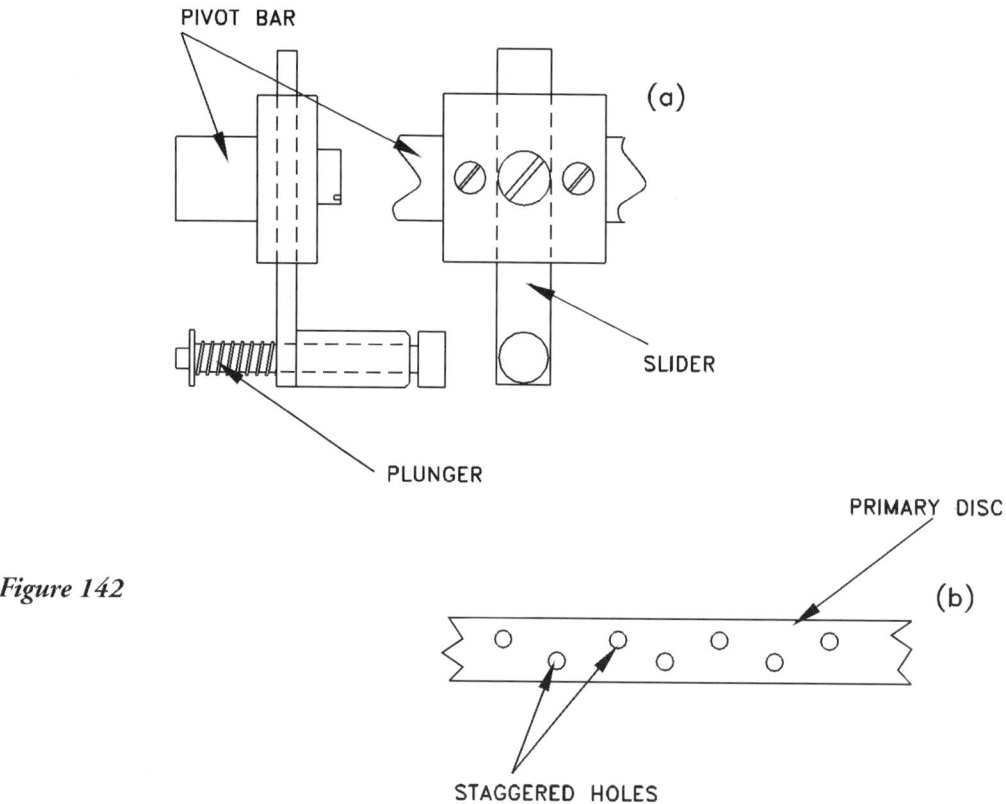

PIVOT BAR

(a)

SLIDER

PLUNGER

PRIMARY DISC

Figure 142

(b)

STAGGERED HOLES

possibilities fully. However, its more obvious attributes are so useful, that it is worth including here. It is basically a simple indexing system, which allows the Pivot Frame to be locked at any one of a number of angular settings around the primary disc. In its simplest form, it may comprise a length of M6 studding, or even a plain metal rod fitted into an existing tapped hole in one of the pivot bars (Fig.141). The rod engages with any of a number of drilled holes around the top face of the primary disc, thus forming a simple indexing system. The simplest application is that of boring sets of

similar holes around a workpiece, at a diameter determined by the position of the router on the guide rods. Woodturners who lack indexing facilities on their lathes will find this useful in many ways, and in particular when making the popular mushroom-style holders for ladies' earrings . A rather more advanced application is that of machining sets of radial slots in a workpiece by locking the Pivot Frame and sliding the router on its guide rods, against stops set on the micro-adjuster. This gives rise to a number of decorative possibilities, one of which is featured in Project 1.

For occasional use, the arrangement is quite acceptable as it stands, provided that the fit of the rod in the pivot bar is reasonably tight, since any sloppiness will transfer itself to the work. The only drawback is that the indexing holes tend to become clogged with wood residues, and need to be cleaned out occasionally. For this reason, a rather better arrangement is featured in Figs 142 and 143. This requires an extra item, bolted to one of the pivot bars. My own version is (as always) made in metal, but a simpler version would be possible in acrylic or Tufnol sheet. The only difficult item, in the absence of a metalworking lathe, is the spring-loaded plunger, but this is merely a convenience, and may be supplanted by a simple plain rod. The vertical slider is necessary however, since the device must cater for changes of 'ride height' of the router. The indexing holes are bored in the edge of the primary disc, conveniently by means of the jig described at the beginning of this chapter. It is also convenient to bore two or more sets of holes around the disc, staggered as illustrated in Fig.142(b). In use, the plunger is simply set to the required set of holes, which may then be used freely, without risk of confusion with the remainder.

As described, the device is capable of producing rather interesting effects. The reader is also invited to explore the possibilities of using it in conjunction with the indexing and offset arrangements afforded by the secondary disc system described in Chapter 1. In particular, the machined slots, although radial with respect to the primary disc, need not be so with respect to the workpiece, due to the secondary disc offset facility. Moreover, the possibility of using two different sets of indexing on the same piece is very interesting indeed, but the reader is warned that it can also become a little confusing.

Figure 143

7

SAFETY

The camera cannot lie! Fortunately, it can occasionally be persuaded to refrain from telling the entire truth. Fig.144 looks (and is intended to look) extremely dangerous. In fact there is no danger at all – the router isn't even plugged into the mains socket. The entire set-up was contrived to illustrate a number of rather silly practices. The cutter is unguarded and protrudes well beyond the top of the workpiece, which is being constrained by a fence whilst being fed in the wrong direction. To cap it all, there is no dust extraction. The photograph gives notice of the fact that I intend to deal with the subject of safety in a slightly unusual (and I hope, interesting) way, rather than embark on a boring treatise which nobody will bother to read.

Many aspects of safety are very straightforward. One doesn't, for example, put one's fingers too close to a revolving circular saw; the possible consequences are quite obvious. To pursue the circular saw topic for a moment however: the purpose of the riving knife behind the sawblade is perhaps a little less obvious; that is, until one has been hit on the head by a piece of wood which has been picked up by the back of the saw. (There should of course be a sawguard present also, to prevent this, among other things, but the essential principle remains).

Router safety considerations may be approached in a similar way. It is not at all a good idea to put the fingers too near a revolving cutter. With most routers used in

Figure 144

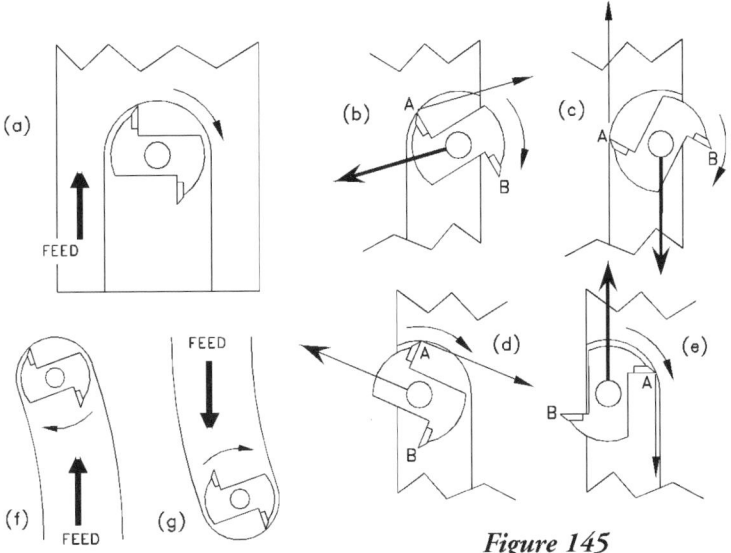

Figure 145

the hand-held 'overhead' mode, it isn't all that easy anyway. On the other hand, if the router happens to be mounted upside-down beneath a spindle-moulding table as in Fig.144, access to the protruding cutter is much easier and special measures have to be taken, not only to guard the cutter itself, but also to hold the work firmly against the table and the fence (if fitted). Moreover, 'safety' can refer not only to the user, but also to the piece being made (nobody likes to waste time or material), and by no means least, the well-being of the router and its cutters.

Most of the rules covering the safe usage of the router are based on plain commonsense, and require very little in the way of understanding of the 'internal workings' of the machine. There is one aspect of the router however (arguably the most important), which depends essentially upon the way in which timber is removed by the revolving cutter, and it is this which I wish to cover in detail. The related general rule is usually expressed along the lines of 'always feed the router in the direction of cutter rotation'. This is undoubtedly a very sound rule but, like most, is better for a little understanding of what

it means and the underlying reasons for it. Incidentally, unless specifically stated otherwise, *all* operations to be described refer to the use of the router in the normal hand-held 'overhead' mode, whether constrained by a jig or not.

Fig.145(a) shows a plan view of a 'straight' router cutter machining a shallow channel in a workpiece. The cutter is revolving in a clockwise direction from the operator's viewpoint (this is the standard direction, regardless of make or type of router or cutter). The direction of feed is shown by the arrow, and the reader is asked to imagine the router being pushed in this direction by the operator. The actual removal of timber is carried out by the leading semicircle of the cutter profile; the trailing half is revolving in free space, in the area where timber has already been removed. Regardless of cutter sharpness, there is bound to be some frictional resistance between the cutter edges and the workpiece. Considering the left-hand side of the cutter only for the moment (imagine a rebate), and taking a brief 'snapshot' of the action (b), point 'A' on the revolving cutter is moving to the right at the instant shown.

Frictional resistance will therefore try to pull the cutter (and the entire router with it) to the left, as shown by the barbed arrow. Consider now, a different instant on the same rebate (c). Here, point 'A' is moving in the direction of manual feed; in this case, friction will cause the cutter to resist the manual feed direction, and try to push the router back towards the operator, again as shown by the barbed arrow. This is actually what 'feeding against cutter rotation' means. Referring now to the right-hand rebate (d): by the same reasoning, point 'A' on the cutter is pushing sideways to the right against the workpiece, again producing a tendency to move the entire router to the left. Finally, the snapshot (e) shows perhaps the most important action: point 'A' on the cutter is attempting to enhance the direction of feed; in other words, there is a tendency for the router to be snatched along the line of the cut; this can be a real

Figure 146

'nasty', but can be controlled and actually beneficially used in certain, very specific, circumstances. When machining a full channel, the combined pushing and pulling effects of (c) and (e) tend to cancel one another out. However, the effects shown in (b) and (d) actually add to one another since, when point 'A' is cutting the wood, point 'B' will be moving through the region where the wood has already been removed, and will therefore be doing no work. The tendency for the router is therefore to move to the left (f), as a result of the *combined* effects of (b) and (d). By a similar mechanism, if the feed direction is from top to bottom, the router will drift to the right (g). The effect is enhanced as cutter diameter is increased. The foregoing explains, to some extent, why freehand operation of a router demands a high degree of skill. The effect is shown 'for real' in Fig.146, where the only manual force is in the feed direction indicated; the router is free to move laterally as it pleases. In this photo-graph, the router is actually being pulled, for clarity's sake. I can think of no better way to introduce the reader to this aspect of router behaviour than to suggest an experiment on these lines, using a cutter of about $\frac{3}{4}$" diameter and a very shallow feed of about $\frac{1}{16}$".

Most router operations are however, carried out under some kind of mechanical guidance in the form of a jig or a fence. It might be thought that an addition of this kind takes care of all things, and the operator has no further worries. Surprisingly perhaps, the presence of a fence or similar restriction can make operation rather more risky than its absence. This statement obviously requires justification. Consider now Fig.147(a), where a rebate is being machined at the edge of a length of timber. The side of the router is being guided by a simple timber batten fence. The router will be pulled against the fence as it is moved in the direction shown, some resistance to applied feed will be felt, and all is well. If the router is moved in the other direction (b), the rotating cutter will tend to push it away from the fence. There is no very great personal danger here since, although there will be a tendency for the cutter to snatch, the tendency to push itself away from the work will eventually stop the cutting action altogether. There isn't much risk to the workpiece either, but it will require further machining, with the router held firmly against the fence. A feed of this kind is often regarded as bad practice, due to the snatching tendency (and it is if used unwisely). I would contend however, that it has its uses; indeed it will be positively recommended as the 'safer' option in one or two project activities, as will be seen. This type of feed relative to cutter rotation is described as 'climb milling' by metal machinists. For convenience, the term is borrowed for use elsewhere in this book. There is an associated rule which, in my own view at least, should be adhered to *absolutely without reservation*, regardless of feed direction, and that is limitation of cutting rate. The rate of removal of stock is very much under the control of the user; the router may well protest at the treatment it is receiving, but will nevertheless do its best to meet the task imposed on it, however ill-judged.

Fig.148(a) shows a different set-up. In order to make the discussion point more forcefully, it is shown in a slightly unusual way (one would not normally set up a fence system quite like this). The feed, combined with cutter rotation will cause the cutter to snatch at the timber, but the associated tendency to pull itself away from the work is prevented by the presence of the fence. In this case, the snatching tendency is quite severe, because the cutter has no option but to pull itself further along the length of the timber and, if the depth of cut is large enough, it becomes quite uncontrollable. This can be dangerous for the operator, dependent upon severity; it is positively guaranteed to do the workpiece no good at all. As noted, this set-up is not a normal one, but it would be quite easy, in an absent-minded fashion, to set up a router with its own fence against a straightedge as in (b). This arrangement may appear safe enough on the face of it, but in fact it is essentially the same as (a), and carries exactly the same risk. Thus, it does pay to give these matters some thought prior to a machining operation. Fig.148(c)

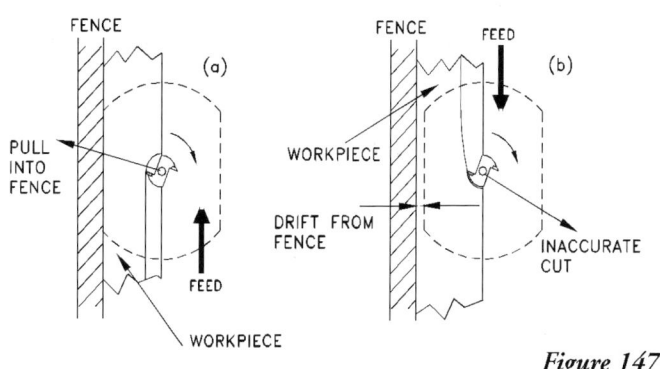

Figure 147

Figure 148

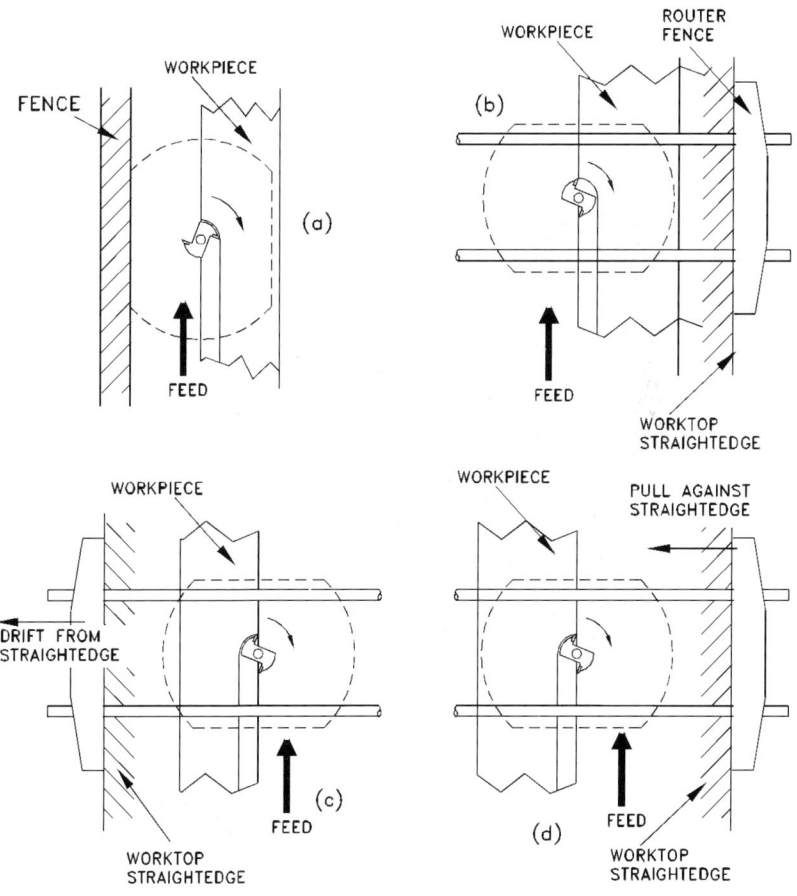

shows a left-handed version of (b). This puts the feed in an apparently safe direction relative to cutter rotation. In my own view, this arrangement is highly unsafe. It may well be that the operator, in the interests of safety, is machining a series of passes at small depth increments. This is fine in principle, but there is a tendency for the router to drift to the left (the fence won't stop it) and, even after a series of successful passes, there could be a sudden, very savage bite into the work. This could cause the operator to lose control, and will also tend to pull the cutter out of the collet, giving an even deeper bite. Even if the operator gets away with it, the workpiece will suffer irreparable damage. An arrangement which satisfies all requirements is shown in (d). Here, the feed is in the safe direction, and the fence/straightedge combination prevents overcutting of the work.

Even the kind of constraint imposed by a trammel system, where the cutter is locked on a circular path, does not escape the snatching tendency of an unwisely fed cutter. In this case, the feed direction must be anticlockwise (Fig.149(a). A clockwise feed is quite likely to drag the router around the work, due to the path restriction imposed by the trammel, which acts rather like a fence in much the same way as Figs 148 (a) and (b). Similarly, when cutting the inner edge of an annulus which has been pre-sawn, the feed direction must be clockwise (Fig.149(b)). Feed direction is of little importance if the cut is being made from the solid

Figure 149

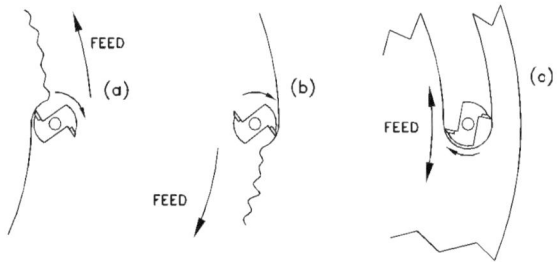

(c), since the cutter is engaged with the work on both sides, and the snatching and resistive effects tend to cancel.

Four factors govern stock removal: cutter speed, lateral feed rate (applied by the operator), depth of cut and, by no means least, cutter sharpness. Cutter speed, although generated by the rotational speed of the router motor (ie. rpm), is also associated with cutter diameter. For a given rpm value, the outer edge of a large-diameter cutter will travel faster than that of a small one. For example, for a single rotation, a point on the edge of a $\frac{1}{2}$" diameter cutter will travel about $1\frac{1}{2}$". A point on the edge of a 1" diameter cutter will travel about 3". Thus, for a given value of rpm, the cutting edge of the larger cutter will travel at twice the speed of the smaller. The speed at the edge of the cutter is referred to as the 'peripheral speed'.

Peripheral speed limitations will, in effect, be dealt with by the cutter maker, who will, for the larger cutters at least, generally specify the maximum recommended speed for a given cutter. Smaller cutters (generally those with $\frac{1}{4}$" diameter shanks) may be run at the maximum speed which the router will give. Computer-controlled systems aside, lateral feed rate is manually applied, and is therefore very much under the control of the individual user. Excessive feed is rather difficult to define, since it cannot be observed or measured under normal workshop conditions, but it *can* be heard. Under no-load conditions, the router motor will make a distinctive noise (invariably a cross between a hoot and a scream – routers are not particularly noted for quiet behaviour). As a cut is applied, the speed will drop, and this will be indicated by a drop in the pitch of the sound produced by the machine (ie. the 'note' will be lower). The same effect may be produced on variable-speed machines by means of the speed control. A small drop in note under load is perfectly normal and is to be expected. A marked drop, particularly when accompanied by a 'growling' noise from the router (caused by 'arcing' in the motor), indicates that the machine is being severely overloaded. The load may be curtailed by a reduction in lateral feed rate or (usually better) by a reduction in the depth of cut. The foregoing noise is easily noted and recognised, by the way, even when wearing ear-defenders.

The professional user may well want to take relatively heavy cuts to save time – fair enough; he or she is probably using one of the larger machines anyway. To my mind however, there is little or no justification for heavy cuts where the amateur worker is concerned, particularly in the form of an unduly large 'depth of cut' setting, this last being, to my mind, the worst crime against the router which can be perpetrated. Overload brings with it a number of unpleasant effects: lateral pressure on the cutter as it is forced against the workpiece will strain the cutter, the collet and the router bearings (and in extreme cases may break the cutter). It will also demand extra power from the machine, which can only come from one source – the electrical supply, in the form of increased current. This, in combination with the inevitable reduction in speed, will generate electrical arcs between the motor commutator and the brushes supplying the current. These arcs are not the same thing as the sparks one might expect, for example, when tool-grinding. They have more in common with the effect produced by electric-arc welding and, over a period, can be very damaging to the motor. The work-rate demanded can also produce excessive heat in the cutter (particularly if it is a relatively small one). Cutter heating is perhaps the least important as far as 'the machinery' is concerned, particularly for tungsten-carbide cutters, which will stand a great deal of abuse. The workpiece may suffer quite severely however. All things considered, a heavy rate of stock removal has very little going for it, and certainly has absolutely no place in the making of the relatively small objects covered in this book.

Finally, the question of cutter sharpness needs to be considered. The blunting of a cutter over a period of time is an insidious business, and can creep up on the user, who may well continue to use a cutter well beyond the point at which it should be re-sharpened. If it can be managed as an experiment, a salutary lesson can be learnt from the use of a blunt cutter followed by a brand new one of the same type on the same operation. Easily the most dramatic effect of a really blunt cutter (which will do the workpiece no good at all) is the production of blue smoke – a sharp cutter will not normally produce this effect, even if it is abused. This effect, by the way, is not to be confused with the limited local burning of the workpiece which can occur if the rotating cutter (even a sharp one) is allowed to dwell in one place for too long. This is a matter of technique rather than safety. The real safety hazard likely to arise from a blunt cutter however, is simply a requirement to increase lateral pressure, and thus risk cutter breakage in the short term. In the longer term, it will also add to the wear and tear on the router (particularly the collet).

There can be some advantage in feeding the cutter in the 'wrong' direction, in some circumstances. It is only after a good deal of thought (and some hesitation) that I feel prepared to deal with this matter at all. I cannot stress too highly that the practice is *only* to be attempted with the benefit of an understanding of what is actually happening between the cutter and the work, and then only with light cuts. This said, the benefit can be obtained in two ways: The first concerns finish. Referring to Fig.150(a), a cutter fed in the normal direction will, due to friction, tend to break away cross-grain timber as the cut is completed. The effect is basically due to the fact that the timber is unsupported (by more timber) at the point where the cutter bites into it. The fitting of a 'spelch block', typically as in (b) can help a great deal. Reversal of feed direction, thus producing a climb milling cut will also tend to eliminate these effects, as shown in (c). The method works by virtue of the fact that, at the point of entry, the cut is very light,

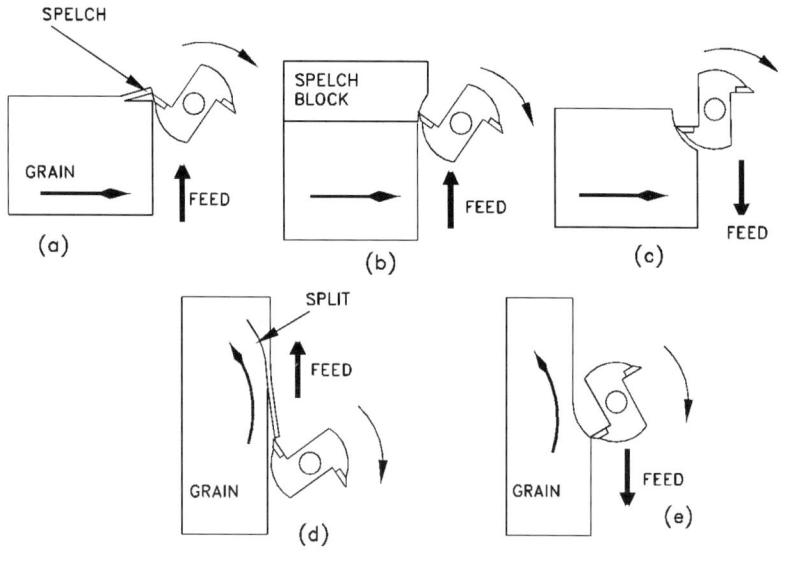

Figure 150

ie. the unsupported area is very small. Continuation of the cut works in such a way that the workpiece is always offering support at the cutting point; finish is usually improved as a result. A similar tearing effect is shown in (d). Here, the cutter is removing a relatively thin sliver of timber which, by virtue of slightly 'wild' grain, tends to run into the work and spoil it. As can be seen from (e), grain direction does not affect a climb milling cut.

Mention was made earlier of the tendency of the cutter to push itself away from the workpiece when climb milling. The tendency can be used to advantage when using the router as a light planer. Figs 151 and 152 show how a series of back and forth planing cuts can be taken, starting at the sides of the workpiece and gradually working towards the centre. When used in this way, the sideways feed into the workpiece must be applied by the operator, against the tendency of the cutter to push itself away from the work.

Figure 151

Figure 152

To return to the 'growling' noise: this can also be generated by vibration of the workpiece (with experience, it is possible to distinguish between this and 'arcing'). Vibration can indicate that the work is inadequately held for the cutter load applied. The same noise can occur, even for work which is held firmly, under conditions such as shown in Fig.153(a), where a disc is being produced from a square blank. In this case, the cut is fairly deep, leaving waste timber at the edges. Despite the fact that the cut is (or should be) made in several stages, the tendency of timber to 'relax' or decompress after cutting will ensure that some contact remains between the cutter and the waste material, causing the latter to vibrate. There is an element of risk here: if the cut is taken almost to the bottom of the work, contact with the cutter can cause the waste to fly off, and possibly ricochet back into the cutter, with rather unpredictable consequences. The effect may also cause tearing-out of the timber at the bottom face of the workpiece. It is by no means a bad idea to trim the waste down with a chisel as the work proceeds. Either of two techniques may be used, dependent upon grain direction, as shown in (b) and (c), and involve some element of deliberately splitting the timber. A far better general solution, wherever possible, is simply not to allow the problem to occur, either by sawing away most of the waste before routing (the better solution from the cutter's viewpoint), or by arranging for the cutter to remove the waste as work proceeds.

The router collet bears a little examination. There may be a tendency to regard it as simply 'the thing that holds the cutter". So it is, but it is also a very carefully-engineered device, and deserves respect. The general idea behind a collet of any type is to generate as much 'gripping area' between the collet and the tool shank as possible and, at the same time, to ensure concentricity of the cutter with the router mandrel. For a parallel-shank cutter, it follows that the bore of the associated collet must also be parallel (Fig.154(a)). In view of the fact that

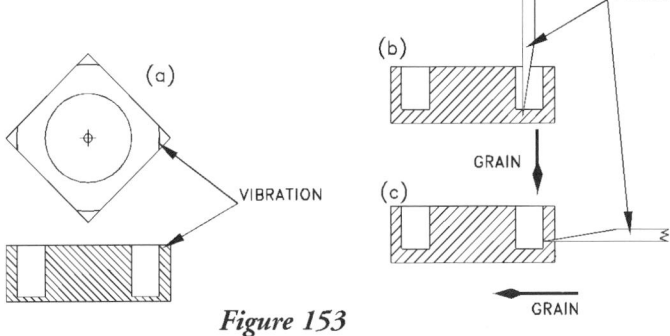

Figure 153

the collet must be tightened on to the shank, the reduction in bore of the collet to allow this to happen must be carried out in a special way. The action is achieved by slitting the collet along its length. Relatively simple collet designs will be slit in four places, from one end only; better-quality pieces will be slit in eight places, four from each end (b). The action relies upon the fact that the difference in collet bore diameter from open to closed is very tiny. It follows that both the collet and the cutters designed to fit it are machined to very close tolerances. The action of tightening the collet nut, is to push the tapered collet into its matching housing on the machine rotor, and thereby cause it to close *very slightly*. From the user's point of view therefore, a collet designed to fit, say,

Figure 154

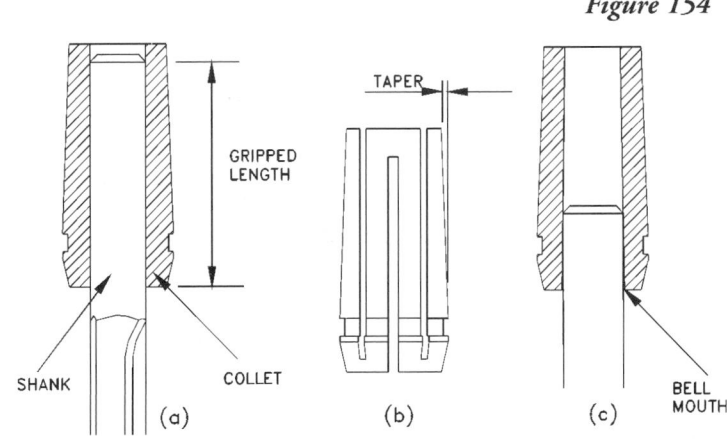

$\frac{1}{4}$" diameter cutter shanks should be used for these and nothing else. Forcing a collet to accept a larger or smaller size is to court almost certain damage. To be sure, this kind of practice is unusual; more common, perhaps is the usage shown in Fig.154(c) and Fig.155. In this case, the cutter is inserted insufficiently far into the collet, in an attempt to gain a little extra working length. This causes the collet bore to close in a tapered fashion, rather than truly parallel. There are a number of unpleasant side effects arising from this practice: the cutter will not be accurately centred to begin with. As work proceeds, the inevitable sideways pressure on the cutter from the workpiece will increase the off-centre effect and, sooner or later, the cutter will 'walk out' of the collet, with unpredictable consequences. Persistent use of this practice will inevitably cause the collet to wear at the point of cutter insertion, and become 'bell-mouthed'. At this point, the collet is of no further use, even if subsequently treated correctly. Care of collets may be summed up quite simply: keep them (and the cutters) clean; use the correct cutters, and make sure that most of the shank is inside the collet (Fig.156).

A further rule applied to collets is 'do not overtighten

them'. Whilst making sense, it rather begs the question of how tight is 'tight'? This is not an easy question to answer in print anyway, but the technique illustrated in Fig.157 may be of some help. The pressure required (on a $\frac{1}{4}$" collet; I have no experience of larger ones) is about that which can *comfortably* be applied with the little finger on the end of a spanner at about 4" from the collet (despite the appearance of the photograph, this is not a 'white-knuckle' job). I do not normally go in for deep cutting in a single pass but, for the purposes of demonstration only, a 1" diameter cutter inserted in this way can be seen comfortably taking a cut about $\frac{1}{2}$" deep in hard timber in Fig.158. In passing, a wise safety precaution when changing cutters, or indeed carrying out any operation involving touching the cutter, is to pull the mains plug from its socket. This may appear to be overdoing things somewhat, but switches can go wrong (albeit very rarely), and with the plug pulled, the cutter *can't* suddenly whizz around.

One possible situation involving unscheduled cutter rotation is shown in Fig.159(a). This is where a cutter is used in conjunction with a guide bush, and the cutter diameter is larger than that of the bush. Inadvertent

Figure 155

Figure 156

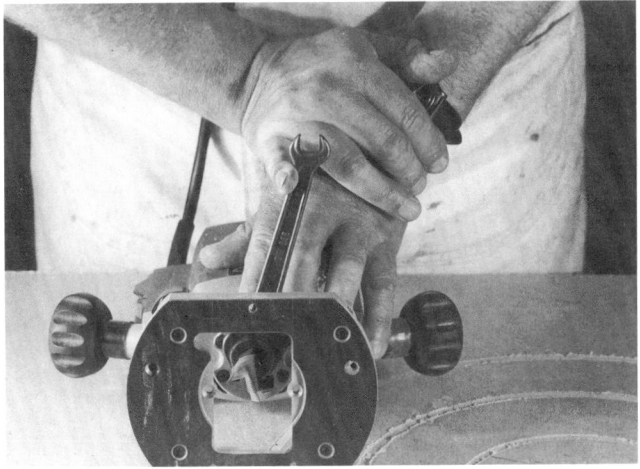

Figure 157

Figure 158

release of the plunge knob during operation, thus retracting the cutter, can produce quite spectacular results. This arrangement of cutter and bush is positively not recommended, but certain dovetail jigs of the 'metal finger' type may render it necessary (b). In such cases, a plunge depth control which operates on a screw thread both ways, and therefore locks the depth of the cutter regardless of control knobs, is to be preferred. It must be borne in mind however, that, in these circumstances the cutter cannot be easily retracted, and very great care must be exercised when putting the machine down after use (preferably in a holder of some kind).

A further precaution, for overhead manual routing, is to ensure that the electrical cable is lifted well out of the way of the work in progress by looping it over a hook in the ceiling, or if this cannot be managed for some reason, at least over the shoulder (this can be rather less convenient). There is rarely a great deal of risk of the router cutting its own cable, but interference with operation, particularly when carrying out trammel work, involving rotation of the router about the workpiece can be a nuisance. Much the same argument applies to

dust extraction hose although, with many existing router designs, dust extraction is not particularly easy anyway.

There is also the question of personal protection against dust, chips and noise, in the form of masks/respirators, goggles and ear-defenders. Even normally safety-conscious workers will regularly neglect these, especially for the quick job where 'it doesn't really matter'. The problem here of course, is that the effects are cumulative and not immediately obvious, and I can only suggest that personal protection is always a good idea.

Figure 159

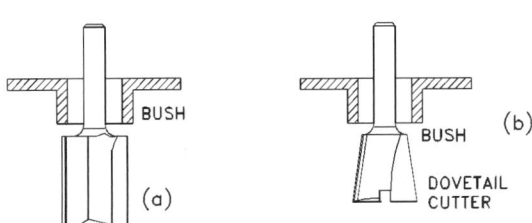

This book is not particularly concerned with the operation of the router in the 'spindle moulder' configuration. For the uninitiated, this is an arrangement whereby the router is mounted inverted beneath a worktable, with the cutter protruding above it. The workpiece becomes the moving component in this configuration, being fed by the operator, usually against a bearing or fence of some kind. In view of the fact that the making of a spindle moulder table, using a router as prime mover, is well within the capabilities of the home worker (and a very useful device it is too, particularly where repeat work against a template is involved), it might be as well to indicate the major safety hazards associated with this type of machining.

The normal overhead hand-held mode of router use is really very safe, largely because the operator is, to some extent at least, shielded from the cutter by the body of the router itself, plus the fact that the hands are normally on the control knobs or some associated jig, well away from the cutter. In the spindle moulder configuration,

Figure 160

the first and most obvious problem is that the cutter is exposed (notwithstanding any guards that may be fitted), and thus poses a far greater threat. Coupled with this, is the fact that the workpiece is moved across the cutter manually. It is usually fairly easy to keep the fingers well out of the way, even when machining complex profiles but, even so, it is normal for both hands to be on the work, which means that the router cannot easily be switched off unless special measures are taken. Personally, I would not even consider spindle moulder work without the benefit of an external push-button 'no-volt' switch. This can be operated quickly by taking one hand off the work, or even by one knee in emergency.

The foregoing comments, along with dust extraction, ear defenders etc., might be seen as obvious safety precautions, and will doubtless be applied by readers to suit their own circumstances. My present concern is with the less-obvious, beginning once again with cutter rotation. To begin with, the direction of cutter rotation in the spindle moulder configuration is in the opposite direction (from the operator's point of view) from the manual overhead mode, ie. anticlockwise. This means that, where the cutter is behind the work, from the operator's viewpoint (see Fig.160), the preferred direction of feed is from right to left, against cutter rotation. Despite my earlier comments on certain advantages to be accrued from 'climb milling' (in this case, left to right), I would state quite categorically that, for the spindle moulder, the practice has *absolutely nothing* to recommend it. It is quite true that the tendency remains for the cutter to push the work away from it, as well as snatch it. This is more than counterbalanced by two things: The natural stance of the worker at the table will generate greater sideways pressure against the cutter, thus overriding the 'push away' tendency of the cutter. Also, the workpiece is, in many circumstances, fairly light in weight. Both these effects will tend to shoot the work off the table to the right. This is bad enough; worse is the possibility that the cutter is exposed, and that the pressure previously exerted can bring the fingers dangerously close to it. Of course, the presence of spring loaded hold-down and side-fence devices (where it is possible to use them) may at least keep the fingers safe, but the general risk remains as stated. Incidentally, side-fence pressure, coupled with the wrong feed direction (remember Fig.144?), poses exactly the same hazard as that shown in Figs 148(a) and (b). If the cutter is in front of the workpiece (Fig.161), the feed is from left to right. Note the presence of a small block of wood clamped to the fence to the left of the cutter in Fig.160. This is an additional anti-snatch measure, used even when feeding against cutter rotation. The idea is to press the work against the block, which is then used as a pivot to feed

Figure 161

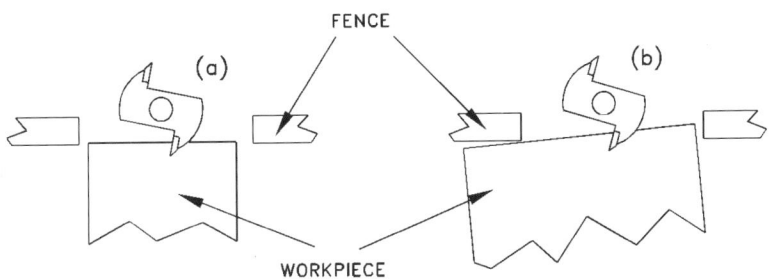

Figure 162

the work into the cutter, followed by normal traverse. It is far less easy to use the same technique on certain types of 'inside' work, and it may be necessary to work by 'feel' as shown in Fig.161. However, the cut in this instance is very light. It is very important to note that, in both photographs, the cutter is bearing-guided; it is unacceptably dangerous to use a naked cutter in this way.

Even when feeding in the preferred direction, there is scope for error. A particularly silly mistake is shown in Fig.162. Admittedly the drawing is highly exaggerated, but does illustrate a general problem, particularly that of sideways tipping. I do not perform work of this type on a spindle moulder, preferring the overhead configuration, and cannot therefore offer any 'tried and tested'

Figure 163

Figure 164

solutions. On the other hand, the cutting of biscuit housings in small workpieces is a very safe business, as illustrated by Figs 163 and 164. There are two important safety precautions. The first is a plywood stop block clamped to the fence, thus allowing the work to be pivoted against it into the cutter.; the second is simply ensuring that the left hand side of the fence is set to provide a depth stop. Although not illustrated, a third requirement for very small work is some form of indirect feed, by means of a suitably shaped wood block.

I reiterate my contention that the router is a very safe machine to use. It simply requires a little thought and understanding. Treat the machine with respect by all means, but don't be afraid of it.

8

DESIGN

This chapter deals with the geometry underlying the design of the projects and jigs described elsewhere in the book, and is primarily intended for readers wishing to develop their own ideas. It is by no means essential to the completion of the projects; these are complete in themselves. Even so, I hope the chapter may be of interest to all readers, particularly with regard to the way in which the router cutter itself can affect the shape of the workpiece.

From Chapter 7, it can be seen that the geometry of the cutter has a distinct effect on its behaviour. Safety matters aside, much the same applies to the results produced in the workpiece itself, particularly when using templates and guide bushes or bearing-guided cutters, or where ellipses are involved. The basic effect arises from the fact that the cutter has a finite diameter and therefore produces a finite width of cut. The diameters of guide bushes and bearings also have to be allowed for. All very obvious of course, but the effects can be a little surprising nevertheless.

Consider the effect of a cutter under the control of a guide bush against a template (Fig.165(a)). The usual calculation made in respect of such templates is shown alongside the drawing, regardless of whether the cutter is guided by a bush or a bearing. Obviously, the value of 'g' must be allowed for when designing a template to produce a workpiece of given dimensions; moreover, the effects upon external and internal (ie. re-entrant)

shapes will be different. Consider first the external profile shown in (b). In this case, the sharp corner of the template is followed by a guide bush of diameter greater than that of the cutter. The effect is to produce a rounded corner on the workpiece of radius 'g'. Whether the template has a sharp corner or is itself radiused makes no difference to the general principle; the radius

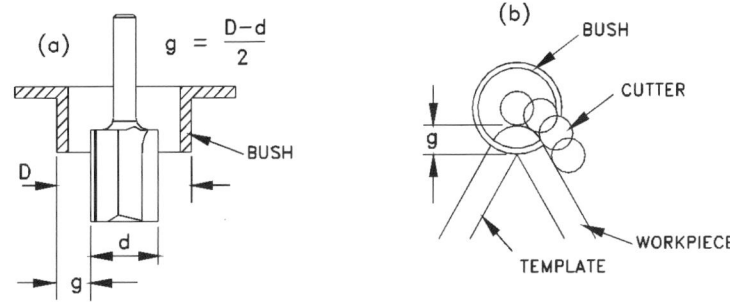

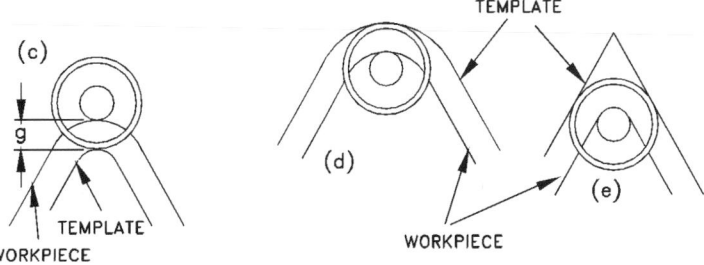

Figure 165

at the corner of the workpiece will always be greater than that of the template by the value of 'g', as shown in Fig.165(c). Re-entrant shapes are also affected but, in this case, the radius of the workpiece is *reduced* by the value of 'g' (Fig.165(d)). It is clear however, that the radius at the workpiece can never be less than that of the cutter. Where the actual cutter radius is acceptable as a workpiece profile, the template may be simplified at this point, simply by not bothering to produce a radius in it (e). As a matter of technique, where such a point is encountered in operation, the cutter will be obliged to dwell for a moment, however carefully it is fed; this will produce some risk of light burning or indentation of the workpiece.

Figure 166

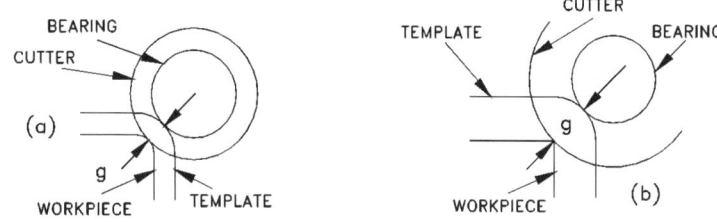

Figure 167

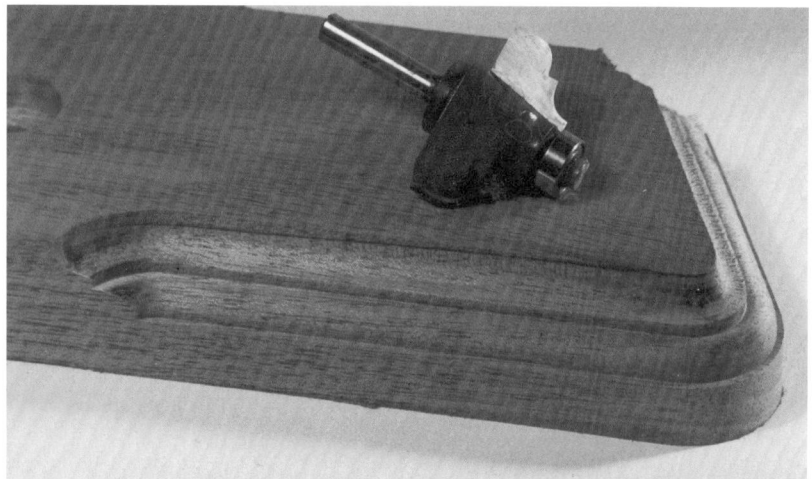

Fig.166 shows the effect produced by a bearing-guided cutter, where the cutter diameter is greater than that of the bearing. On external corners (a), the workpiece radius will be reduced by the value of 'g' and, where the template radius is equal to or less than 'g', a sharp corner will be produced (b). For internal work, much the same considerations apply as given in Fig.165(d) and (e), with the difference that the radius produced by the cutter will be greater than that of the template. To conclude this section, it is as well to remember that a cut produced under the control of a guide bush or bearing will be parallel to the guiding member at all points along the path traversed. This is also true of the individual paths produced by a stepped or multi-profile cutter. Thus at a corner, for example, the radius of each step profile will be different, as can be seen from Fig.167.

When using trammel jigs for cutting circles or parts of circles, there is no real problem in terms of consistency of profile since, apart from diameter, one circle is very much like another – a most important consideration where inlay work is involved. Ellipses are a different proposition entirely and, given an interest in making woodware of this shape, deserve separate consideration since they present a number of pitfalls. It is perhaps as well to give a few definitions to begin with: referring to Fig.168, the longest dimension (on the horizontal centre-line as drawn) is referred to as the 'major axis'. The

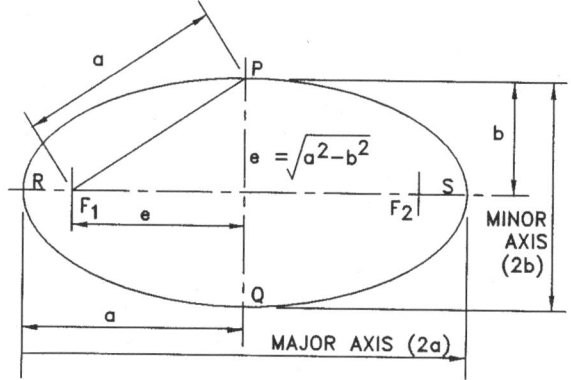

Figure 168

shortest, on the vertical centre line is the 'minor axis'. There are two points within the ellipse, known as the 'foci' (ie. two 'focuses'), shown as 'F1' and 'F2' on the drawing; these have mathematical significance but, for the practical user, their only use perhaps is as locations for the two pins which would be needed for the 'pins and string' method of drawing ellipses (more of this later). It is conventional in geometry and mathematics to use and identify 'half-distances' in calculations and constructions of ellipses; these are labelled 'a', 'b' and 'e' respectively on the drawing. As a matter of passing interest, the circle is but a special case of the ellipse, where 'a' and 'b' are equal, and the two foci sit on top of each other at the centre. The straight line may be considered as another special case of the ellipse, where the major axis has some finite value, and the minor axis is zero. Not that it matters much, but the foci in this case are located at the extreme ends of the major axis (ie. 'e' = 'a'). The only other definition to note is that of 'aspect ratio'. This is a measure of the major axis length relative to that of the minor axis. A long thin ellipse will have a higher value than a short fat one (the minimum value being unity, in the case of the circle). The convention is useful when specifying ellipses; for example, an aspect ratio of '2' simply describes an ellipse which is twice as long as it is wide. With practice, one can mentally visualise the approximate shape of an ellipse if the aspect ratio is stated – a useful attribute when initially dreaming-up designs. To pursue the example, this kind of information is sometimes presented as '2:1', which simply means 'two to one'. Ellipses are sometimes referred to as 'ovals', by the way. This is not strictly accurate; an 'oval' would, on a drawing, be egg-shaped. In the solid (ie. a real egg) it would be an 'ovoid'. Even so, the term 'oval' is often quite loosely and commonly used to describe an ellipse.

To state the obvious, the circumferences of any pair of concentric circles will be parallel to one another at all points. A good test of parallelism for any pair of lines is

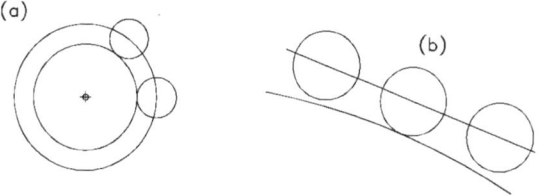

Figure 169

given by drawing a series of small circles, with their centres located on one of the lines. The circumferences of the circles can be arranged to touch the other line at all points if the lines are parallel (Fig.169(a). They will either miss or overcut the second line if the lines are not parallel (b).

Fig.170 shows a series of ellipses based on the same major and minor axes. Each ellipse is the same distance from its neighbour at both the axes (ie. at points 1,2 and 3,4). At point 6, the small circle overcuts the inner ellipse by a considerable amount; that at point 5 shows a tiny overcut. Two important points can thus be deduced by inspection: the ellipses are *not* parallel at all points, and the effect becomes more marked as the aspect ratio is increased. In the case of a mirror frame or similar object using a fairly low aspect ratio, the difference is of no real importance and will generally go unnoticed. Where precise inlay work is required it can spell trouble.

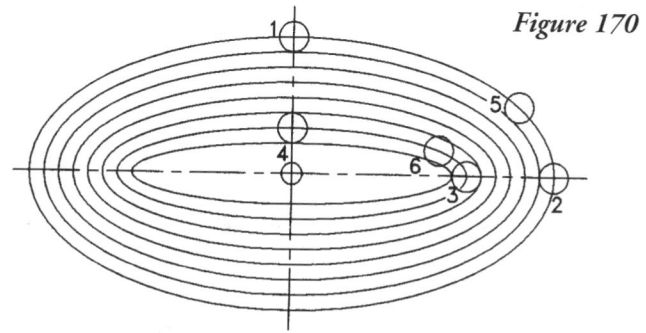

Figure 170

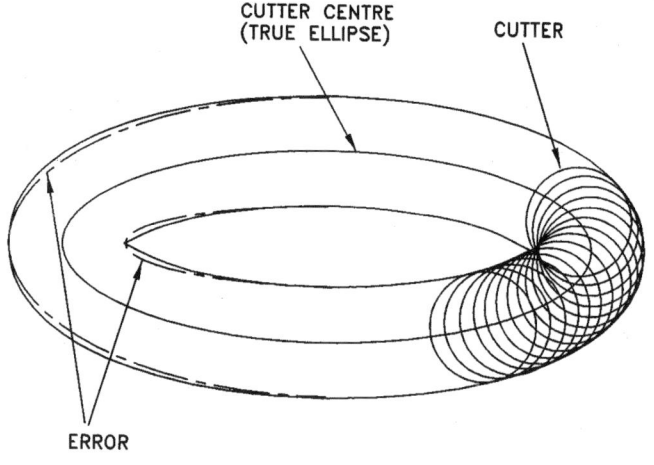

CUTTER CENTRE
(TRUE ELLIPSE)   CUTTER

ERROR

Figure 171

There is an associated problem. Fig.171 shows the path taken by a fairly large-diameter router cutter, guided by an ellipse jig. The nature of the jig is unimportant for the moment; it is sufficient only to know that the path or 'locus' of the centre-line of the cutter is a true ellipse. The paths of the inner and outer edges of the cutter, which represent the actual channel cut in the work are, by definition, parallel to the centre line path and to each other. From the earlier discussion (see Fig.170), it follows that *neither can be a true ellipse.* Quite clearly the inner path in Fig.171 is not an ellipse, since it is quite sharply pointed at each end. The outer path, although less obvious perhaps, is rather more bulbous at the ends than a true ellipse would be. Although a nuisance in many cases, the effect can be made use of, since it allows the generation of regular shapes which would be quite difficult to generate by any other means. The shape generated by the inner path can in fact be quite attractive, if the dimensions are carefully chosen. To my mind, the outer shape tends to look rather ugly, whatever one does with it, but this is only a personal view. The foregoing information is based upon inspection only. However, I do have in my possession an

elegant detailed mathematical analysis (not performed by me), which proves the correctness of the observations made.

The ellipse may be generated in a number of ways. I am personally aware of two 'mechanical' methods (I invented the router version of one of them), which constrain a stylus or, more importantly perhaps, a router cutter to follow an elliptical path; the underlying geometry of both is described later. For the benefit of readers who may be limited to manual methods however, one or two ways of drawing ellipses by hand are offered.

To begin with the 'pins and string' method: this is quite widely known in principle, but is generally employed in a somewhat 'hit and miss' fashion, involving a number of guesses at pin position and string length. This needn't be the case; it is quite easy to obtain the necessary values, either by simple geometry or equally simple mathematics. The geometric method is described first. Referring back to Fig.168, it is first necessary to draw the major and minor axes, shown in the drawing by the two chain-dotted lines. The required minor and major dimensions are then marked on the axes, at points P,Q,R,S. A pair of compasses is set to the value of 'a' (half the major axis length) and, with their centre at 'P', an arc is drawn across the major axis at two points. The two intersections locate the foci at 'F1' and 'F2', and the two pins are placed at these points. For low aspect ratio ellipses, the arcs will cut the axis at an acute angle, and the positions of the foci may be difficult to determine precisely. Where high accuracy is required, the formula given in Fig.168 may be used instead. Referring now to Fig.172, a complete 'pins and string' construction is given (this is in fact one of the ways of defining an ellipse). The drawing shows the pins and string in place, and two arbitrary positions of the stylus are shown at 'P1' and 'P2'. The length of string between 'F1' and 'P1' is shown as 's1'; that between 'P1' and 'F2' is shown as 't1'. It can be shown mathematically that, for any given ellipse, the sum of 's' and 't' is a constant value, regardless of the position of 'P'; this is why the pins and string method works. As a rough check, the reader just might like to try a ruler on the drawing. Since the distance between the pins is fixed, the length of string between them remains constant. For a fixed loop length, it follows that the remainder (ie. 's+t') is also constant, regardless of how it is divided up by the position of the stylus. Point 'P2' shows another position of the stylus. If now the stylus is placed at point 'P3', on the major axis, it is clear by inspection that the string length between the minor axis and 'P3' is equal to 'a'. The remaining length, on the left-hand side is equal to 'e'. Thus the total is 'a+e'. Since the string is actually a loop, its total length is twice this value, ie. '2a+2e'. Thus there is absolutely no need for guesswork.

Two practical hints may be of some help: it is one thing to calculate the exact loop length of string required, and quite another to tie a knot such that this is actually managed. A further simple set-up makes this easy. Two extra pins are set such that the distance between them is exactly half the required loop length (ie. 'a+e'). The string may now be tied tightly around these with no real problem, although a helping extra finger may be necessary. One of the pins is removed and the loop, the exact length required, thus freed. The second point concerns the rather annoying tendency for the string to slip off the stylus when actually drawing the ellipse. This can be prevented by a small piece of rubber or card slipped over the stylus, below the string. Finally, a cautionary note must be added: any form of thread or string employed will almost certainly have some 'stretch' or elasticity; it is difficult therefore to obtain a high order of accuracy. On the plus side, since all the items necessary to generate the ellipse are contained within it, the stock material need be only a trifle larger than the ellipse required. Fig.173 shows an ellipse being drawn and, in the foreground, the extra pins needed to establish loop length.

Two of many methods of generating an ellipse on the drawing board (or directly on to the workpiece) are now

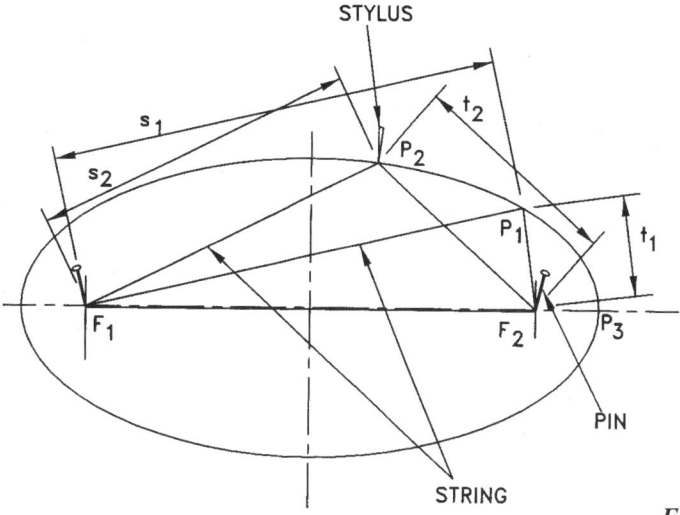

Figure 172

given. Both are capable of a high order of accuracy, provided that sufficient points are generated, but both require a groundwork rather larger than actually needed by the ellipse itself. The first is, to my mind, the simplest of all the possible methods. It requires a rectangle to be

Figure 173

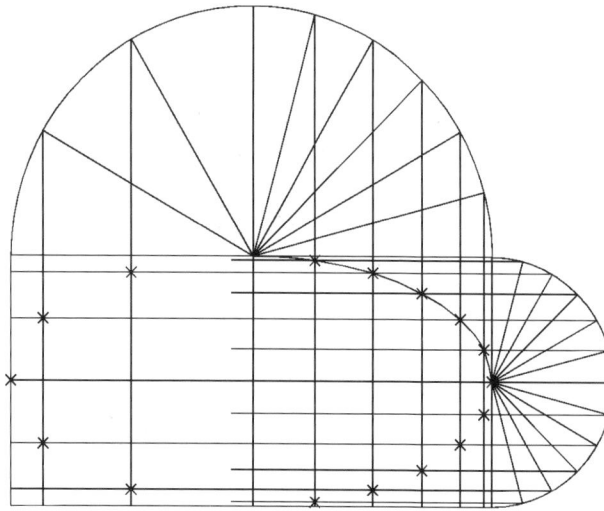

Figure 174

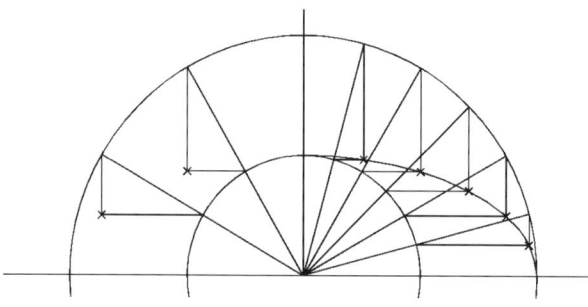

Figure 175

where the segment lines cut their respective circles. The intersections of these within the rectangle are points on the required ellipse. The second method is essentially similar, but requires the drawing of two concentric circles, of diameter equal to the major and minor axes of the ellipse. These are divided into segments as before (Fig.175), although in this case it is not necessary for the segments to be equal. Taking each segment line in turn, a vertical line is drawn from its point of intersection with the larger circle, and a horizontal line from its intersec-

drawn of the same dimensions as the major and minor axes of the required ellipse. Two semicircles are constructed on the long and short sides of the rectangle respectively, and each divided into the same number of *equal* angular segments (Fig.174). Vertical and horizontal construction lines are drawn at each of the points

Figure 176

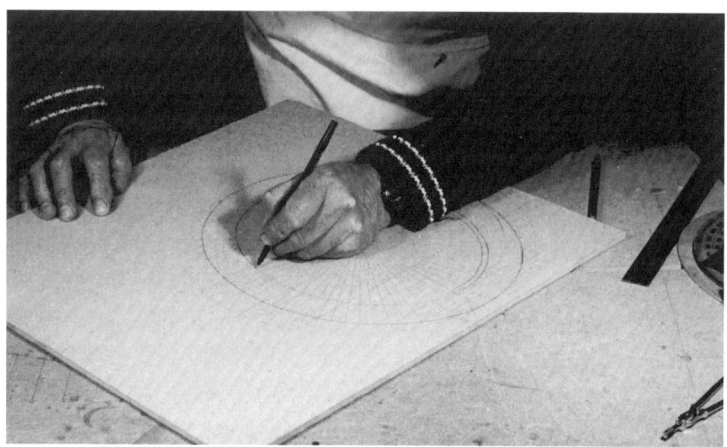

tion with the smaller circle. The intersection of these lines gives a point on the required ellipse. The drawing shows two points only on the-left hand side, to illustrate the method clearly. The right-hand side employs more points, for greater accuracy. Perhaps the only real disadvantage of the method lies in the degree of concentration required, particularly if a large number of intersections is used; it is very easy to make mistakes. Fig.176 shows a template being generated by the second method.

The first 'mechanical' method to be described is available commercially, and is illustrated in Chapter 3, Figs 56-59. Fig.177 shows the essential features. The system is designed around a baseplate which is fixed to the centre of the workpiece by some suitable means. The baseplate carries a pair of channels cut at right angles to one another, across its centre. Two sliding shoes are fitted into the channels, such that they run freely but without undue play. The shoes each carry a stud on the top face which permit a plain trammel bar to be fitted over them. Finally, the trammel bar contains a location for a stylus of some kind which actually draws the ellipse. In the commercial design, the 'stylus' is a router, although a pen can be fitted in place of the router for

Figure 178

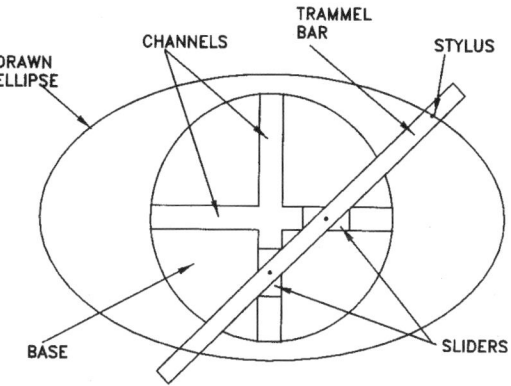

Figure 177

pure drawing purposes if required. The positions of the sliders on the trammel bar can also be adjusted and locked to permit different sizes of ellipse to be drawn. In use, the stylus is simply moved in a more or less circular motion around the baseplate. The sliders move back and forth, crossing each other's path four times in a complete revolution, and thereby move the stylus on an elliptical path. Fig.178 shows a simple home-made version, used to draw small ellipses. The commercial device invariably generates a great deal of interest at woodworking exhibitions, since its movement is quite fascinating to watch. In my experience, most people walk away shaking their heads (whether they eventually buy one or not), as though they have just witnessed some piece of magic. Actually, the device is a mechanisation of a very simple geometric principle.

The principle is known in geometry as a 'trammel' method of generating ellipses. Fig.179(a) shows a bar containing two points, called sliders for convenience. The bar is free to move, with the proviso that the top slider must always lie on the 'y' axis, and the lower slider on the 'x' axis. Given these constraints, it can be shown mathematically that *any* point on the bar will describe a true ellipse, ranging from a circle to a straight line. The paths of the points 'P1'-'P4' in Fig.179(a) are shown in (b). It is of interest perhaps to note that the points outside the sliders go one way, and those inside go the other (but all are true ellipses). Ellipses can be drawn quite accurately on paper with a very simple set-up, using a trammel bar of fairly substantial card. Long pins may be used as the 'sliders', perhaps the only difficult

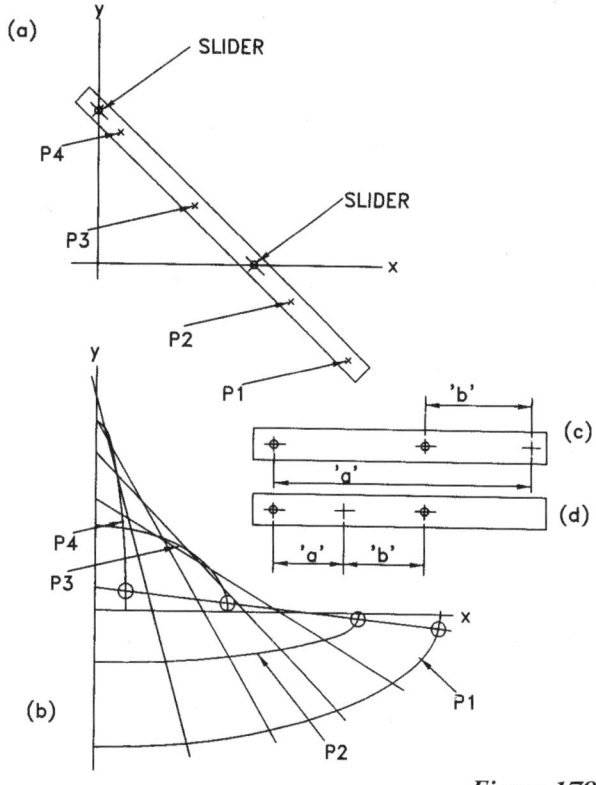

Figure 179

Figure 180

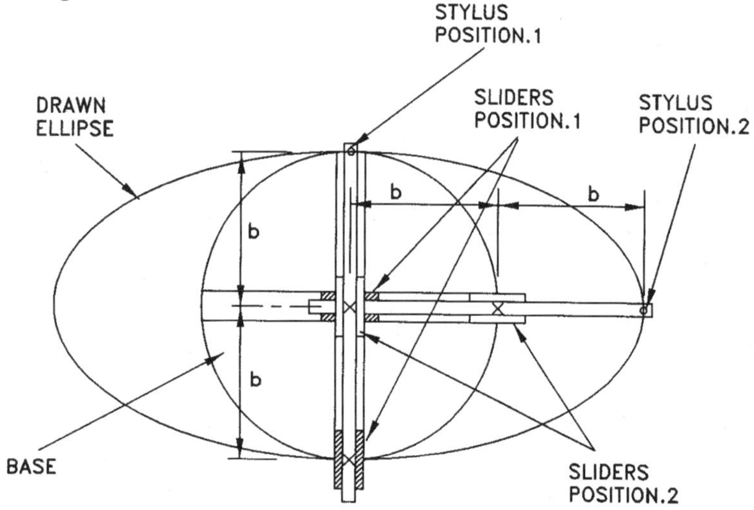

part of the operation being that of ensuring that the points are always located precisely on the axes. For readers wishing to avail themselves of the method, Figs 179 (c) and (d) show the necessary dimensions for 'outside' and 'inside' ellipses respectively.

All jigs and fixtures are bound to be limited in one way or another, usually on maximum or minimum dimensions, and this one is no exception. From Fig.180, it is clear that it is not possible to generate an ellipse, even with a simple point stylus, any part of which lies beneath the baseplate. Slightly less obvious perhaps, is the fact that the device is limited to a theoretical maximum aspect ratio of 2:1. In position 1, it is clear that the minimum value of 'b' cannot be less than the radius of the baseplate. Rotation of the system to position 2 can only double the value of 'b', thereby defining the maximum aspect ratio. The practical maximum will be rather less, because some fixed amount must be added to the length of the slider, to accommodate the router, or even any simple stylus mount. It follows that, as the trammel bar is lengthened, and the size of the ellipse thereby increased, the aspect ratio is also reduced. Thus, for a given baseplate size, larger ellipses must look rather more and more like circles, and project design should be undertaken with this in mind. A change of range may be obtained by changing baseplate size (two sizes of the commercial device are available).

The second device is based upon the Pivot Frame jig. Although I claim this device as it stands to be an invention of mine (the Pivot Frame is my invention also), the basic geometric principle is well over two hundred years old. The device was used on the mandrel of an ornamental turning lathe and was described (somewhat oddly) as an 'oval chuck'. In that form, it comprised a pair of parallel bars rotating about a fixed eccentric disc, which caused the bars (and their support) to move laterally as they rotated. This in turn caused any fixed point on the support to describe an ellipse. The router version is described fully in Chapter 3, which gives full instructions for making it. Only its outline, plus the essential geometric principles are given here therefore.

It is necessary to refer back to Chapter 3, Fig.60, which gives a plan view of the complete jig. As the Pivot Frame rotates about the primary disc, it also rotates the control disc which is attached to the router base. Since the disc sits between the two parallel bars attached to the worktable, the rotary movement also causes a lateral movement of the worktable on the slider system let into the primary disc. Thus the path described by the router cutter *relative to the worktable* is no longer a circle. It is not immediately obvious however, that the path is actually elliptical. Fig.181(a) shows the control disc in the position which places the guide bars on the worktable parallel to the guide rods. This may be regarded as the basic position. The centre of the control disc is indicated by the heavy black dot; it moves under the control of the Pivot Frame on a circular path indicated by the barbed arrow. The cutter is offset from the centre of the control disc by an amount 'b', equal to *half* the required minor axis dimension. It can be seen that the path of the cutter relative to the primary disc is, as always, circular. However, the worktable is being moved by the control disc, via the parallel bars, one of which is shown on the drawing as a short heavy black line. The rather obvious annotation 'r' to the radius of the control disc is actually quite important. The control disc sits between the two bars at all times. Its centre is therefore always on the horizontal centre line of the worktable, regardless of how it is moved by the Pivot Frame. Because this line is also the major axis line of the ellipse being drawn, it follows that the centre of the control disc will always lie at some point on the major axis, again regardless of Pivot Frame operation. The reader is invited to make quite sure that this point is fully understood before proceeding, because it is crucial to the remainder of the explanation. Turning now to Fig.181(b), the control disc is shown rotated anticlockwise by 90° The axis of the

worktable (and therefore the ellipse major axis) is shown by the heavy chain-dotted line. The position of the cutter relative to this line is now quite obviously 'b' (the half-minor axis). Because the position shown is exactly halfway between the two extreme horizontal positions, the vertical line through the centre of the cutter is also the ellipse minor axis.

An intermediate position of the disc, at 30° to the horizontal, is shown in (c). In this case, the cutter lies on a point of the ellipse denoted by 'x' and 'y', measured as distances from the minor and major axes respectively. Note that 'y' is again with respect to the horizontal centre line of the worktable. A further intermediate position is shown in (d), at 45° to the horizontal.

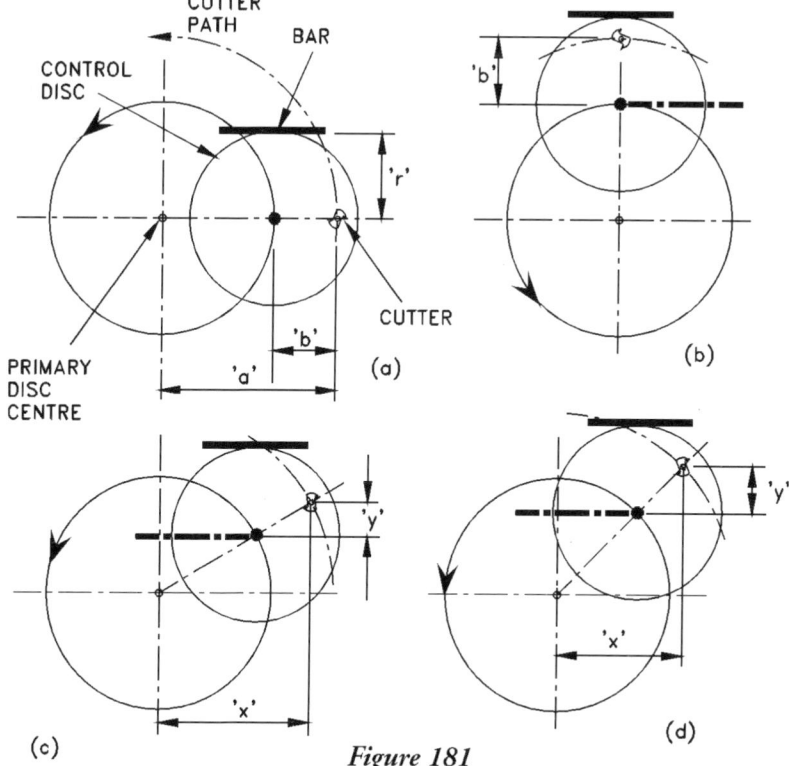

Figure 181

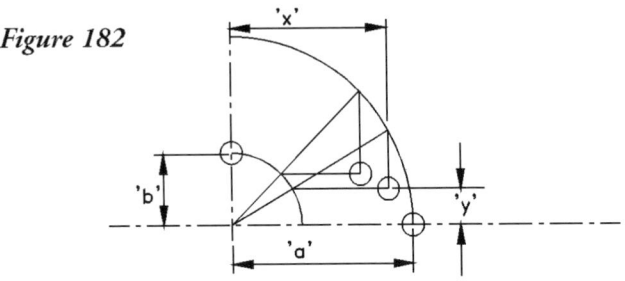

Figure 182

Fig.182 shows how the mechanism has a good deal in common with the manual construction shown in Fig.175.

I am perfectly satisfied that the device generates a true ellipse, having proved it mathematically (readers with the necessary interest will find it easy to derive the 'parametric equations' of the ellipse from the drawings). I am also satisfied that the explanation given here is correct; I can only hope that it is also reasonably clear, since the action of the device is quite complex and difficult to describe in words.

The jig suffers from the minor snag that it works without reference to drawn major and minor axes, although it may always be set to a value of 'b=0', to draw a straight line on the major axis. This is not particularly convenient and, for this reason, a manual method of finding the axes of any given ellipse is offered here. Referring to Fig.183(a), a ruler is applied (very carefully) in the general major axis area to find the maximum dimension, and the position on the ellipse profile lightly marked at each end (i). A similar exercise is carried out for the minor axis, to find the minimum dimension. It is now possible to strike arcs from the four points thus found and, with a little trial and error, to find the centre of the ellipse (ii). This may then be checked (and adjusted if necessary) by drawing a couple of circles which just touch the ellipse profiles at their maximum and minimum positions (iii). Once the centre has been found accurately, a further pair of arcs

which actually cut the ellipse profile are drawn (iv). It is then possible to bisect these accurately, again with the aid of compasses (v). Referring now to Fig.183(b), a line is drawn joining the two centres; this should also pass through the previously found centre of the ellipse (vi). For the sake of accuracy, the major axis is bisected with compasses, to check the position of the minor axis (vii); it is then a relatively simple matter to draw a line at right angles to the first, passing through the centre (viii). The method is in fact both simple and rapid, and is also very accurate. Given the nature of the ellipse however, it needs rather more care in the case of 'fat' (ie. low aspect ratio) ellipses.

Figure 183

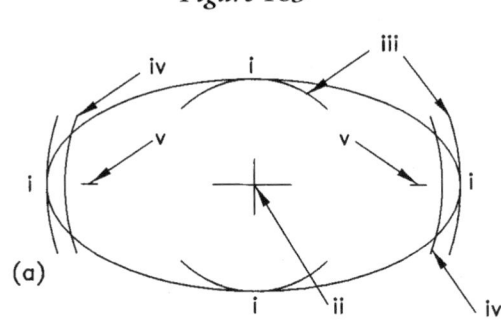

(a)

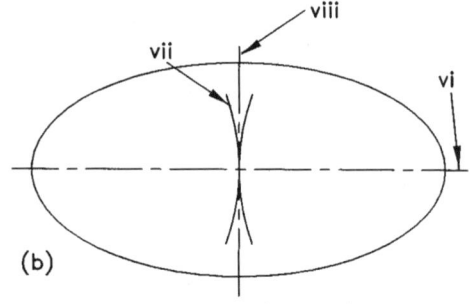

(b)

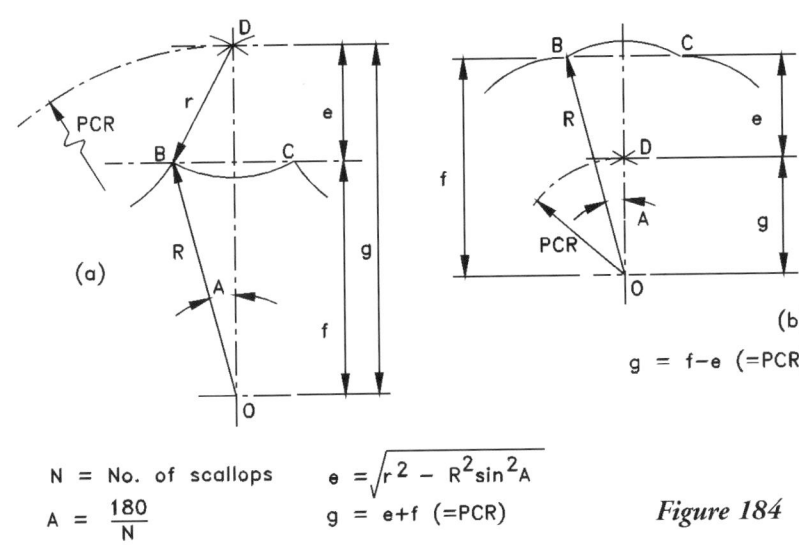

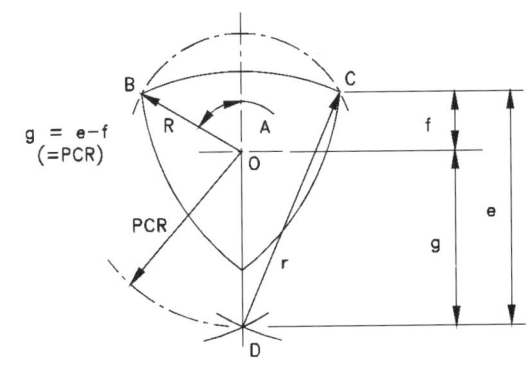

$$N = \text{No. of scallops}$$

$$A = \frac{180}{N}$$

$$f = R.\cos A$$

$$e = \sqrt{r^2 - R^2\sin^2 A}$$

$$g = e+f \ (=PCR)$$

Figure 184   *Figure 185*

$$g = f-e \ (=PCR)$$

Finally, a general method is offered for dealing with dimensions related to circular arcs. The three drawings comprising Figs 184 and 185, although dealing with slightly different aspects of construction, are nevertheless identical in basic concept. A geometric method is given, together with mathematical formulae which may be used instead if desired.

The method is developed with reference to Fig.184(a). Three dimensions must be initially chosen. The first is the maximum 'diameter' of the piece to be made. This is actually the diameter of the circle which circumscribes the piece, ie. all the scallop points touch the circle. The *radius* of this circle is given as 'R', and its centre is at 'O'. The second requirement is the number of scallops, denoted by 'N'. A simple calculation based on 'N' gives the value of 'A' which is *half* the angle subtended at 'O' by a single full scallop. Finally, the scallop radius must be chosen; this is denoted by 'r'. As can be seen, it is not at all necessary to draw the entire piece; if a vertical centre line is drawn through 'O', and a pair of lines at angle 'A' drawn on each side of it, also centred at 'O', this will suffice. A short arc of radius 'R' is drawn (omitted from Fig.184 for clarity); its intersection with the two angular lines gives points 'B' and 'C'. With

compasses set to the value of 'r', two short arcs are struck from 'B' and 'C', to give point 'D'. An arc drawn with 'D' as centre will produce the required scallop. The distance 'OD' is measured, and can then be used in either of two ways: it may simply be used as the 'offset' value for the beam trammel or Pivot Frame as shown in Chapter 1, Fig.13. If on the other hand, a full drawing is required to check appearance, the compasses may be set to this value to draw a circle, centred on 'O' as the 'pitch circle radius' (PCR). The appropriate angular intersections, based upon 'N' are also drawn and, from their intersections with the circle, the remainder of the scallops drawn. If the formulae are used, it is not necessary to make a drawing of any kind.

Fig.184(b) represents a set of internal scallops, as might be required as the cutout portion of a mirror frame (see Project.1, Fig.187). All annotations are the same as for the previous drawing and the construction is, I think, self-evident. The only difference lies with the formula for 'g'. Finally, the general principle may be applied to shapes of the type shown in Fig.185, with any number of sides which, for this analysis may be regarded as 'scallops'. Once again, the only difference lies with the formula for 'g'.

PROJECT 1

THREE BASIC PROJECTS

Figure 186

The first project (Fig.186) is a very simple exercise indeed, and may well regarded as a practice piece, on the way to something a little more interesting. The techniques required to make it are described in Chapter 1. Suggested dimensions are given in Fig.187, which illustrates a design suitable for a 6" diameter mirror. The outer twelve scallops are best suited to the use of a beam trammel with secondary disc indexing and offset as illustrated in Fig.24(b), Chapter 1. The inner twelve scallops can be machined on either a beam trammel or a Pivot Frame, dependent upon scallop radius; that drawn is suited to the Pivot Frame (Fig.188). The rebates for the mirror and its backing are machined as illustrated in

Fig.4, Chapter 1, with the result shown in Fig.189. The design allows the use of a straight cutter to machine both scalloped profiles, followed by a cove cutter, used at exactly the same radius setting of the jig, thus sparing unnecessary setting-up. The same idea is featured in Project 2 (see Fig.209). There is however, no objection to the use of a bearing-guided cove cutter if this method is preferred. Note that the mirror and backing rebates are given only indirectly. Precise dimensions will depend upon the actual mirror used.

Pieces of this type are best machined from a single piece of timber, since there is not a great deal of joint area for a segmented construction. It might be a little

$11\frac{9}{16}$ PCR

8 RAD

$1\frac{1}{4}$ RAD

$1\frac{1}{2}$ PCR

(a)

$5\frac{1}{4}$

$7\frac{1}{2}$

HANGING SLOT

$\frac{1}{4}$

$\frac{1}{8}$ $\frac{3}{8}$

$\frac{3}{4}$

$\frac{5}{8}$

$\frac{1}{8}$

$1\frac{1}{8}$

(b)

TRAMMEL PIVOT

CUTTER

8 RAD

OFFSET $11\frac{9}{16}$

(c)

WORKPIECE CENTRE

PIVOT FRAME CENTRE

WORKPIECE CENTRE

OFFSET $1\frac{1}{2}$

$1\frac{1}{4}$ RAD

CUTTER

(d)

Figure 187

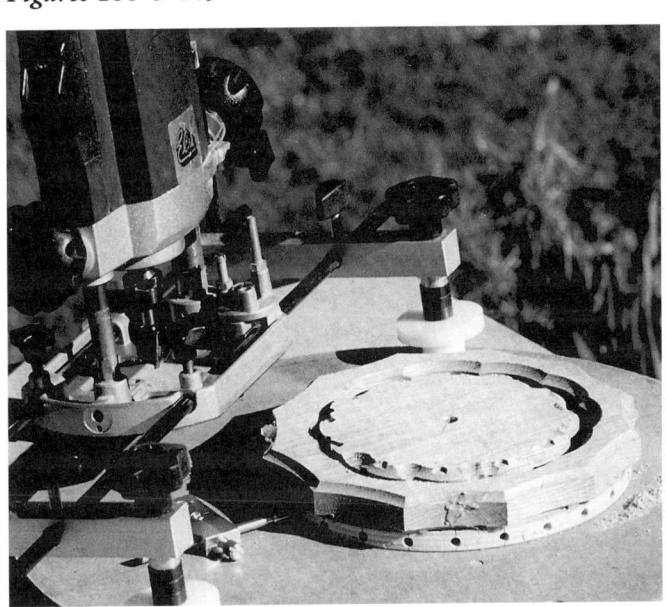

unwise for the newcomer to embark on a segmented project this early in the game anyway. It is most important that the chosen timber is well seasoned and therefore stable. The plywood mirror backing is unlikely to move much and, if the frame itself shrinks in any way, it is liable to split across the short grain (this has happened to me). The reader is referred to the second project in this section for details of fitting the backing. Although this second project is a little more challenging overall and uses a smaller mirror, the backing procedure is the same in both cases.

The second project (Fig.190), designed to fit a 4" diameter mirror, is a much more interesting exercise. I have actually lost count of the number of these I have made, to precisely the same basic dimensions, differing only in form of decoration. They appear to be very popular and I can strongly recommend the design as a suitable gift, particularly as it is so easy to make. Both

Figure 190

the frame and the base are of a three-segment construction. An optional decorative feature is the inlaid stripe.

The main frame segment is shown in Fig.191(c). Note from the drawing that the full length of each segment blank is not strictly required; areas shown shaded may be omitted. A full length segment does however have one or two advantages: obviously, the longer the joint line, the easier it is to check mitre angle accuracy; registration between segments is also materially assisted by the sharp external corners which provide an accurate equilateral triangle. All this is of some importance when setting up for machining, since the appearance of the piece is materially improved if the junctions of the curves fall exactly on the timber joint lines (this isn't always as easy as it may seem). If these advantages are dispensed with in order to save timber (no overpowering reason why not), then the inner triangle formed by the aperture in the centre may be used for registration instead, albeit with slightly more difficulty. In this case, it is important that all segments are of exactly the same width. Whatever the method chosen, the small triangular offcuts are not thrown away. They are useful cramping blocks, used as shown in Fig.192. The idea here is to glue the blocks to the main segments with superglue, to provide parallel faces for cramps when gluing the segments together. The blocks are bandsawn off afterwards, and the segments gently disc sanded back to their original profile. If full-length segments are used, one of the offcuts will be found sufficiently large (even after temporary service as a cramping block) to make the pedestal (Fig.193). Segmented assemblies of this type benefit from a dry run to ensure that the joints are accurate. With a three-piece assembly it is quite easy to check all three pieces against a light source. Only one joint is glued initially, using the method illustrated in Fig.192. If aliphatic 'fast grab' glue is used, the remaining joints can be made very soon afterwards (following a further check on joint accuracy), provided that the initial joint is re-cramped

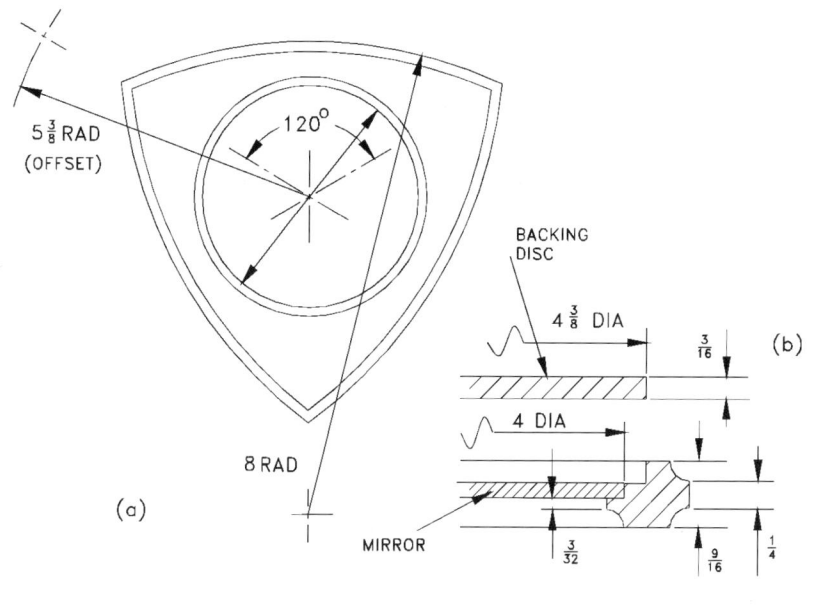

5 3/8 RAD
(OFFSET)

120°

8 RAD

(a)

BACKING
DISC

4 3/8 DIA

3/16

(b)

4 DIA

MIRROR

3/32

9/16

1/4

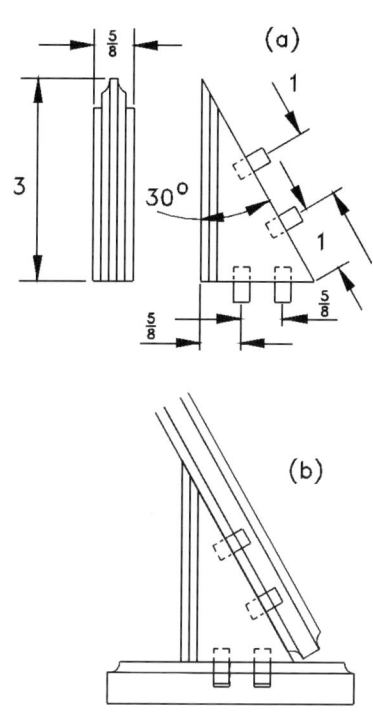

(a)

5/8

3

30°

1

1

5/8

5/8

(b)

Figure 193

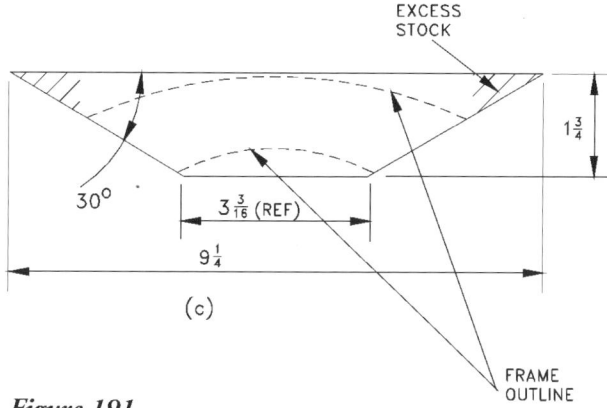

EXCESS
STOCK

1 3/4

30°

3 3/16 (REF)

9 1/4

(c)

FRAME
OUTLINE

Figure 191

Figure 192

as shown in Fig.194, to relieve any possible strain on it imposed by the others. The method of cramping as illustrated may look a little overdone but, in my experience, it is vitally important to ensure that joints do not buckle vertically under cramping pressure, hence the need for cramping to a flat baseboard. Where many cramps are used together, a dry run is essential, to ensure that the cramps can actually be applied as needed without mutual interference. Note also the use of polythene sheet to avoid unwanted adhesion to cramps or worktop. Particular care should be applied to the gluing process, since there is not sufficient room for any mechanical joint reinforcement or protection in the form of biscuit joints. Dowels cannot be used for odd numbers of segments, since there is a registration problem when fitting the last piece, as illustrated in Fig.195. There is perhaps the saving grace that the acute mitre angle (30°) does offer at least some element of side grain, with arguably a stronger bond than a plain end grain joint. Some joint protection is also offered by the presence of

Figure 194

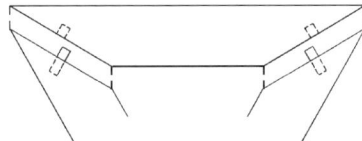

Figure 195

the backing disc which traps the mirror in position, since this is firmly glued into position in a circular rebate in the main frame on final assembly.

External profiling may be carried out with a simple beam trammel and an indexed secondary disc. Dependent upon the make of router used, it may be necessary to cut off the unwanted corners, as shown in Fig.196, to allow the assembly to be moved sufficiently close to the pivot point to provide the necessary offset distance. With the set-up given, it is an equally simple matter to provide the top outer cove profile, and also to cut the channels to receive the veneer inlay. In the latter case, it is advisable to set lateral stops against the outer ski of the trammel to prevent the cutter from over-running at the corners. It is important to ensure that this does not happen, since the result is a mess and impossible to correct. If the work is done carefully, the $\frac{1}{16}$" diameter cutter will leave only a tiny radius at the outer corners, which is very easy to sharpen-up with a craft knife.

Knife-cut veneers as purchased appear to be remarkably accurate in terms of thickness; I have never obtained a reading greater than .025" or less than .023". Router cutter diameters are also highly accurate. In fact, the only parameter likely to throw up the occasional surprise is the timber itself, since the compressibility will vary from species to species, giving rise to an easy fit in one case, and a tight fit in another, even when machined with the same cutter. Such problems are by no means insuperable, but it is as well to be aware of the likely causes. Three veneers in a sandwich will be about .010" oversize for a $\frac{1}{16}$" diameter cutter, and must therefore be thinned down a little before they will fit the channel comfortably. Easily the best way of doing so is with the home made veneer thicknessing jig described in Chapter 6. Failing this, the veneers may be manually sanded down before assembly, but this method can scarcely be expected to produce consistent results. Another way of dealing with the problem is to increase channel width slightly, by a very tiny *reduction* in machining radius, to avoid disturbance of the outer channel profile at the corners. The method requires very great care; if overdone, the resultant sloppy fit cannot be improved. A further drawback is that adjustments of this type need to be re-made every time the project is repeated. Although it is possible to set trammel devices very accurately indeed, I do not care for the method; one can always discard a spoilt strip of veneer. The reader will note that no dimensions are given on the drawings for the inlays. These can be arranged to choice, the only point to watch being that the overall trammel set-up must be maintained for both the inlay and outer profile machining

Sycamore veneer will be found quite excellent as an inlay timber. The centre slice is blackened on a hot-plate as described in Chapter 5. Any thicknessing operation on the veneer must be carried out before blackening; the timber becomes too fragile to enable this to be done afterwards. The veneers are laid up as a sandwich over a caul machined from MDF to about the same radius as the channel. This is quite easily done by hand (Fig.197) and, as can be seen, the assemblies retain sufficient curvature after gluing to enable them to fit the channels easily. The first strip is held down to the caul at both ends with adhesive tape, after which, succeeding strips are glued and held in place until the glue sets. The photograph also shows an inverse caul, which I made to cramp the entire assembly for a while; in practice, I found it totally unnecessary. The preferred adhesive, to my mind, is superglue, since it acts quickly.

A word about superglue: for the task illustrated, a slightly viscous formulation is preferable; the thinner

Figure 196

variety soaks into the timber, to the detriment of the joint. Surprisingly, the glue appears to add nothing to the final thickness of the sandwich. Unwanted adhesion is always a problem with superglue; that to the caul is easily dealt with by a barrier of polythene strip. Finger-sticking is something else; I can only suggest due care, in the awareness that this is really no help at all. I am often

Figure 197

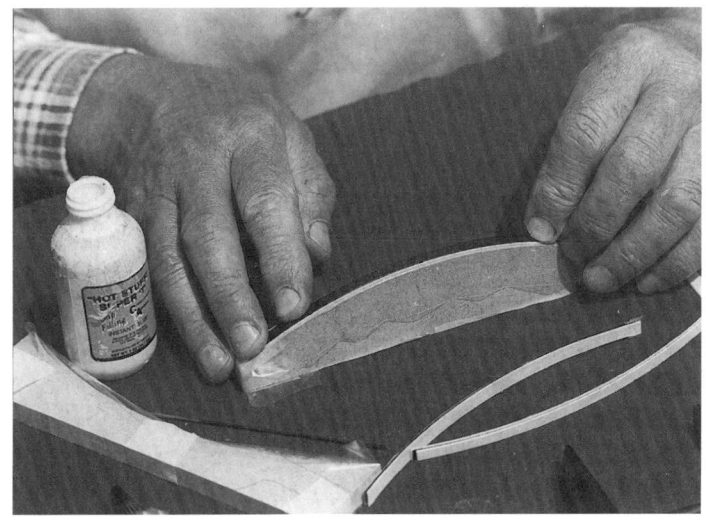

asked what to do about the problem of nozzles becoming clogged with partially-set adhesive. My solution is simple; I don't use them, preferring instead a small metal rod, visible in Fig.197. This of course leaves an open pot. Although rather carelessly omitted from the photograph, I normally put a small toolmaker's clamp on the base of the pot, to prevent it from being knocked over.

An extra sandwich is made (not necessarily with a black veneer), for the purpose of trial and error fitting of the mitred joints, which can be formed on a disc sander quite easily, by the way. The inlays are glued in place by applying superglue to the channels, and then pressing the inlays rapidly into them. The trial pieces are valuable as end stops to guide the main inlays during this operation, but they must be very rapidly removed, to avoid unwanted adhesion. Finally the inlays are chiselled and sanded down to the level of the frame. I strongly advise that the inlays are fitted as early in the proceedings as possible, since they prevent accidental damage to the edges of the channels once they are fitted.

The workpiece, still on its secondary disc, is fitted to the centre of the Pivot Frame, and the central hole

Figure 198

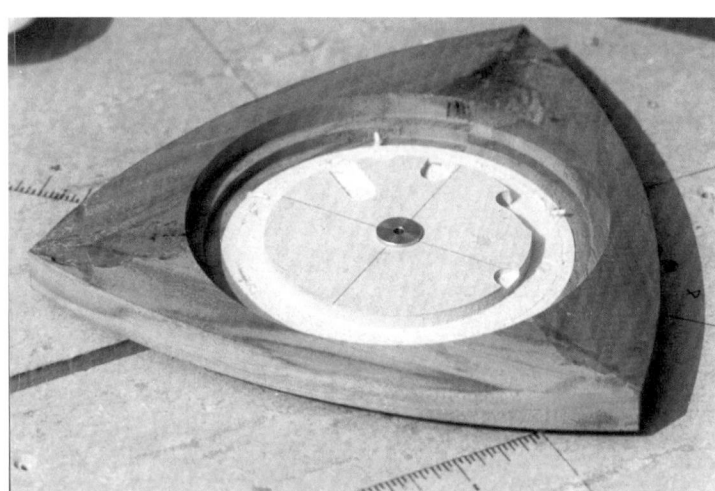

Figure 199

routed. The central decorative cove cut can also be made at this time. The workpiece may now be removed from the secondary disc. A plain plywood disc, about $\frac{1}{4}$" thick is cut on the Pivot Frame (and left in place for subsequent operations). It is made a fairly tight fit in the central hole of the workpiece, which may be tried for fit as it is brought down to size. The workpiece is then fitted with a few strips of double-sided adhesive tape on the upper inlaid face, and placed face-down on the primary disc, using the plywood disc as location. The remaining rebates may then be cut in the rear face of the workpiece (Fig.198). Finally, the workpiece is removed and the underside outer cove profile cut with a bearing guided cutter.

A further plywood disc, which is required to sit in the outer rebate, to trap the mirror eventually, is also cut on the Pivot Frame. Initially, it is made slightly oversize, to permit either a plain sheet of veneer, or a simple parquetry pattern to be laid on it, by any preferred means (Fig.199). It is then trimmed to a precise fit in the workpiece rebate. At this stage, it should stand a little proud of the rear face of the workpiece, and may be brought to final thickness by reversing it on a flat worktop, holding with double-sided tape, and using the router in planing mode.

The base is made in much the same way as the main frame, using the dimensions given in Fig.200. After assembly, the piece is rebated on the underside, and fitted with a plywood joint protection disc, the dimen-

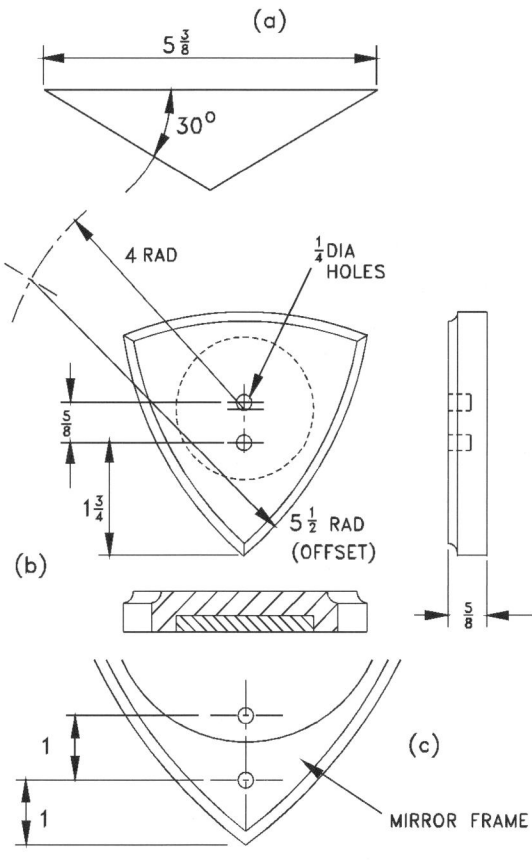

Figure 200

sions of which are not particularly important. The three arcs forming the profile will be found difficult on a beam trammel, due to their radius, although they can be done easily on a Pivot Frame. If only a beam trammel is available, the arc radius may be increased somewhat, without requiring larger segment blanks. The pedestal may be formed, as mentioned earlier, from one of the main frame offcuts. It is simply disc sanded to its basic triangular shape, and then profiled on its vertical flank with a bearing-guided cutter. This is easily achieved by holding the piece on a flat worktop on each face in turn, with double sided tape. The dowel holes in the base, main frame and backing disc, may be drilled with a pillar drill. Those in the pedestal may be cut with a router, mounted in a jig of the type described in Chapter 6 (see Fig.123). Note that one of the dowel holes is actually cut in the backing disc for the main frame.

This arrangement requires a certain order of assembly: the main frame is finished and polished on its front face. The base and pedestal may be similarly treated. The mirror is fitted with some form of adhesive felt backing, simply to stop it rattling in its housing, placed in its recess, and the backing disc glued into place. At this assembly point, it is important to have dowels fitted, at least temporarily, in the pedestal. These are inserted into the frame and disc at the time of gluing, to ensure that the latter is in its correct position. The rear face of the mirror frame can then be finished and polished once the glue has set, after which the complete assembly may be carried out. Note that, with this design, which is a fairly simple one, the mirror cannot be removed once fitted.

Other designs are possible, as can be seen from Figs 201 and 202. No dimensions are given for these, and the reader is invited to experiment (on paper first perhaps). I would call attention to an error on my part, shown in Fig.201, which has in fact spoilt the piece. The ebony used for the inserts was not completely seasoned, and has split at the joints. Be warned!

Figure 201

Figure 202

The third project is basically a very simple scalloping exercise, with a routed profile as illustrated in Figs 203 and 204. It will be found convenient to rout the scallops on a beam trammel with associated secondary disc, as shown in Fig.24(b) Chapter 1 and Fig.206, using a pre-bored central hole as location; this hole will eventually be needed for the shaft of the clock movement also. The main disc and outer ovolo profile are more easily routed on a Pivot Frame.

The remainder of the exercise is to some extent at the discretion of the reader. It would be a very simple matter to overlay or inset the platter thus made with a commercial clock face, or to bore a series of holes around the periphery to provide a simple indication of the hour positions. The exercise illustrated, although just a little more difficult, provides a very rewarding result, with the additional satisfaction that the entire project is home-made. It is also a useful introduction into the use of the indexing jig described in Chapter 6 and illustrated in Fig.143. All the information necessary to produce the hour markers and the decorative star pattern is con-tained in Fig.205(a). Note from this drawing that the

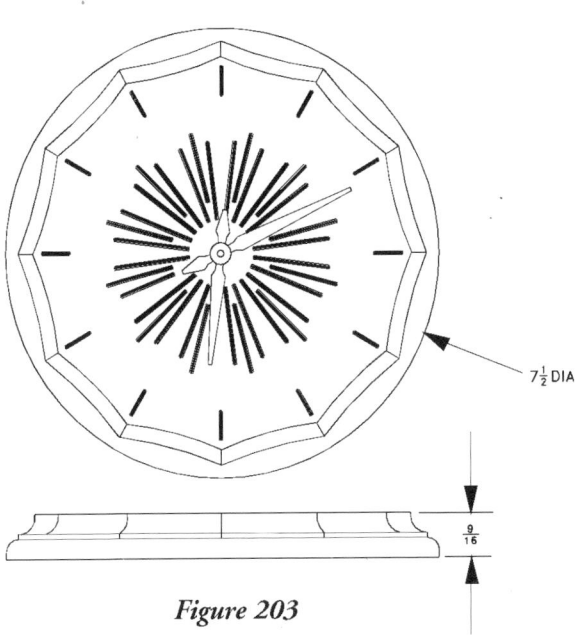

Figure 203

Figure 204

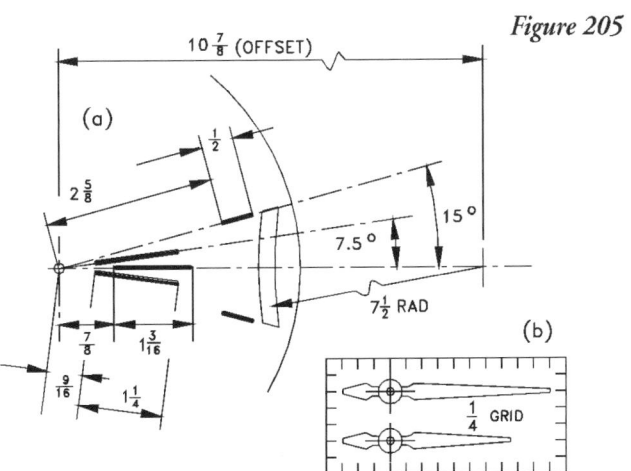

Figure 205

Figure 206

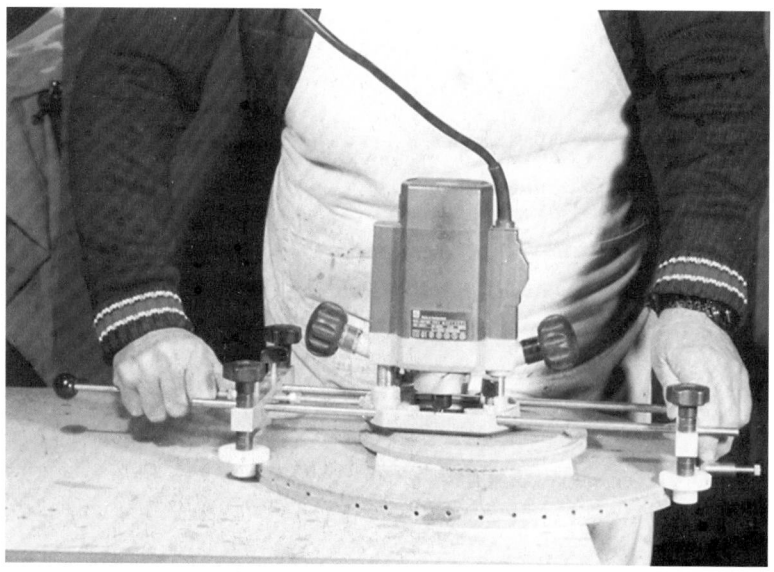

Figure 207

minimum angle specified is 7.5°, which implies 48 indexing stations around the primary disc. In order to minimise the possibility of errors with regard to routing the slots at the wrong stations, this is best managed with two sets of 24 stations, staggered as shown in Fig.142 Chapter 6. In this way, a given group of routed grooves can be set up on one or other of the groups of indexing holes. Even so, some care is needed, because the hour markers for example, need alternate indexing holes to be skipped to produce the twelve stations required. Although the actual operation of routing the grooves is quite easy, there is plenty of potential for silly mistakes. Any uncertainty in this respect is best dealt with by routing a given set of grooves in a very shallow pass with the cutter; if errors are made, the offending cuts can be lightly skimmed off with a pass over the entire platter, once all the grooves have been cut to full depth. The length of the grooves may be set up by means of reference locknuts on the Pivot Frame micro-adjuster. This is clearly seen in Fig.207, which also illustrates a further important point of technique: the horizontal traverse of the grooves is provided by means of finger pressure on the micro adjuster, and *not* by pushing the plunge knobs on the router. In this way, control of lateral feed rate is improved. The cutter used is $1/16$" diameter, and is therefore fairly fragile. Each groove, which is about $1/8$" deep, is cut in a series of not less than three passes, with extra care taken on the last cut, to ensure complete clearance of cutting residues. Each groove is filled with a sandwich of three veneers, more or less as described for the second project in this series.

Sets of clock hands can be bought, together with battery-operated quartz movements, from suppliers of craft materials. For the interested reader, the hands illustrated in Fig.204 are home-made by fretsawing a sandwich of sycamore veneer and thin brass sheet, stuck together with superglue. Dimensions are given in Fig.205(b).

2

TWO INTERLINKED RING PROJECTS

Both projects described here are really exercises in the production of inlaid interlinked rings. They may be completed from the dimensions given, but are easily modified to suit individual requirements. Moreover, the basic operations lend themselves readily to the production of other (and larger) pieces, such as cheeseboards and, for that matter, clock-faces. The first project, illustrated in Fig.208, is a penholder, and features a proprietary product; this requires only a single central fixing however, and makes no demands upon the design, either in terms of size or shape. Two basic techniques are involved; that of producing the external profile, and that of making and fitting the inlaid rings.

Layout dimensions of the basic shape are given in Fig.209, and of the interlinked rings in Fig.210. The rings used for the inlays are made from scraps of suitable timber and are mounted at the centre of the primary disc for machining; a description of this process is given later. The base blanks may be triangular in plan and are readily sawn from lengths of stock of suitable width. Some saving in timber is possible however, by making a card or acrylic template of the required shape, but slightly larger than finished size, and using this to mark out available stock. In view of the fact that I have made over a dozen pieces to this design, I found an acrylic template very useful; this is shown in Fig.211.

The two values required for the outline, that of radius and offset are given in Fig.209. Machining is straight-

forward, following practices described earlier. Note from the drawing that the cove may be machined simply by replacing the cutter; no adjustment of the jig itself is needed.

The layout of Fig.210 is used to machine the recesses for the interlinked rings; it is essentially the same as Fig.209, but with different values of machining radius and offset. A $^1/_8$" diameter straight cutter is used, and set to cut a recess about $^3/_{16}$" deep. When machining these recesses, it will of course be necessary to use the router knobs to plunge to the preset depth over the recess itself; in other words it is not possible to set the actual cutter to the required depth off the workpiece. This will result in a slightly uneven bottom to the recess, due to spring in the rods but, as the recesses are to be inlaid with solid rings, it doesn't matter in this instance. Note that each recess should be machined in about three passes, due to the relatively small cutter diameter.

The first recess may be machined in a straightforward fashion (Fig.212); after this, things get a little more involved. There are two essential considerations: the first is that the joints in the rings themselves are curved, and must also be very precisely positioned.

Figure 211

Figure 212

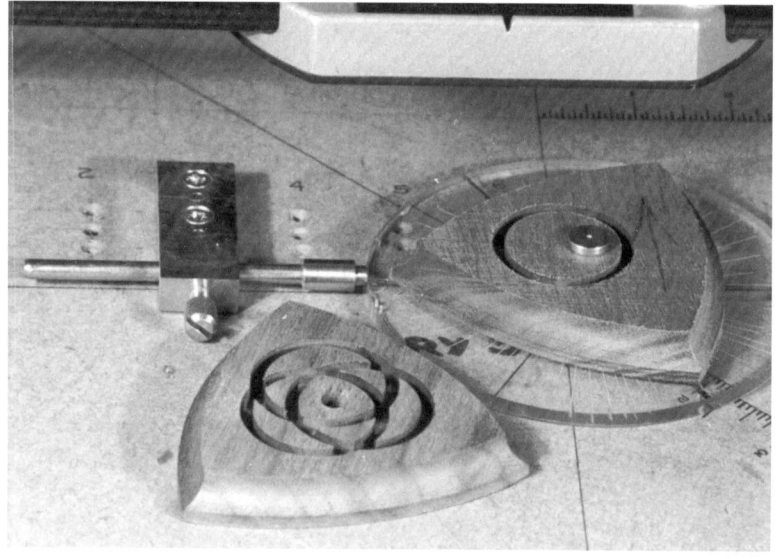

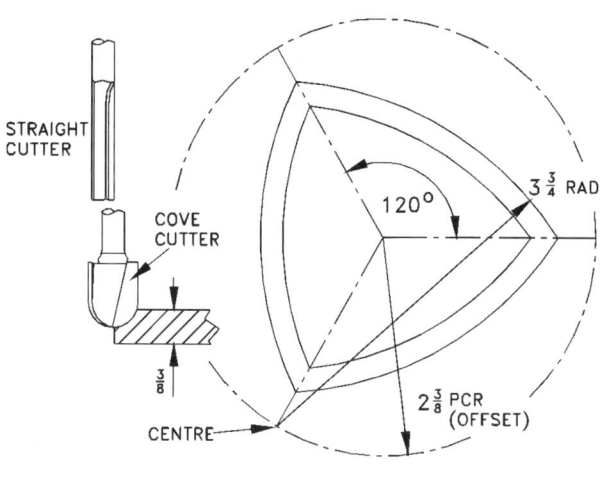

Figure 209

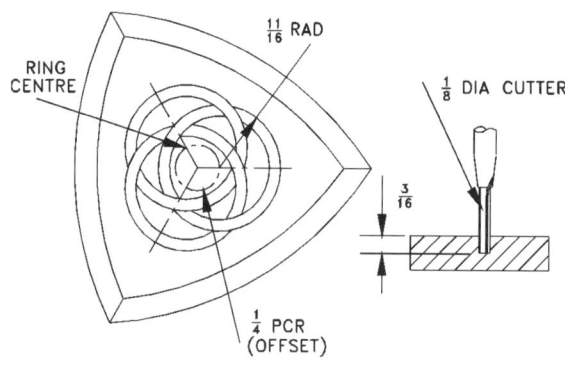

Figure 210

They must therefore be machined with the router; any attempt to cut them by hand carries the risk of poor joints. It therefore makes sense to machine the joints at the same time as the recesses; (it is necessary to assume for the moment that the rings have actually been made). After machining the first recess, the piece is rotated to machine the second, but before actually doing so, the first ring is fitted into the previously-machined recess, and firmly held there with hot-melt glue fillets or adhesive tape (Fig.214), thus machining the joints for the first ring, whilst cutting the recess for the second. It is stressed that the ring is *firmly* held, since the slightest vibration during machining may wreck it. Each ring will end up in two pieces, and herein lies a small but very useful tip: provided that the *width* of the ring is correct, a small discrepancy in *diameter* either way can be accommodated since, even if the ring won't fit the recess to begin with, it can be sawn at a suitable point. It can then be sprung sufficiently to fit the recess, and subsequent machining will remove the sawcut. It helps to number the base and the component parts of each ring for subsequent fitting. Strictly, this shouldn't matter since all parts should match, but at least it ensures that the different types of wood used for the inlays follow the same order if several pieces are to be made.

Figure 213

The second problem arises from the fact that the interlinking process quite obviously requires that the recesses break into one another at several points (Fig.212). This leads to the possibility of breakaway of the short grain at various points if the router cutter is traversed laterally. A great deal depends on the timber chosen; yew, for example, is very tolerant, walnut rather less so. I find that it is preferable to make a series of very rapid full-depth plunge cuts at the appropriate points, the steps being sufficiently small as to present a smooth curve. When all three recesses have been cut, one uncut ring will remain. This can be dealt with simply by removing the second cut ring, replacing it with the last, and repeating the machining in the joint areas.

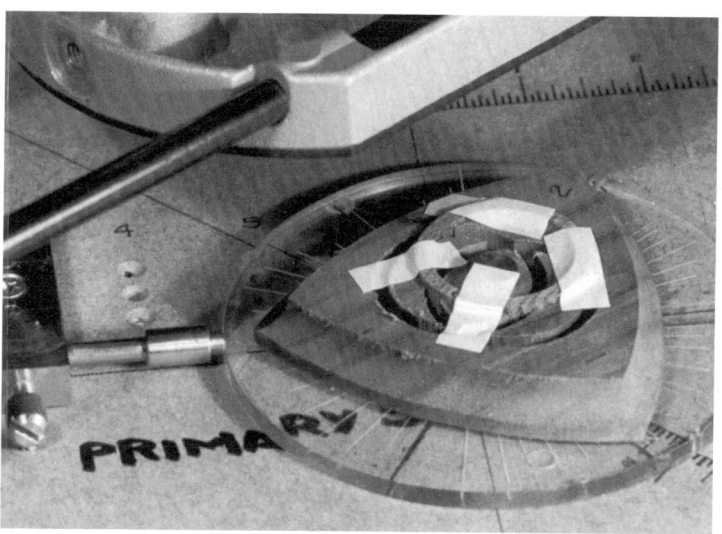

Figure 214

The inlay rings are made from small sawn scraps of timber, each with a central hole of the same diameter as that in the centre of the primary disc; three different timber types are used, chosen to contrast with one another and also with the base. The thickness should be sufficient to allow the rings to stand proud of the recesses in the base, thus allowing handling with tweezers or pliers. Making the rings and recesses is something of a chicken and egg process, since both must be done more than once, and of course, they must fit well. My own method involves making the rings first (as many as I feel are necessary, plus a few spares). They are machined with a $\frac{1}{4}$" diameter cutter, by holding them with a bolt through the centre hole of the primary disc (Fig.215). Note that in the drawing, the blanks are shown as squares. This is undoubtedly the simplest way of preparing blanks, but the routing process will be made easier if they are sawn into rough oversize circular discs. The cutter must be placed in two positions, the first to machine the outer diameter and the second, the inner. The two positions (Figs 216(a) and (b) may be locked by means of pairs of reference locknuts on the Pivot Frame adjuster studding, on either side of the pivot bar. My own method of checking the ring width when setting up the jig is to use an engineering Vernier caliper. In the absence of equipment of this accuracy, it

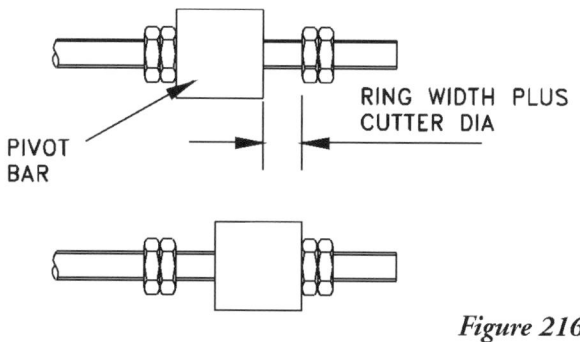

Figure 216

is perhaps wise to machine a trial circular recess in a piece of scrap timber, and check the rings for fit in this way (this can be a fairly tedious business). Note from Fig.215 that the rings are not machined to full depth, since complete removal of the central scrap will result in the ring flying off and getting smashed. About .010" should be left at the base. When the blank is removed, it can be rubbed against a coarse sanding block (Fig.217), and the ring will eventually fall away, with a nice clean finish. The Pivot Frame radius for the base recesses will be found exactly half-way between the two pairs of locknuts. This may be found quite accurately by inserting a $\frac{1}{8}$" thick metal bar between the pivot bar and each

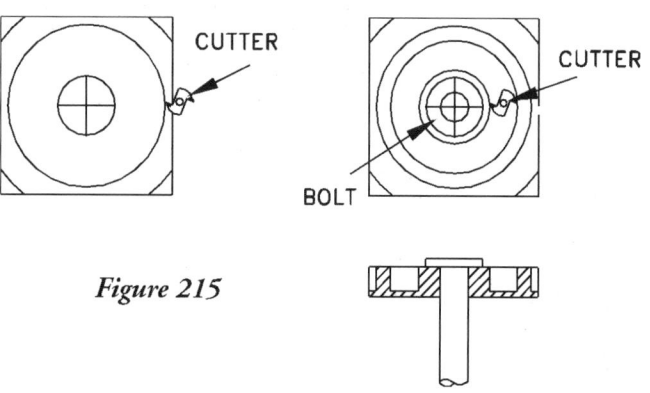

Figure 215

Figure 217

Figure 218

Figure 219

pair of locknuts, and then locking the router on the guide rods in this position.

Assembly of the rings is simple in principle, but can be a little tricky in practice dependent upon the adhesive used and the fit (which must be free from gaps, but not tight). It is possible to use PVA or similar water-based adhesives but, if these are used, assembly must be very rapid and efficient, since the water content of the glue will cause the rings to swell a little and render assembly (particularly of the last one) well-nigh impossible if progress is too slow. I have used such adhesives successfully in the past, but my current preference is for cyanoacrylate (superglue), despite its tendency to stick my fingers to the work. The trick is to apply the glue with a thin metal rod, working it into the recess only where it is needed to hold the particular section being fitted. It also helps to use a spare ring section as a guide for fitting and gluing the first section. After gluing, the guide ring is removed, and the remaining rings fitted and glued, each ring using the preceding one as a guide (Fig.218). The completed assembly is shown in Fig.219. It only remains to chisel and sand the inlays down flush with the surface.

The second piece, illustrated in Fig.220 is a yo-yo. The design and construction, particularly the addition of the metalwork, may appear to be somewhat exagger-

ated for such a simple item, but the piece was actually made for a competition, which required both appearance and performance. The complete design is given in Fig.221, but may of course be modified to suit individual preferences; the real object is that of showing how other sets of interlinked rings may be generated (in this case, five), to provide decoration. In passing, the body of the piece was actually turned on a lathe after finishing the inlay work. This, I think, illustrates two points. The first is that the lathe and the router, even when used as separate pieces of machinery, can complement one another rather well. The second is that the fact that the profile of the inlay work is obviously embraced by the curvature of the body of the piece, and is therefore produced by solid inlaying, and not by the rather simpler application of veneer.

I have made no attempt to detail the metalwork, since this is optional and will, in any case, depend upon available facilities. Rather, the piece may be seen as an exercise in laying out and cutting a group of *five* interlinked rings. These may be applied to more or less any chosen object.

Figure 220

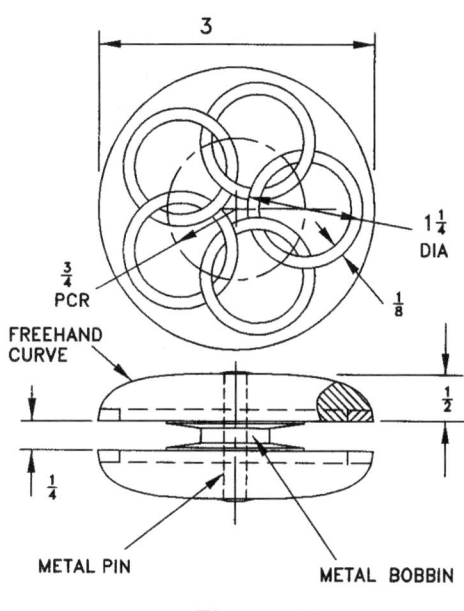

Figure 221

3

NAPKIN RINGS

One of life's major woodworking pleasures for me, is finding a use for waste pieces of timber. This project was initially conceived for this reason and will be found to place very light demands on timber stocks. It does however, demand deep cutting of relatively small workpieces, which in turn implies very careful hold-down practices. In common with many of the projects, the dimensions on the drawings, although they may be followed if desired, merely indicate one particular version of the general idea, and may be altered to suit available material without undue difficulty.

The basic concept is really nothing more than a piece of wood with a large hole through it. It is one of the staple 'Christmas present' ideas among woodturners, myself included. Short of rather complex set-ups however, the woodturner is restricted to variations on the longitudinal profile of a cylinder. The use of the indexing system outlined in Chapter 1, together with a Pivot Frame or beam trammel allows the outer profile to be varied considerably. It must be stated however, that the Pivot Frame is to be preferred for work of this nature, simply because it allows small-diameter circles to be machined, and will therefore cope with the bored hole quite easily.

Basic dimensions of the design offered are shown in Fig.222, together with the Pivot Frame and indexing system settings. Almost any hardwood may be used although, in view of the lie of the grain, those with a

tendency to tear are perhaps best avoided. It is also sensible to choose a timber which takes a finish without becoming excessively dark on end grain as compared with side grain. Regardless of how the grain is chosen to run on the blanks, there will be an appreciable area of end grain, either on one flank, or at both the top and bottom faces. It is a relatively simple matter to insert a

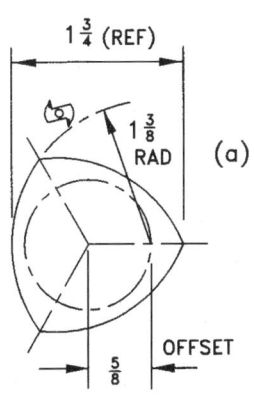

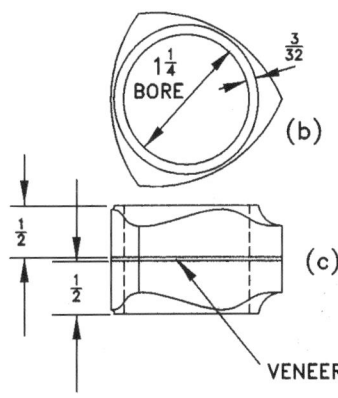

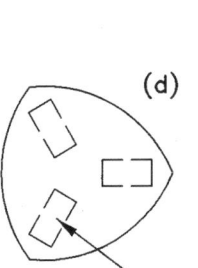

Figure 222

Figures 223 & 224

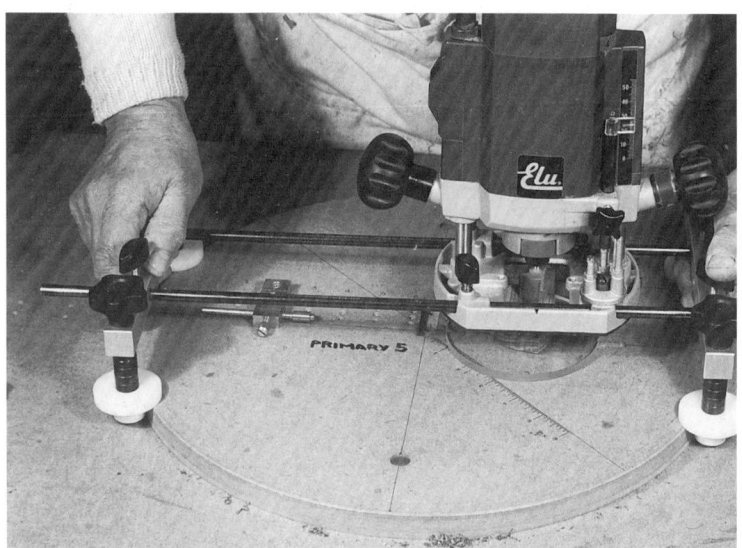

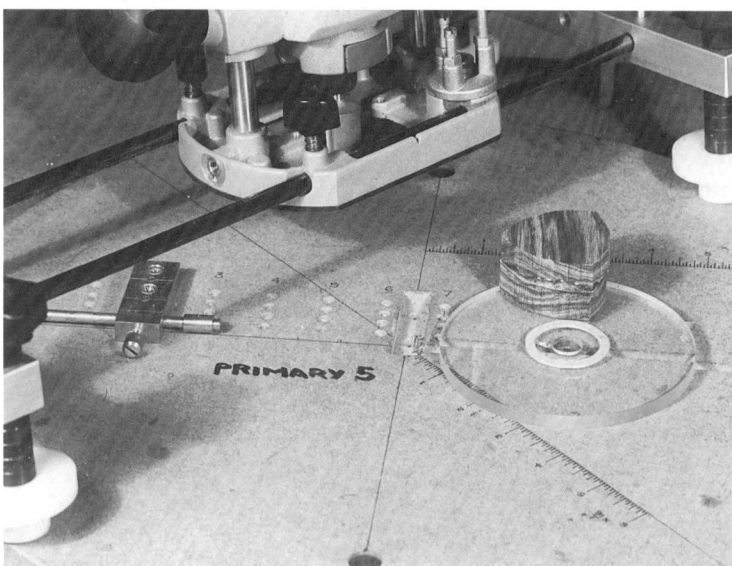

small piece of contrasting veneer between two pieces of timber, to provide a decorative horizontal line through the finished piece (c); the method also allows smaller scraps of timber to be used initially.

It is very important that the blanks are all of the same thickness and that the two opposing faces are parallel. This is quite easily managed by disc-sanding one face of each blank dead flat, and then mounting them on the Pivot Frame one at a time, skimming the other face flat and parallel, using a cutter of large diameter. It is then a simple matter to assemble as many pairs as required, with veneer between them. It is sensible to make at least one more than actually required for a full set. The blanks are roughly sawn to shape prior to assembly, partly to ensure that they will yield the full required final profile (the rings shown *were* made from odd scraps), and partly to limit the load on the router cutter on final profiling. After assembly, they are again checked for parallelism between faces, and re-skimmed if necessary; this is a very important step, as will be seen and is, incidentally, easily managed with a vacuum chuck (Figs 223 and 224).

The next task is to drill or bore a $\frac{1}{4}$" diameter hole right through the centre of each blank to take the bolt which will hold the workpiece for all routing work. This must be done either with the router or on a drill press, to ensure that the hole is at right angles to the faces; manual drilling simply isn't sufficiently accurate. The work may then be set up on the Pivot Frame indexing system. Machining is a simple matter of sweeping the cutter in an arc across each of the three faces in turn, setting the depth in very small increments *off* the workpiece. Although the indexing system will prevent the secondary disc from rotating during machining, the central holding bolt may not be adequate to prevent movement of the workpiece on the disc. For this reason, it is suggested that a piece of veneer is attached to the secondary disc with double-sided adhesive tape, and similar tape applied between workpiece and veneer. In the latter case, the tape can be in the form of three small strips arranged as shown in Fig.222(d), to facilitate easy removal of the workpiece from the veneer after machining, and also to ensure that the workpiece remains level. In passing, veneer can normally be relied upon to be of constant thickness, and is therefore unlikely to be a source of tilting error. It is *not* sound practice to feed in the climb-milling (clockwise) direction for this operation. This is because almost the entire length of the cutter is potentially in contact with the work, even though small depth increments are used. If the workpiece does move during machining, the cutter will snatch it severely. When all pieces have been profiled, the Pivot Frame set-up is changed to provide a central mounting position for the workpiece (the secondary disc and indexing system are no longer required), and both outer edges profiled with a cove cutter to choice. Due to the inevitable spring in the guide rods (which should, in any case be kept as short as possible), it is very difficult indeed to plunge the cutter into the work and then complete a full rotation without indenting the workpiece at the point of entry. For this reason, the cutter is fed in *laterally* after presetting the minimum cutting radius with the aid of a couple of reference locknuts on the micro-adjuster against the outer edge of the pivot bar, and a further pair inside, to limit the withdrawal distance (this latter pair is not essential, but will be found convenient in practice). At this point, the reader is invited to study the three photographs, Figs 225–7, noting the position of the hand in each case. In Fig.225 the knob is being pushed inwards, but the forefinger is being used to restrict inward movement. This is to limit lateral cutting depth, thus allowing a number of cuts to be taken. The finishing cut is taken with the adjuster pushed to the limit, as shown in Fig.226. Finally, the thumb is used to withdraw the cutter, as shown in Fig.227. All three actions are made simultaneously with rotation of the Pivot Frame around the primary disc, to ensure smooth

Figures 225 to 227

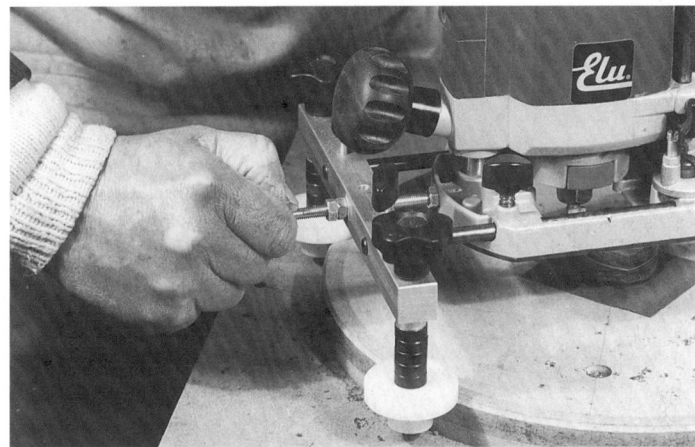

Figures 228 &229

entry and withdrawal of the cutter. At no time is the router handled directly, other than to switch it on and off, all hand pressure and guidance being generated at the pivot bars (Fig.228). The process is swift and simple, and allows many pieces to be completed in a very short time (Fig.229).

The router is now fitted with a $\frac{1}{4}$" diameter straight cutter, set to machine the inner bore. A small piece of veneer which has been pre-drilled (or preferably punched) with a $\frac{1}{4}$" diameter central hole is attached to the primary disc with double-sided adhesive tape. The machined side of the workpiece is attached to the veneer, also with double-sided tape. The first series of cuts are taken to within about $\frac{1}{4}$" of the base (Fig.230), at which point the workpiece is removed, together with the veneer on the primary disc. Further sacrificial pieces of veneer are prepared with central holes; one piece of veneer is required for each workpiece. The previously machined face of the workpiece is now attached to a piece of veneer, with a full unbroken piece of adhesive tape, and the assembly mounted on the primary disc with the central bolt. The purpose of the tape is to prevent movement of the outer part of the workpiece

Figures 230 & 231

relative to the central plug on final breakthrough. This series of cuts is taken at very small depth increments, with the final breakthrough increment being about $^1/_{32}$". Note that it is *not* a good idea to make this final increment wafer thin, since it is required to maintain the position of the outer ring during the final cut. Also, this final pass is taken in an anticlockwise direction. This is because the combination of cutter and Pivot Frame rotation will give the cutter a tendency to nudge the workpiece away as the last shred of the final cut is completed, rather than snatch it inwards. Fig.231 shows the general idea. If the cutter is allowed to make its final pass with its bottom face about $^1/_8$" below the level actually required to remove the material, it should trace exactly the same circular profile as the initial set of cuts. It is for this reason that the two opposing faces of the piece were made parallel to begin with and that the bolt hole was made square to the faces.

Pieces of this nature are somewhat difficult to finish, essentially because the quality of the inside must match that of the outside, giving rise to handling problems. The matter is given detailed attention in Chapter 5.

4

CIRCULAR BOX

Figure 232

The design illustrated in Fig.232 is one of the easier projects but, for the dimensions given, requires the use of the Pivot Frame. If a beam trammel is used, the box diameter must be increased to provide access to the pivot point, and some other device, such as a lathe, will be required for the knob. The entire project may be carried out on a lathe in fact, since only circular profiles are involved. It may be noted however, that the machining of dead-straight circular flanks at depths of the order of an inch or so, may be carried out far more easily with a suitably guided router. The design is actually related to Project 3, since it will comfortably hold a set of six napkin rings of the size and shape given in that project (Fig.233).

Construction is very straightforward, comprising a base, an open (annular) ring for the outer 'wall', and a lid. The ring may be given a simple decoration, in the form of a contrasting veneer sandwiched between two rings of the chosen timber (Fig.233). In view of the very thin wall of the annular ring, a radially segmented construction is *not* recommended, since the joint area between segments would be very small and in end grain. Instead, it is recommended that all components are cut from boards of appropriate size. It is also recommended that, on assembly, the grain of the timber is arranged to run in one direction for all component parts. In addition to enhancing the appearance of the finished piece, any stresses due to differential shrinkage will be minimised by this means.

The stock boards may be planed flat and thicknessed

with the router in planer mode, after which, fairly generous circular profiles are drawn directly on to them with compasses. Rather than waste the material at the centre of the rings, they may be fretsawn to the drawn profile. A ring of similar size is cut from veneer, and the annulus assembled as shown in Fig.235.

It will be seen from Fig.234 that the depth of the assembled ring is rather greater than the reach of most standard $\frac{1}{4}$" shank cutters. This means that machining must be carried out partly from each face, a procedure which demands accurate location of the workpiece. Two extra pieces of timber are required for this task. The first is a sub-base, made from a sheet of plywood or MDF with a $\frac{1}{4}$" diameter hole at the centre, its purpose is simply to protect the face of the primary disc. The second is a 'locating disc' of MDF, about $^3/_8$" thick, also with a $\frac{1}{4}$" diameter hole at the centre which may be machined on the Pivot Frame, using the central hole in conjunction with a suitable bolt and also using the protecting ply sheet. The ply sheet is held in position with a few fillets of hot-melt glue around the edges, once it has been centralised on the primary disc; both the sub-base and the locating disc are also shown in Fig.235. Note that, for this and remaining work, the Primary disc

Figure 233

must itself have a similar hole at dead centre (which it will have if machined as outlined in Chapter 1). The locating disc is machined to the required final *inside* diameter of the ring, and then removed from the work station. The ring is now centralised on the ply sheet (essentially by manual adjustment with the aid of a steel

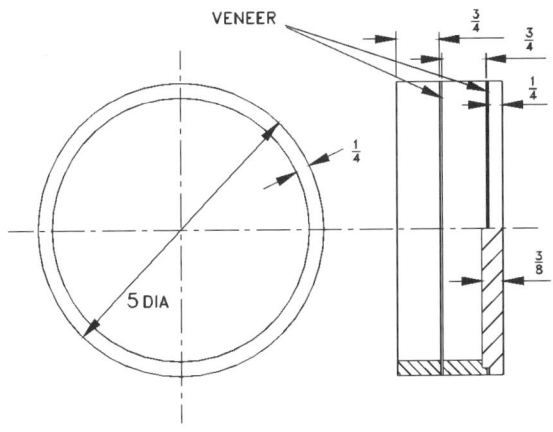

Figure 234

Figure 235

Figure 236

Figure 237

rule), and held in place with a generous application of hot-melt glue around the *outer* periphery. In view of the fact that the ring is a rather deep workpiece, it must be very firmly held down. The inner diameter of the ring is now very carefully machined to a depth of only about $1/8"$, increasing the diameter very slightly with each pass, until the locating disc fits it. The fit should be fairly

tight, and there must certainly be no sloppiness. At this point, a pair of reference locknuts are set on the micro-adjuster to limit any further increase in diameter. As a final check, the router is slid inwards on the guide rods, and then moved out again until limited by the locknuts. A further tiny trial cut is then taken, to ensure that the locknuts have been set correctly. The ring may now be machined to about three quarters of its full depth, taking very light cuts, both in depth and diameter, until the final sequence of cuts is made against the locknuts. The hot-melt glue joints are then broken and the ply sheet cleaned up. The locating disc is then placed on the ply sheet using the central bolt to hold it down, and the inverted workpiece fitted over it. More hot-melt glue fillets are placed around the outside of the workpiece and the machining of the inner surface completed. However accurately the foregoing procedures have been implemented, it is possible that a tiny shoulder will appear as the cutter machines away the last of the waste. This will almost certainly be due to tolerance build-up in the various parts of the entire system and must be carefully sanded away during finishing. The outer surface of the ring may now be machined in a similar way, using the locating disc. Since the outer diameter is merely a figure set by the drawing, and does not require to be machined to fit anything in particular, the locknuts are reset to the necessary dimension on the adjuster, and left alone until machining is completed. Finally, the small rebate is cut; this will accommodate the base rebate.

The base is machined by fixing it to the plywood sub-base with double-sided adhesive tape. The outer periphery is machined to full depth, but slightly oversize on diameter to begin with. The rebate to take the ring is machined as shown in Fig.234, working carefully down to a diameter which provides a good fit with the ring. At this point, the micro-adjuster is set, and a final cut taken at a very tiny depth increase. The depth of cut is set off the workpiece, and the adjuster slid inwards against the locknuts to actually make the cut. Any depth error due to spring in the guide rods is thereby negated, resulting in a dead level surface. The ring is fitted to the rebate, and a line drawn with a sharp pencil around the outer periphery. The ring is then removed, and the base machined to the line (Figs 236 and 237). The lid (Fig.238) is dealt with in a similar way, providing a tight initial fit to the ring. After completing the outer diameter of the lid, the rebate is reduced in diameter slightly, to allow the lid an easy fit to the ring. It must be borne in mind that some wood movement is likely to occur over a period of time, and this may result in the lid jamming if the initial fit is made too tight. The final cove profiling on top of the lid should be made with a bearing-guided cutter, since it is highly unlikely that the lid can be reversed and replaced with sufficient accuracy to enable the Pivot Frame to be used directly for this purpose. The lower veneer ring is fitted and the waste sanded away after gluing. This (optional) feature must be allowed for when machining the base.

It is not my intention in this book to suggest that the woodturning lathe can be replaced by Pivot Frame or trammel techniques. My own activities encompass both woodturning and routing, and I regard the two

Figure 238

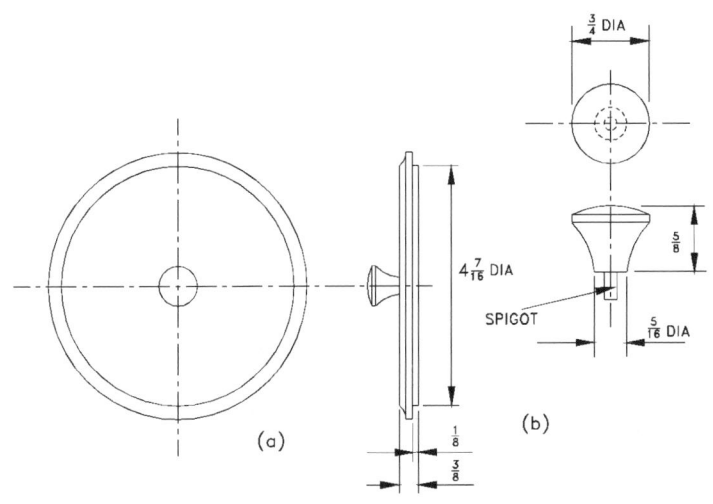

techniques as complementary rather than competitive. It may well be however, that the reader does not possess woodturning equipment. For this reason, a plain circular knob, of the kind which is actually much easier to make with a lathe than a router, is offered in Fig.238(b). The greatest difficulty with small work of this kind lies in prevention of the workpiece flying off its mounting when machining. This implies firm fixing, but this is by no means the whole story. To obtain a solid base for the work, it is necessary to use a piece of timber considerably larger than would appear to be required, and to attach it to the baseboard with double-sided adhesive tape, backed up by generous fillets of hot-melt glue around the outside (Fig.239). A fairly large straight cutter (about $\frac{3}{4}$" diameter) is used, and the depth of cut set to about $\frac{1}{8}$" short of the baseboard. The waste timber is now removed in a series of plunge cuts, to provide a cylinder about $\frac{1}{4}$" greater in diameter than actually required. The procedure will give a somewhat scalloped finish on the work but this does not matter for the moment; the object of plunge cutting is to limit sideways pressure on the workpiece. The cutter is then moved inwards on the Pivot Frame and a very light skim cut taken over the top face of the workpiece, to ensure that it is straight and level. The straight cutter is replaced with a suitable cove cutter, set to give the same depth of cut. This too is moved around the work in a series of plunge cuts, to produce a profile slightly oversize on diameter. A pair of reference locknuts on the micro-adjuster are now set to give a 'minimum diameter' stop slightly less than that of the workpiece as it stands, and a full sweep taken around the work, moving the micro-adjuster inwards to the stop, as the Pivot Frame is rotated. This will give a smooth profile. The cutter is now replaced with a small straight cutter of about $^{3}/_{16}$" diameter, and the profile machined to its final dimension, stopping the cutter about $^{1}/_{32}$" short of the base board. Finally, the central $^{1}/_{8}$" diameter hole is bored, either on the Pivot Frame or on a pillar drill after removal of the work-piece.

A piece of $^{1}/_{8}$" diameter steel or brass rod, about 2" long is now fitted into the hole in the knob with superglue. This will eventually be trimmed and used to fit the knob to the lid but, for the moment, it will serve both as a mandrel and a convenient handle. The surplus material left by the router is first removed, and the knob then roughly domed on a disc sander . It is then placed in a pillar drill or suitably mounted portable drill and the dome completed with abrasive sheet on a block (see Fig.108, Chapter 5). After final finishing and polishing, the metal rod is trimmed to protrude about $\frac{1}{4}$" and used to fit the knob to the lid after the box has been finished.

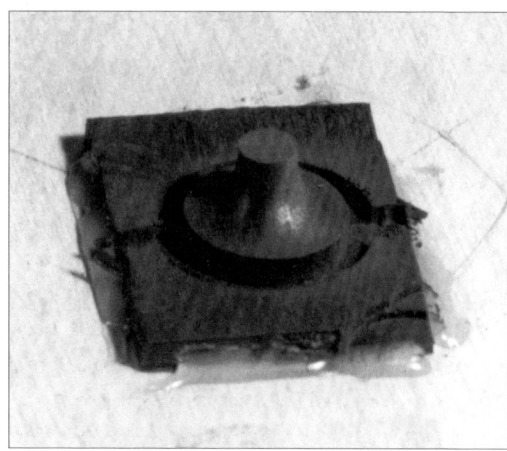

Figure 239

SCALLOPED BOXES

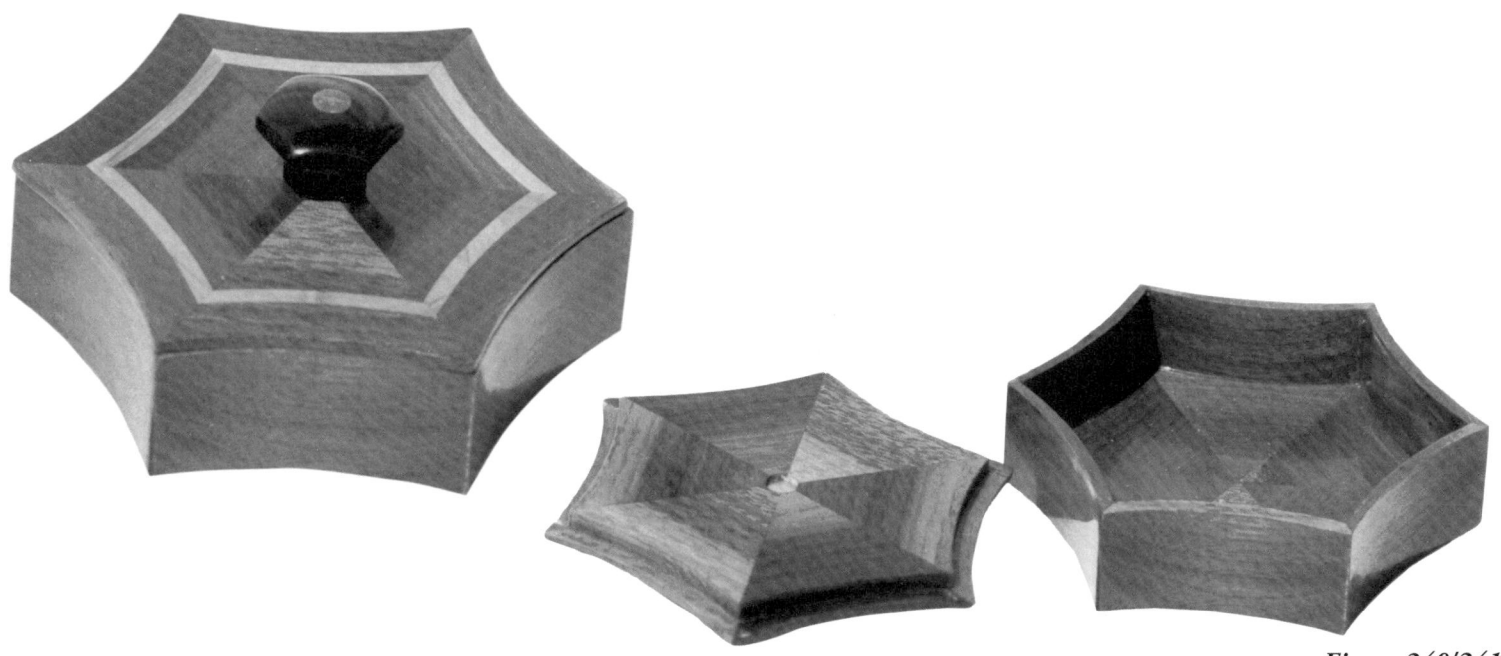

The projects described here are nothing more than an advancement of the techniques employed in Project 1, and may be carried out either with the Pivot Frame jig or with a beam trammel. In the illustrations, the Pivot Frame is used in its beam trammel mode, but any trammel offering similar facilities may be used instead.

The designs feature sharp internal corners, which cannot normally be completed with a router in a single solid workpiece due to the finite diameter of the cutter. The effect can however be achieved with segmentation, but a high order of machining and assembly accuracy is required. Much of this will be offered directly by the jig used, but the initial machining of the segment joints must be done by other means. My own preferred technique relies upon disc sanding. This can give very

accurate results, provided that the stock material is carefully prepared beforehand. Before proceeding further, I would state quite categorically that it is *not* essential that all segments are cut from a single piece of timber. Indeed, the projects described can be an excellent way of using up scraps of timber, provided that they are all of the same type, and that they match reasonably well in terms of colour etc. It is however, necessary to work with stock which is of uniform *thickness*. The stock material can quite easily be thicknessed with the Pivot Frame in planer mode, even if the material is in the form of individual segments which have been roughly prepared to begin with. Work of this nature is indeed very easily handled with a simple vacuum chucking system. Alternatively, the workpiece may be held down by

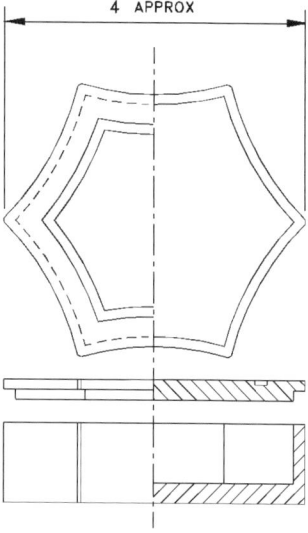

Figure 242

4 APPROX

adhesive methods. It is assumed in the following that stock material comprises segments of roughly the required planform, but not necessarily the same thickness.

The easier of the two projects described in this section is illustrated in Figs 240 and 241. Construction details are shown in Fig.242; Only one dimension is given on

Figure 243

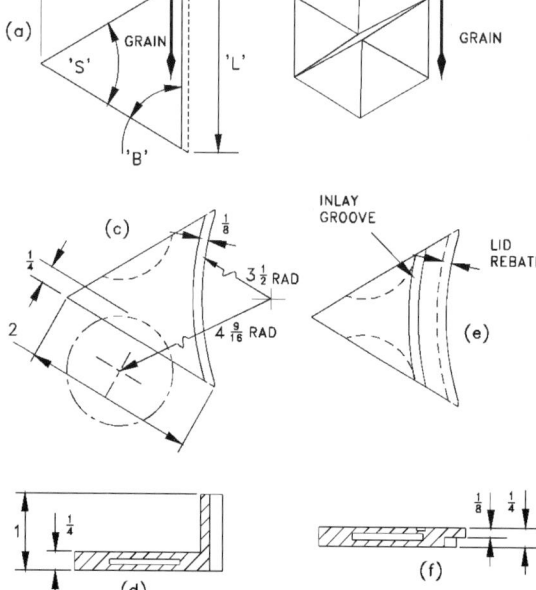

this drawing, merely to indicate overall size, since the machined segments actually determine the size of the finished piece.

The first task is to prepare one dead flat face on each segment, to be regarded in the following as the 'face side'. This may be carried out simply by placing one face of each segment on a disc sander. The material is then thicknessed with the Pivot Frame in planer mode, or with any similar form of ski system. The outer edge of each segment is then sanded straight and square to the face side, to provide a 'face edge' for marking out. The sander table should initially be checked with a trial scrap of timber to ensure that the sanded edges will indeed be dead square. When mitring frames or segments where the joint lengths are fairly small compared with the overall segment length, such as the second of the two mirror frames featured in Project 1, it is usually only possible to work with the mitre angle formed by the mitre and the outer edge of the segment, shown as 'B' in Fig.243(a). This is at best an indirect measurement; the angle that really matters is the centre angle S' and, wherever possible, this is the angle which should be given the closest attention when sanding. My own preference for dealing with this type of problem is actually described and illustrated in detail in Project 6 which, although employing much the same techniques, is slightly more demanding. I would suggest therefore that the reader studies Project 6 before attempting any of the work described here. It may be seen that the stock width, shown as 'w' in Fig.243(a), although vitally important in some segmented work, is of secondary importance for this task, since the machining of the scallops will eventually ensure that all are alike.

A further problem arises with any form of segmentation, that of joints popping open due to environmental changes and consequent timber movement. Note that the work is assembled with the timber grain in the direction shown in Fig.242(b). It is also reasonable to assume that most workshops will feature a rather more

Spartan environment than normal living quarters, and it is therefore more likely that the timber will dry out and shrink slightly, rather than to acquire moisture and swell. Without going into great detail, the combination of grain direction and drying-out will place the greatest stress on the centre part of the joints which are rather likely to end up as indicated (b). The problem is particularly significant for the designs given here, since the bases and lids are quite thin, and do not in themselves allow much joint area, which will in any case be in end grain and therefore not of the best. It is highly desirable therefore, to strengthen the joints in some way. Moreover, if the piece is intended to be available for inspection on all surfaces, the bottom cannot be covered with the ubiquitous green baize; it follows that the joints must be either decorative or invisible. Dowels are difficult to place accurately in thin material, which leaves joints of the 'biscuit' type. Even these cannot be successfully managed with standard biscuits which, at about $^5/_{32}$" are too thick. Fortunately, it is possible to acquire for the router individual slotting cutters of the biscuit type which are rather thinner than the standard item. I strongly recommend, and use in work of this type, a 36mm. diameter by 2.5mm. thick slotter. This is used in conjunction with home-made biscuits, made from four thicknesses of veneer, glued together with superglue. A sandwich of this kind will end up about 2.2mm. thick, which allows an easy fit in the housing, and a very sound joint when glued. Alternatively, the stock material from which the biscuits are to be made may be bandsawn to the required thickness. Either way, the grain direction should run approximately at right angles to the longer dimension of the biscuit; this will give maximum mechanical joint strength. A close-grained timber is to be preferred for the biscuits, which may be profiled by marking to a suitable template, then fretsawn roughly to shape and finished on a disc sander.

To return to the base segments for the first, and simpler project: two possible courses are open when making these. They can be cut from the solid (d), or they can be fabricated as pieces which are essentially 'L' shaped in elevation prior to any form of machining. The latter technique is quite possible; I have used it many times. Moreover it is used, albeit in a rather special way, in the second design to be discussed. In the interests of taking things a little slowly to begin with, this arrangement is avoided for the present, since it does add a further element of risk in terms of jointing. It is therefore left for the more adventurous reader to pursue if so inclined. Machining from the solid on the other hand, although it does waste material, is at least safer for the workpiece.

After sanding the segments to the required internal angle it is important to make a dry assembly check; a method of doing so is described later. At the risk of appearing pedantic, I would suggest that the standard to aim for is a first-class fit first time; this is entirely feasible, given accurate angular checking equipment. It should certainly not be necessary to make any *significant* angular adjustment although the tiniest of adjustments may be made as required. This may be achieved by placing the segments on the sanding table and pulling the sanding disc around by hand. It is, in any case, advisable to make one or two extra segments of each type, partly to allow for future accidents or errors, and partly as sacrificial pieces when setting up the trammel or Pivot Frame. As a general rule I find that, if I need six items and start with six, I end up with five. If I start the same requirement with seven, I end up with seven; there is probably some obscure law of physics at work here! Even with a generous supply of segments, I would still advise the production of one or two pieces of identical planform in MDF or similar material, for experimental purposes; thickness doesn't matter particularly. If the biscuit housings are to be cut with the router in normal overhead mode on a trammel or Pivot Frame, it is also necessary to make one further, somewhat thicker, segment of the same planform, again in MDF, to act as a pedestal when machining the biscuit joints. The use of this item will be explained later, but it may be noted here that it will not be required if the biscuit housings are to be cut on a spindle moulder.

Each segment must be profiled separately with the router, but all must end up alike. For maximum accuracy, the same operation is carried out on each segment in turn, with all jig and router settings fixed and locked;

Figure 244

Figure 245

this means that the segments are removed and replaced a number of times. It is therefore essential to organise a system of location so that the segments are always replaced in the same position relative to the trammel. For ease and cleanliness of working, a vacuum chuck is normally to be preferred but, for very small segments, the vacuum area cannot be made sufficiently large to permit really safe attachment. I would suggest instead, the simple adhesive system shown in Figs 244 and 245. In both illustrations, the visible hot-melt glue fillets are reinforced with small pieces of double-sided adhesive tape on the underside of the workpiece. They comprise a base, made from a scrap of MDF or plywood, or a secondary disc, carrying a pair of thin guide battens, set to the segment centre angle, which allow each segment to be placed precisely in the desired position, and temporarily held with adhesive. It is important that the battens are firmly fixed; they will have a lot of work to do. I strongly advise therefore that they are initially fixed in position with superglue, and then permanently held with small brass screws, which may be 'spotted through' after assembly (Fig.246). The choice of brass rather than steel is important: the battens should be arranged to be well out of the way of any cutting action but, if the router is inadvertently allowed to cut into them, brass will be kinder on the cutter. If a secondary disc is used, angular adjustment is easy, even if final adjustment precludes the use of the indexing holes. The arrangement shown in Fig.245 does not use a secondary disc and is therefore described in detail. The base is drilled with a $\frac{1}{4}$" diameter hole to hold it to the worktop with a suitable bolt. The worktop itself should feature a slot $\frac{1}{4}$" wide and a few inches long to provide lateral adjustment for the base. (To digress slightly, a design for a 'universal' worktop is given in Chapter 6, which features a number of slots). The trammel is set to the radius required to machine the outer flank of the scallop, and the jig positioned beneath the cutter (a $\frac{1}{4}$" straight cutter will be adequate) such that the *smallest* segment blank may

Figure 246

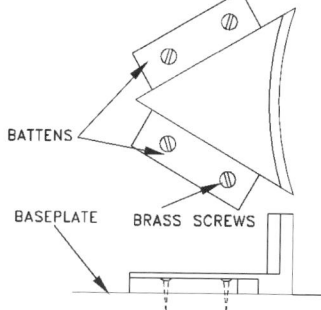

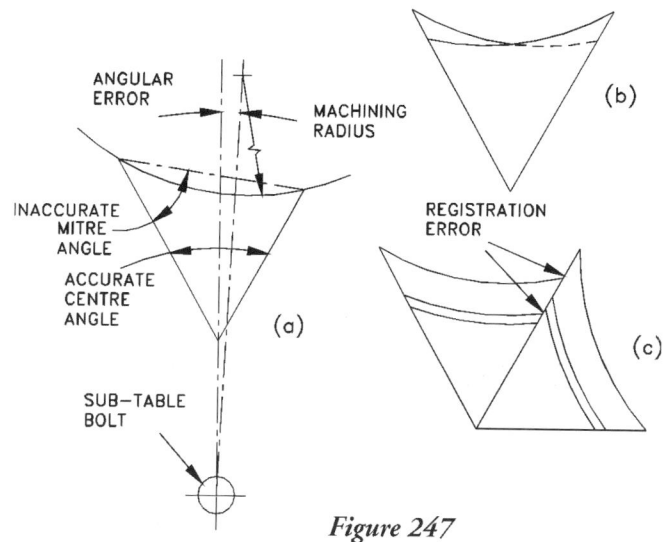

Figure 247

be fully machined. It is worth recalling at this point that the segment width was stated to be unimportant. It can now be seen that, regardless of initial segment width, all will be machined identically, provided that the smallest is used to set the jig position relative to the cutter.

Each segment is now machined in turn on its outer flank only. The positioning of the segments beneath the cutter requires a little thought: it must be borne in mind that the segment machining angle is the centre angle. Although this may be correct, it is possible that the overall machining process will have produced outer mitre angles which are not quite identical, as shown in exaggeration in Fig.247(a). This can give rise to difficulties when attempting to set the jig since, if the outer corners of one of the segments are used for initial setting, it may well be that this introduces an angular offset error (c) which will be repeated on all segments, and which will show up as a mismatch on assembly, particularly at the inlays. A much better plan is to use one of the sacrificial segments (the central angle must be as accurate as those to be ultimately used). This may be initially set at its outer corners, the jig locked firmly, and a radiused cut taken to *half* the depth of the segment, which is then flipped over, and the remaining half machined. Any setting errors will be evident as steps at the extremities, as shown in (b). The operation is repeated as necessary, tapping the jig one way or the other, to rotate it slightly on its bolt, until both sides match. At this point, the bolt is very firmly tightened and, as an

additional measure, a couple of fillets of hot melt glue applied, to prevent further rotation of the jig. This set-up is now left undisturbed until all operations have been completed on all segments, the only permissible alteration being that of the trammel radius as necessary.

The outer profiles of box and lid are much the same, but with one small but important difference: The trammel radius is reduced by about $1/_{32}$" for the lid only. This will have the effect of making the lid very slightly larger than the base, a feature which will be found very important when finishing. It is allowable to set the jig such that the cutter is just a little short of the sharp corners of the segments since, for safety's sake, these will eventually be removed anyway. It may be of interest to note at this point that the grain direction of the timber produces rather weak points on the scallops. This is rarely a problem, given sufficient care in machining, but the finish obtainable on the outer faces of the scallops is a rather different matter. Fig.109, Chapter 5 shows that this can be quite poor. In my experience, it is more a function of timber type rather than cutter sharpness or direction of cut. The finish can of course be subsequently improved by means of a little hand sanding with a suitably shaped sanding block, as described in Chapter 5. For this reason, it is suggested that, at the time of machining the scallops, a set of concave and convex blocks are made, whilst the trammel is more or less set up for the task.

The next task is the machining of the inner flank of the box scallop and clearing away all waste at the same time. For this purpose, a large diameter cutter is very useful, since it can remove much of the waste (using very small depth increments) at the same time as the flank is cut (Fig. 245). The minimum trammel radius (which machines the inner edge of the vertical scalloped side of the box) is set as a stop on the trammel by means of a pair of reference locknuts. Thus, the waste may be machined away from the inner part of the segment simply by sliding the router away from the stop, and then returning it to the stop to machine the flanks accurately for each segment in turn. Note that any steps due to variation in base *thickness* will be very difficult to remove after assembly. It is most important therefore, that the depth stop on the router is securely set to the required position, and that the final cut is set *off* the workpiece, taken from one side to the other in a single sweep and machined with the hands guiding the trammel and not holding either router knob (to avoid over-depth cutting due to spring in the rods). It is equally important that, when placing each segment in position, the surface beneath it is completely free of dust and shavings, thus ensuring that the segment is not tilted in any way.

The scalloped inlay channels in the lid segments are machined with a $1/8$" diameter straight cutter. The channel need be only about $3/32$" deep, and must certainly not be sufficiently deep as to break into the biscuit housings when these are cut. The rebates at the outer edges of the lid segments are machined next with a cutter of about $3/8$" diameter. This is a simple exercise, although it is very easy to make the mistake of machining them on the side as the inlay channels, which will

place the decorative inlay inside the box (yes, I did it!). Only a little freedom of movement is required between lid and box. One of the box segments may be replaced on the jig and used as a reference to set the cutter edge about $1/32$" inside the inner profile of the scalloped web.

It remains to cut the biscuit housings. This task is relatively easy if a spindle moulder configuration is available. A machining technique suitable for standard or home-made biscuits is shown in Fig.164, Chapter 7. If a spindle moulder is used for small work of this nature, it is essential to handle the work indirectly, for safety's sake. Manual overhead routing, although simple enough in principle, does require one special measure: the arbor for slotting cutters normally bears a plain shank with a threaded portion at the lower end, to enable cutters and bearings to be secured by means of a nut. In order to keep the slotter and its guide bearing on the plain part of the arbor, there will inevitably be some projection of the arbor beneath the slotter, as can be seen from Fig.52, Chapter 3. It is not therefore a simple matter of placing the workpiece direct on the worktop; a pedestal is needed. The arrangement illustrated in Figs 248–250 serves a dual purpose, using the shaped pedestal which was made at the same time as the segments. This is fitted into the guide battens used to hold the segments and secured firmly with hot-melt glue. The top surface of the pedestal is then skimmed dead flat with the trammel, to ensure that biscuit joint housings will be at the same level on both sides of the segments. A pair of cheeks are now attached to the sides of the pedestal with superglue, which may be enhanced by hot-melt glue fillets at the edges or, where plenty of duty is envisaged, by means of small brass screws. The cheeks provide an accurate means of location for the segments and also allow the segments to be temporarily held in place by means of hot-melt glue fillets. They also provide the very important function of acting as depth stops against the slotter guide bearing, to provide the required amount of slotter penetration into the workpiece. They should protrude above the top surface of the pedestal by a little less than half the thickness of the workpiece; thus, in order to provide the necessary stop function, the slotter bearing must be mounted below the cutter. The router plunge depth is set such that the slot sits about midway between the upper and lower faces of the workpiece, using practice pieces if necessary. Once set, the depth stop on the router is locked firmly and left alone until all housings in both box and lid have been completed. The position of the slotter in relation to the side length of the segment is set as a trammel radius by means of a pair of reference locknuts. This will allow both sides of the segment to be machined in turn, by sliding the router on the guide rods, to clear the workpiece between the two operations. This procedure assumes that the trammel pivot is a rod or bolt in a hole of appreciable depth, rather than a point. True, it is easy to lift a pointed pivot from its housing but, I admit to an intense personal dislike of any form of pivot which can hop off its housing, on the grounds that it is potentially both inaccurate and dangerous. In passing, the Pivot Frame may be set up with the same pedestal arrangement but, in this case, there is no need to set a lateral stop. The Pivot Frame is simply rotated backwards by almost a full circle, to approach the work from the opposite side.

Extensive use of hot-melt glue fillets is made in the foregoing operations (and indeed elsewhere). In my personal view, this is a sound and relatively easy means of temporarily holding the work for machining (and removing it afterwards), and is particularly useful when the position of the workpiece is fixed by side battens. I would agree that double-sided adhesive tape is also a very useful temporary 'hold down', particularly as a reinforcement for glue fillets, but removal is normally effected by a sideways wrenching action, which is not possible where side cheeks are used. I am aware that leverage with a chisel between work and mounting surface can also be used, but this may cause damage. For

Figure 248

Figure 249

this reason, I would suggest cautious application of the tape (ie. in small pieces).

It is a fact however, that small hot-melt glue fillets can break loose, particularly on MDF, leaving the work vulnerable to movement. Apart from the obvious procedure of ensuring that the joints are good to begin with,

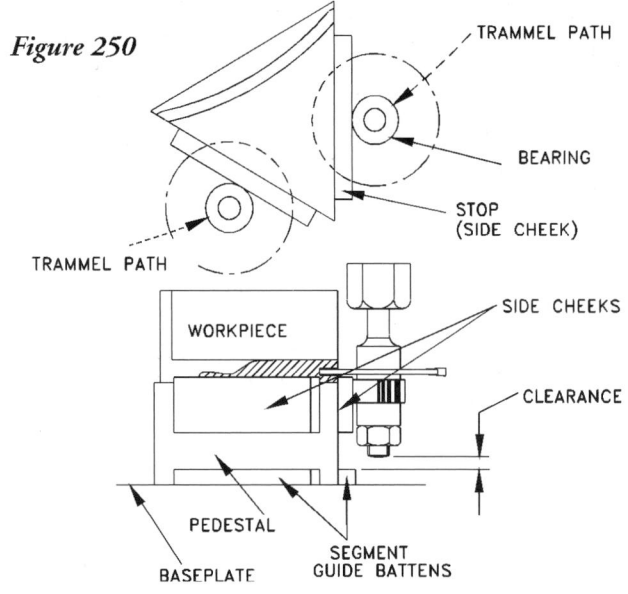

Figure 250

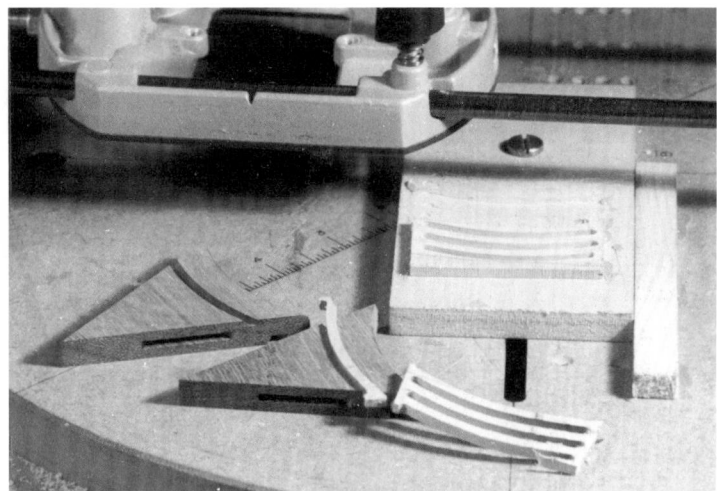

Figure 251

it pays to listen to the sound of the machining process. Even one loose fillet out of a set of say, four, can be heard as a distinct buzz, over and above the sound of the router itself, and even when wearing ear-defenders. A noise of this nature should be taken as due warning and the offending joint located and repaired.

It remains to cut and fit the inlays into the box lid. These should be made about $1/8$" thick; this will give a little machining/sanding allowance, to bring them flush with the segment faces after fitting. Small curved strips of this kind can be a little difficult to handle with a router if made separately, since they are rather fragile. They can however be made in groups of about three or four quite easily, using the set-up shown in Figs 251 and 252. This comprises a sacrificial base panel, made from a scrap of MDF or plywood, with a $\frac{1}{4}$ diameter hole near one end. The worktop should also feature a slot which allows the base panel to be slid over the worktop as desired and locked with a bolt. A simple batten fence is tacked alongside the base panel to guide it in a straight line. Scraps of the chosen inlay timber, about $\frac{1}{2}$ wider than required by the segment, are tacked to the base with hot-melt glue fillets. The Pivot Frame or trammel is set up, with two pairs of reference locknuts on the micro-adjuster, to machine the outer and inner flanks of the inlays in turn. In use, the trammel is set to the smaller radius, and the first flank machined to full depth; the trammel is then set to the larger radius, and the second flank machined. Note that the machining is not taken right to the edge of the workpiece. This allows groups of inlays to be held together safely during machining and also ensures that the cutter does not become contaminated with hot-melt glue (which doesn't exactly

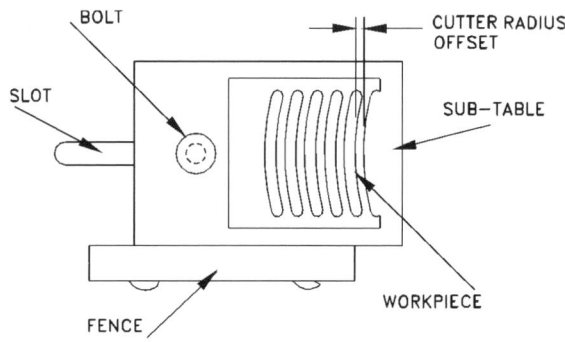

Figure 252

help the cutting action). To machine the second and subsequent inlays, the radius is reset to the smaller size, and the base panel slid inwards, until the cutter is set to remove a whisker of a shaving from the 'scrap' edge of the previous slot (to re-establish the inner radius on the next inlay). The work may then proceed as before, after which, the groups of inlays are sawn apart. For inlays of this type, featuring relatively long gentle curves, the fit in their housings should be 'easy' (but certainly not sloppy). If a water-based glue is used on final assembly, the timber will swell slightly to give hairline joints. This particular task is quite simple. It consists only of gluing the inlays in position under pressure, such that the ends protrude past the flanks of the individual segments. When dry, a little gentle sanding will bring the ends flush with the flanks. The projection of the inlays above the faces of the segments may be dealt with by holding the segments down on a flat surface and using the router in planer mode to bring the inlays flush with the segments.

For dry assemblies of both box and lid, the simple jig shown in Fig.253 may be used. For some constructions, the jig may also be used for gluing, but a little caution is advised. Regardless of any pressure pads which may be placed between the bolts and the workpiece, the actual pressure point is still that where the end of the bolt is located. Thus, if the bolts are located halfway up the jig, and a pair of 'L' shaped segments are being glued, the narrow joints at the top will be subjected to too great a pressure, and the joint will be starved. The rather larger gluing surface at the base, on the other hand, may not receive enough pressure to close the joint completely. For a shallow workpiece, such as the lid, the jig must be fitted with internal packing to bring the edges of the segment opposite the bolts. In any event, no attempt should be made to glue all joints simultaneously, since it is very difficult indeed to obtain perfect all-round alignment this way. Rather, I would suggest the slightly more time-consuming method of using the jig to cramp all

Figure 253

segments, but gluing only one pair at a time. In this way, control of segment positioning may be obtained without matters getting out of hand. I am not aware of any form of mechanical joint enhancement which may be applied to the vertical scalloped flanks of the box however; there simply isn't room, and they will therefore necessarily be plain end-grain butt joints. When assembling the lid segments, the inlays provide very good reference points for alignment. The *inner* surfaces of the vertical flanks of the box may be used in the same way. In order for the joints at the curved flanks to be neat, it is quite essential to work to a high order of accuracy when making the segments; any kind of overlap on the joints will spoil the appearance completely.

Assembly of the lid will not give a great deal of trouble, since its essentially flat surfaces on both sides may be sanded and finished relatively easily. The only area where particular care is required is at the outer rebates, which must be carefully cleaned of excess glue whilst it is still soft. Assembly of the box must be watched carefully, particularly in terms of excess glue in contact with bare timber inside the box. If this is allowed to happen, it may well show up as a discoloration after finishing. If the segments are not of even thickness, and thus give rise to stepped joints inside the box, this will present an even worse problem. I would very strongly recommend that all inside surfaces are very carefully sanded and prepared for final finishing, including sealing if necessary, before the segments are glued together.

In passing, it may be noted that the size of the box does not necessarily determine whether a Pivot Frame or a plain trammel is used, since the only machining operation involving either device is that of the scalloped edges. The only limitation on a plain trammel therefore, is the minimum radius of the scallop, which is not vitally important.

Lids usually have knobs on them. It is undoubtedly a very simple task to turn small knobs on a lathe. I would suggest however, that a good way of 'showing off' is to fit

a scalloped box with a scalloped knob of a kind which would be very difficult to make on a lathe. Knobs of this type are easily handled with the Pivot Frame or even a plain trammel. The set-up must however include an angular indexing/offset system of the type described in Chapter 1. There is one point, concerned with very small workpieces, which must be watched carefully however: due to the difficulties of mounting a workpiece safely on a very small supporting area, it is usually sensible to carry out all the necessary profiling with the workpiece presenting as large a mounting surface as possible, and to finish off the top (ie. the mounting face) by other means. Two suitable designs are shown in Fig.254, comprising six and eight sides respectively. The first will suit the project just described; the second will suit the second project of this series.

One of the harder timbers, such as ebony, will be found to work well for small knobs, since timbers of this type will take a first-class polish. (it is also an excellent way of using up small scraps of such materials). Regardless of timber type however, the work must be approached with very great care, since the 'points' of the scallops are easily damaged during the machining process. It is particularly risky to machine a knob with the grain running as shown in Fig.254(a), since the short grain at the points will break out very easily; the preferred grain direction is shown in the same drawing; this offers the timber the best chance of providing its own support. Even this is not enough by itself, particularly where the timber is very hard and inclined to be brittle. The cutter must be fed in the climb milling direction, as shown in Fig.255. Note that the feed direction indicated for the Pivot Frame in this illustration applies to the right-hand flank of the piece. It is important that the plunge knob is released so that the cutter is clear of the work on the return stroke. Although it is very convenient to swing the cutter back over the cut (with the router switched on) in order to position the trammel for the next cut, it is highly likely that this will cause

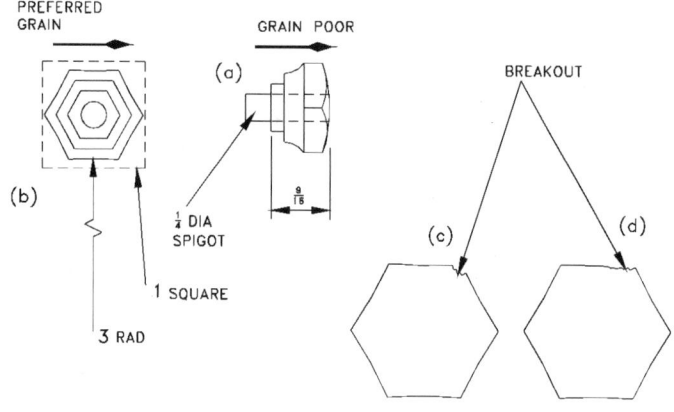

Figure 254

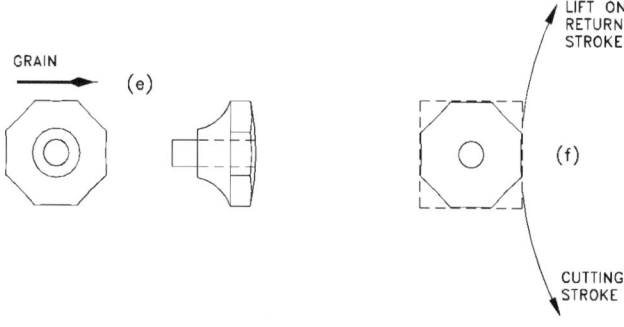

breakaway at the points. Due to the relatively small support area, it is also necessary to take things very gently in a series of small cuts of about $\frac{1}{8}$" deep or less, and to work all round the workpiece at one depth setting before proceeding to the next.

Prior to machining the profile, it is necessary to prepare the workpiece by sanding one face dead flat, mounting it beneath the router in Pivot Frame or trammel mode, and machining the top face parallel to the base with a large-diameter cutter. A $\frac{1}{4}$" diameter hole is then drilled or routed clean through the workpiece. The hole is used to locate a bolt which passes through the workpiece and the secondary disc. The workpiece is also fitted with a small square of double-sided adhesive tape, to prevent rotation on the secondary disc during machining. After machining the scallops, the final face (ie. that used for mounting) is domed as described in Project 4.

The second project, illustrated in Figs 256 and 257, is slightly more difficult and requires an extra home-made jig. This particular design is shown being made on the Pivot Frame, largely to demonstrate it in operation, but

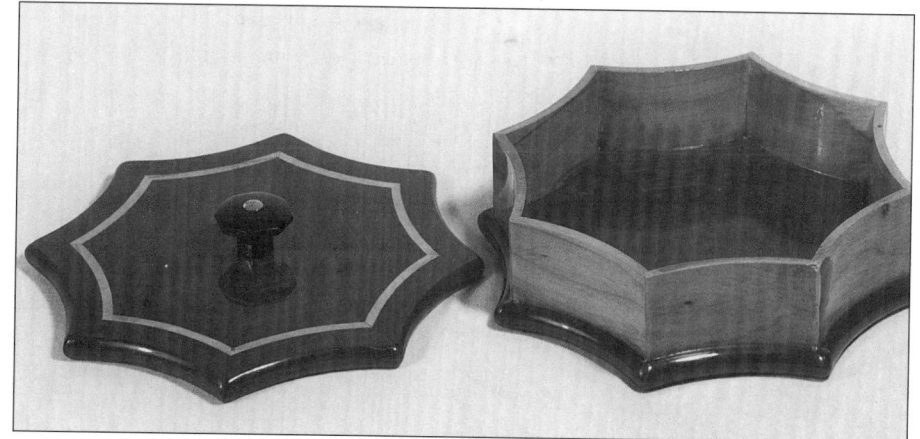

Figures 256 & 257

Figure 255

it may be made on a trammel, with suitable increase in the radius of the scallops. Apart from being an eight-segment construction, the major difference lies in the construction and fitting of the sides of the box. These are made in eight individual pieces from a contrasting timber and glued into machined grooves in the base, prior to assembly of the segments (Fig.258(a)). The lid has a similar (slightly larger) groove, enabling it to fit

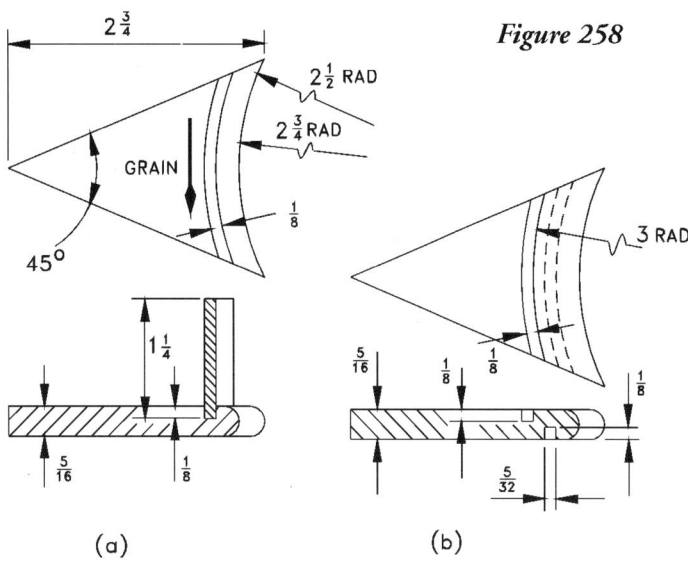

Figure 258

over the completed box. Otherwise, both the lid and the base are made in much the same way as previously, including the lid inlay. One other machining difference will be seen in Fig.259, this being the use of a pedestal vacuum chuck, allowable in this case due to the rather larger vacuum area available. The device is by no means essential however (the previous method may be used), and is featured in this project only to illustrate its use.

The curved flanks require a rather special jig, since their depth is somewhat beyond the reach of a standard cutter. They must also be considered as being a little fragile under the stresses of the machining process, although they are quite robust once completed. The jig is illustrated in Figs 260 and 261. It is quite simple, but must be made accurately in order that the blanks will be a fairly easy push fit into it; the blanks themselves must be made with equal accuracy. The studding illustrated, which may be that supplied with the Pivot Frame, is simply for the purpose of gently nipping the blanks after fitting, to hold them firmly in position. The em-

phasis here incidentally, is on 'gently'. The sides are only $1/8$" thick; excess pressure will spring them slightly during machining, with consequent loss of accuracy. It is always wise to make one or two extra pieces to allow for accidents but, in this case, it is essential to make several spare blanks, since a few will need to be sacrificed to obtain a viable set-up. To begin with, the flanks must be a good fit in the grooves in the base; this will require careful adjustment of the inner and outer radii of the Pivot Frame or trammel, and the appropriate setting of the stops on the micro-adjuster. It is also necessary to make sure that the router is level with the worktop, in order to be equally sure that the cutter is perpendicular to it. The Pivot Frame inherently deals with this problem, but a plain trammel may need a little adjustment with spacers.

It is equally important to ensure that the angular setting of the jig is correct. This is done by means of reversal of a sacrificial blank after partly machining it, in the same way as illustrated in Fig.247(b). Once the jig is

Figure 259

such that no steps appear, the single bolt is fully tightened and the position of the jig is locked with hot-melt glue fillets. There is no need to waste full-depth blanks on the setting up process. One blank may be bandsawn into two more or less equal halves, and mounted on a temporary pedestal of scrap material of the same dimensions. The pedestal should be just a little shorter than the true blank in order to guarantee that only the latter is nipped firmly. Once the jig is set up, the machining of the full blanks will be found a very easy and rapid process. The plunge stop should be set to a little over half the blank depth. I would strongly advise the following machining procedure, using two pairs of reference locknuts, to be followed. The cutting radius is set to the minimum, which machines the inner (concave) face of the blank as positioned in the jig, but which is actually the *outer* face of the sides of the assembled box. The blank is machined to the depth stop limit. The router is

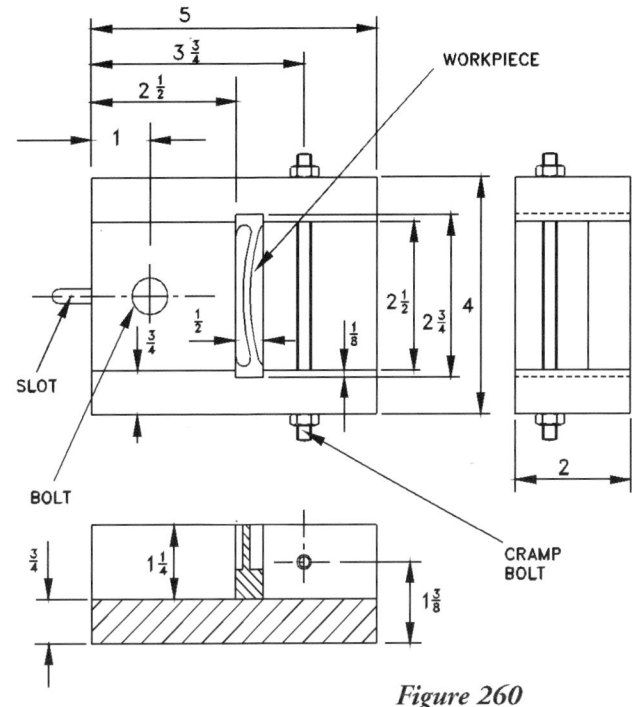

Figure 260

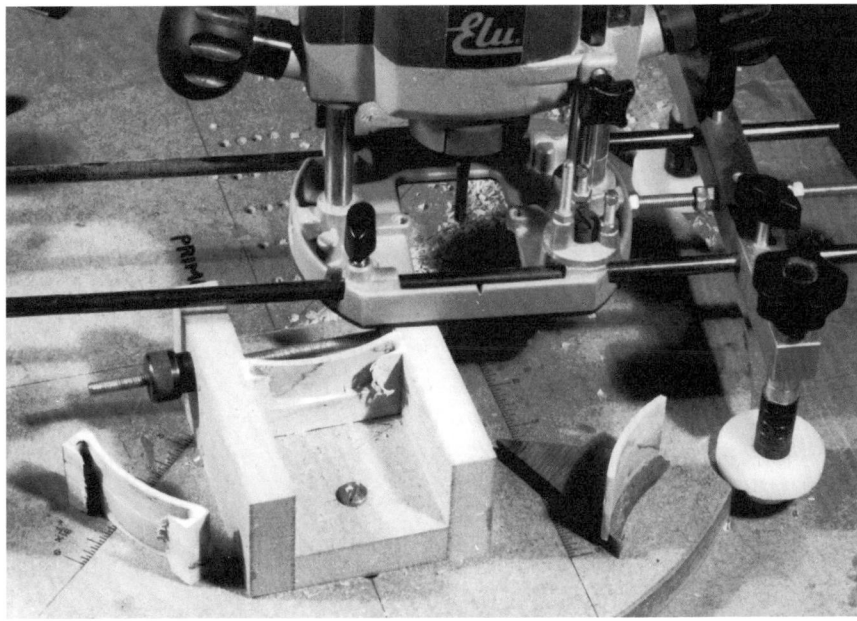

Figure 261

now moved on the guide rods to the outer radius limit, and the other face machined. The router is stopped (essentially for safety reasons) and the work reversed in the jig, such that the machined portion is now on the bottom. The router is moved back to the previous stop, to complete the concave face, and then moved to the maximum radius stop to complete the convex face. This procedure will ensure that the final cuts, which are necessarily made with the workpiece in its weakest condition, tend to compress the convex face of the workpiece (dams are made this shape for much the same reason). The router is reset back to the minimum radius, leaving the set-up ready to receive the next blank. It will be seen from Fig.261 that there is a fair amount of waste to be sawn away at both ends afterwards, but this is necessary to ensure that the work is firmly held, and also to ensure that the jig is not unduly machined along with the blanks. The machined flanks are glued into their individual base segments such that they protrude slightly at each side, allowing a little gentle disc-sanding to bring them flush. It is advisable to use a square-edged guide block against the flanks, to ensure that their sides make a right angle with the bases as they are glued.

The internal channels in the lid are deliberately machined to give clearance on the box sides when the lid and box are assembled. Although it is quite possible to achieve a very satisfactory first-time fit in this way, it so happens that, in this particular instance, I over-sanded one of the box segments, and this threw the whole assembly out (ie. the lid wouldn't fit). This obliged me to widen the slots slightly, using a $1/16$" diameter cutter. The lid was fixed to a secondary disc, the Pivot Frame set to the required radius, and the workpiece very carefully positioned such that the cutter produced the necessary enlargement of the channels. The procedure is not illustrated, since the essential techniques have already been covered, but it is a useful recovery procedure.

6

SCALLOPED SWEET TRAY

Figure 262

This project, illustrated in Figs 262 and 263, may be regarded as a slightly more adventurous follow-up to Project 5. The inlay work may be regarded as optional but, if undertaken, must be done with very great care to ensure that the inlaid strips are in alignment at every one of the twelve segmented joints. The major increase in difficulty lies however in the fact that the outer flanks of the tray are scalloped on both the top and underside, producing a profile as shown in Fig.264(b). Note from this drawing that the cove profiles do not produce a constant web thickness at all points. In the first place, it isn't necessary, since it is not detectable in the finished piece – although there is no aesthetic objection to it otherwise. Most importantly however, the arrangement is not unduly demanding in terms of cutter selection.

Any pair of reasonably matched cove and ovolo cutters will serve; in my case, a matched pair of rule-jointing cutters was used. It will be seen however that, in order to make the jig illustrated in Fig.272, it is necessary to use a cove cutter of the same radius as that used to produce the ovolo profile on the actual segments. It follows incidentally, that the dimensions given in the drawing need not be strictly observed. To avoid over-depth cutting and possible disappointment, the required profiles should be first drawn in elevation, and the derived plunge depths recorded and subsequently used.

It is important that the workpiece is held very firmly, particularly when machining the flank profiles. However light the cuts, the full curved profile of the cutters will always be in contact with the workpiece, represent-

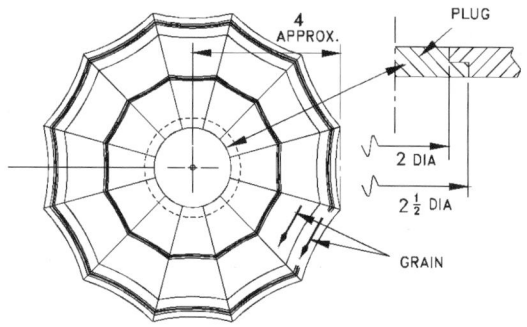

Figure 263

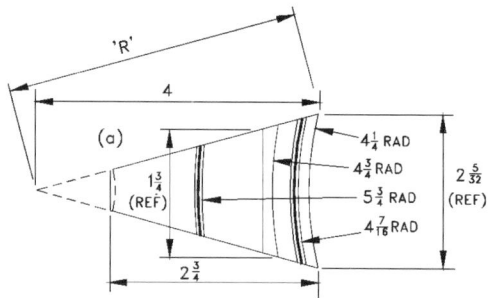

Figure 264

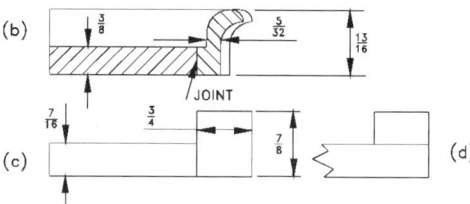

ing a relatively heavy sideways loading on the latter. There is also the further possibility of 'chatter' of the workpiece when the second cut (the underside in this case) is made, due to the relatively flimsy cross-section. This is unlikely to damage the workpiece, but could result in an inferior finish. The jigs to be described will deal with this problem.

It is possible to save timber by constructing the blanks as shown in Fig.264. Note that the joints should be

Figure 265

made as shown in (c) rather than (d), to maximise the final glued area, and of course the timbers should match in terms of colour. Note also that the joint lies well inside the curved profile; this is the reason for the rather generous width allowed on the deeper section of the blank. Prior to assembly of the blanks, the stock material is planed to width and thickness (with the router in 'planer' mode if need be). The segments are sawn slightly oversize, after marking out with a combination square or sliding bevel set to the mitre angle of 75°, with the timber grain in the direction indicated, as shown in Fig.263. After jointing (a useful method is shown in Fig.265), the sides of the segments are disc-sanded to their true profiles. Angles may be checked with the same instrument as used for marking out, but I would suggest another method. Since two mitre angles are required per joint, it follows that any angular error set into the marking device will be doubled for every joint. In my view, it is better to work on the centre angle. The method doesn't actually guarantee the elimination of

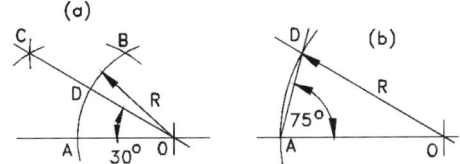

Figure 266

Figure 267

radius for this pair of arcs, to give a slightly more precise location for 'C'. A straight line drawn through points 'O' and 'C' will be at 30° to the base line, and will cut the arc at 'D'. A straight line drawn through points 'A' and 'D' will determine both the size and the mitre angle (75°) of the segment, as shown at (b). The card is clamped to a flat worktop, together with a steel straightedge aligned with the bottom line. The segment may be slid along the straightedge and its angular alignment with the top line observed. It is possible to bring the segment very accurately to both lines, by preferentially sanding one or other of the joint flanks as required. It is of course necessary to ensure that the sander table provides a dead right-angle in elevation.

Note that the segments are, by intent, not long enough to meet at the centre. However carefully the jointing is carried out, it is very difficult indeed to ensure that all the segment points meet exactly at dead centre, and short-grain in the timber at this point doesn't exactly help either. It is preferable to leave a hole at the centre, to be filled later with a decorative plug. It also reduces the width of stock required initially to make the segments.

For any segmented construction which is to be assembled directly after sanding, *consistency* of the outer flank length 'L' is as important as angular accuracy. Any variation in length between segments will eventually show up as an apparent angular error when the construction is assembled. In other projects, I have stated that this does not matter if the segments are to be identically scalloped on the same jig, since scalloping automatically takes care of the problem. If inlay work is to be undertaken however, it is important that the segments are sanded accurately to begin with, and fully checked as a dry assembly, since even the tiniest error when subsequently using the scalloping and inlay jig may cause misalignment of the inlays, which will be readily apparent. Suggested inlay positions are shown on Fig.264(a), but these may be varied. At least two

angular error, but it does at least limit it to one per segment. The centre angle for a twelve-segment construction is 30°. This can be set very accurately on a line drawing, preferably on stiff white card, by the method illustrated in Fig.266. The construction is a very well-known one but, for readers unfamiliar with it, a brief description follows: a horizontal line is drawn near the bottom edge of the card, and the position 'O' marked with a pencil. A pair of compasses is set to radius 'R' (see Fig.264(a)), and a fairly generous arc drawn, centred at 'O', to cut the base line at 'A'. The compass point is now placed at 'A' and a short arc drawn to cut the first, at point 'B'. A further pair of arcs are drawn, centred on points 'A' and 'B', their intersection giving the point 'C'; note that the compasses may be set to a slightly reduced

spare segment blanks should be made at the same time as the main batch. They should be treated as true segments throughout, receiving exactly the same treatment as the rest. Their purpose is simply to cater for possible accidents. Fig.268 tells its own story in this respect. The segment on the right moved on the jig during machining and was picked up by the cutter; the other was caused by forgetting to lock the router on its guide rods. Both were due to carelessness – but it happens in the best of circles. It is also sensible to make at least three $\frac{1}{2}$" thick MDF blanks at the same time. These will be required for making and setting up the jigs.

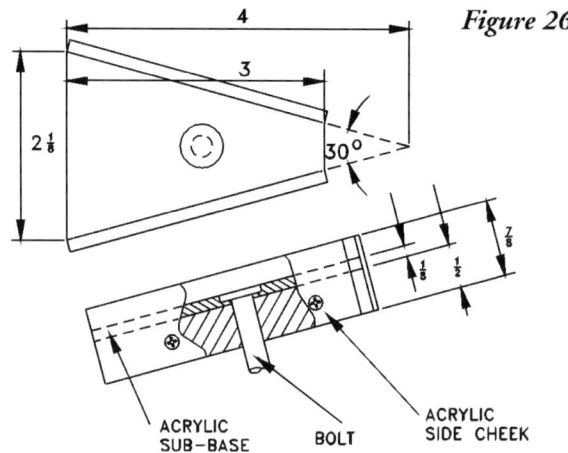

Figure 269

Figure 268

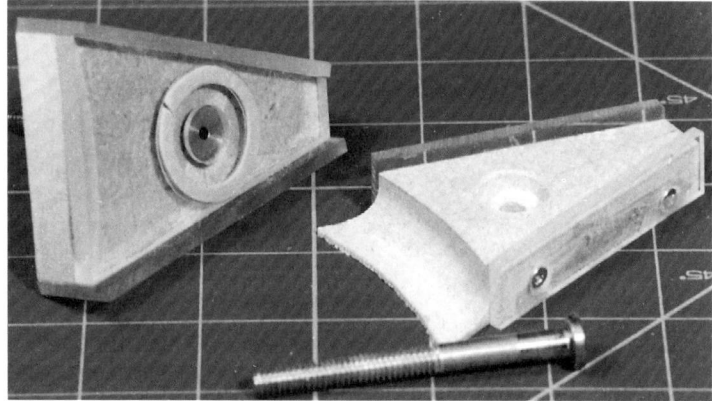

Figure 270

Workpieces comprising eight or more segments imply relatively large mitre angles; this in turn implies joints which are predominantly end-grain, and therefore not of the strongest. This, coupled with the possibility that even well-seasoned timber may move a little over a period of time, ideally requires that the joints are protected in some way. The method chosen for this project is biscuit jointing, using a pedestal jig. The technique is described fully in Project 5, but jig dimensions are given in Fig.269. Note that the angular accuracy of the jig is every bit as important as that of the segments. For my own convenience, I made this particular jig as a vacuum chuck, in the interests of rapid, clean working, but this is by no means essential; this version is shown in Fig.270, together with a further jig, to be described. This photograph also illustrates the effect of 'creep' in the gasket material. Readers wishing to follow this particular line are advised that, in this case, the available vacuum area is decidedly limited, and will yield an effective total pressure of about 12lb. This is sufficient for light machining, but does not, in my view, guarantee freedom from sideways movement, with attendant risk of pickup by the cutter as seen in Fig.268. It might be thought that the raised sides of the jig will serve this purpose, but unfortunately, this cannot be guaranteed. Extra cramping, typically in the form of a bolt and a large washer (Fig.271), will serve the purpose. Note that this must be regarded as *extra* cramping; it is not likely to be adequate by itself. It will however, serve as adequate backup for double-sided tape, if this method is used.

The jig may be used to cut the biscuit housings as it stands (ie. vacuum only) and, with extra cramping, the outer and inner flanks; the extra cramping will need to be removed to machine the centre portions of the segments dead flat. It is wise to replace it however, to machine the inlay slots; if a segment becomes loose, the tiny cutter may be broken.

Before carrying out any of this work however, a decision must be made regarding the choice of beam trammel or Pivot Frame. Both are suitable in principle but, in the case of the Pivot Frame, with the jig set in a position suitable to machine the scallops and inlays, the maximum available machining radius may not be sufficient to machine the entire lower surface flat. On the other hand, the beam trammel may not allow setting of the *minimum* required radius (that of the outer flank) shown in Fig.264(a), although there is absolutely no objection to increasing this slightly; the appearance of the finished piece will not be materially affected. None of this is desperately important; there is simply a need to think about the project before carrying it out.

Whether used as a vacuum chuck or not, the jig itself requires holding to the worktop via a single bolt, more or less at the centre. This runs in a slot in the worktop, enabling the jig to be positioned accurately relative to the cutter. The method of achieving this position is described fully in Project 5, but consists essentially of machining an outer scallop on a dummy MDF segment to a little over half-depth, turning the segment over and machining the remainder. Any angular misalignment of the jig will show up as slight shoulders where the cuts overlap. Once set, the jig is firmly locked in place with hot-melt glue fillets, and left strictly alone until all segments and spares have been fully machined.

Figure 271

The biscuit housings are machined first, using the method described in Project 5. The outer flank of each segment is then scalloped to full depth with a straight cutter of approximately $\frac{1}{2}$" diameter. These flanks will eventually require further profiling on the underside with a cove cutter, but the initial machining serves as a useful setting-up guide for later work. The router is locked on the guide rods for this operation. To digress slightly: where a vacuum chuck is used, or where some risk of lateral movement of the workpiece exists, the direction of traverse should be in the climb milling direction (anticlockwise). This is for the very good reason that climb milling tends to push the work away from the cutter which, in this case, is further into the taper formed by the sides of the jig.

The same cutter is used to machine the inner flanks. The minimum (ie. the actual flank) radius is set by a pair of reference locknuts on the micro-adjuster. The router is thus able to machine the flank itself with the depth stop set to give a slight overcut in depth and then, by sliding it on the rods, to machine the remainder of the lower face of the segment dead flat. When all segments have been so treated, the straight cutter is replaced by an ovolo cutter and the inner flank profile machined on all segments. There is a useful little trick here, by the way: if at all possible (it usually is), the diameter of the straight cutter used initially is chosen to match the smallest diameter of the ovolo cutter to be used, ie. that measured across the bottom straight portion. If this is done, the position of the router on the guide rods can remain unaltered when the ovolo cutter is fitted, since it will automatically traverse the required lateral path, and needs only to be set in terms of depth. Direction of traverse for both cutters on the inner flank remains anticlockwise. This is not the climb milling direction for the inner flank. The net effect on the workpiece is still, unfortunately, to push it away from the jig but the climb milling direction will, in this case, make matters marginally worse.

The router is then fitted with a $1/16$" diameter cutter and set to the outer inlay radius, to machine a groove of about $3/32$" total depth, in not less than two passes. It is not necessary to make the groove any deeper; it serves no useful purpose and may load the tiny cutter unduly. Small diameter cutters are not particularly good at clearing debris from the bottom of the groove and this represents additional cutter loading. After machining to full depth, a couple of further full sweeps are taken to ensure that the bottom of the groove is in fact clean and also to remove any small timber whiskers from the sides of the groove. After all segments have been machined, the inner groove is dealt with in the same way. It is of course a matter of individual preference whether the foregoing procedure is used, or the alternative of machining both inlays on one segment is adopted. The lateral positions of the router are easily dealt with by means of reference locknuts, but the depth stop will need to be reset for every operation.

A further jig (Fig.272) is required to machine the coves on the underside of the scallops. This is much the

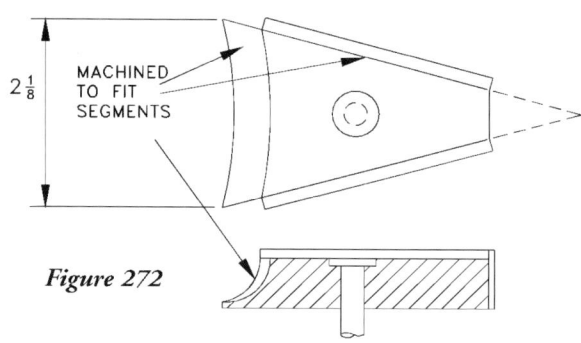

Figure 272

same in principle as the previous jig but, due to the very limited surface area available, I would advise against making this in the form of a vacuum chuck. Rather, I would suggest the use of double sided adhesive tape on the underside of the segment, backed up with a strip of plain adhesive tape, stretched over the top of the segment and embracing both side flanks of the jig (Fig.273). Traverse is again anticlockwise. The initial position of the jig is set with the aid of a sacrificial MDF segment, as described earlier. The inlays are built up from three strips of sycamore veneer, the centre one being blackened by heating, as described in Chapter 5. The veneer assemblies are built up over a curved template, as described in Project 1.

Segment assembly is best implemented with the aid of shaped cramping blocks. I have covered this subject extensively elsewhere and Project 5 also carries a little information. A twelve segment assembly does however provide the opportunity to briefly examine a number of important principles. It is assumed that the segments have been given a final light 'lick' on the sander to establish the angles accurately and to ensure that the flanks to be jointed are dead square with the faces; it also assumes that a dry assembly (easily done by hand) has been carried out to check accuracy. Given careful machining, the outer scallop points, and the inlays will align correctly at all joints. The inlays provide the best visual reference for jointing but, if these have not been provided, the outer points will serve.

The segments are glued in pairs initially, complete with biscuits, with the aid of a pair of shaped cramping blocks as illustrated in Figs 274–276. Block dimensions as given, suit the particular design of tray illustrated. It is important that they are made such that the outer edges are parallel when they are fitted to the segment pairs, thus enabling them to be gripped by a sash cramp without slippage. Small stop blocks are glued to the main blocks with superglue where necessary, to prevent the blocks sliding on the segments. The blocks, are designed to apply pressure at right angles to the joint line, roughly halfway along the length of the joint. It is equally important that the segments are clamped down to a flat worktop, with a flat clamping block on the upper face. If the top block is made from clear acrylic, about $\frac{1}{4}$ thick, this will allow examination of the joint alignment. Additionally, small pieces of polythene sheet are placed in contact with the top and bottom faces of the segments, to prevent unwanted adhesion. My personal preference for this type of work is aliphatic glue. This is much the same as PVA glue, with the additional

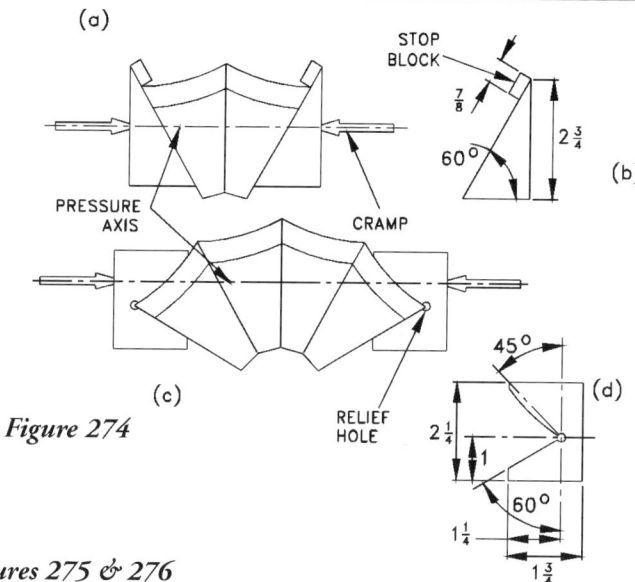

Figure 274

Figures 275 & 276

Figure 273

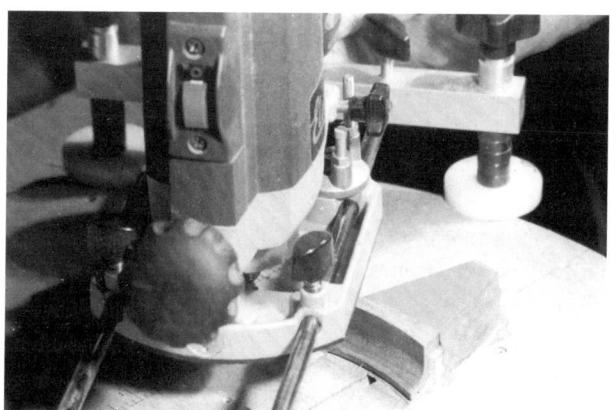

benefit of a 'fast grab' characteristic. It is not necessary to coat the biscuits with glue, but the biscuit housings and both joint faces must be given a fairly generous application, after which the segments are squeezed gently together with the sash cramp, and excess glue wiped from the top face with damp tissue, to allow examination of alignment. Vertical clamping is now applied, and the side and top clamps tightened alternately, a little at a time, until the pressure is judged to be adequate. The joint is left in this condition for about half an hour, after which period, the clamps may be removed. Excess glue is then removed, by wiping or scraping, from the remainder of the joint, and the assembly put aside for about 24 hours for the glue to cure fully. If excess glue is left to fully harden before removal, residues may show up as white marks when final finish is applied.

Pairs of segments are then joined together as sets of four, using similar procedures, and cramping blocks as illustrated in Figs 274(c) and (d), and Fig.276. The curved portion of the blocks may be obtained by tracing around a segment flank. Note that a small relief hole is provided in each block, to avoid damage to the segment corners. The penultimate stage is the assembly of any two of the three sets, to form an eight-segment assembly. Cramping is much more difficult in this case, and I

Figure 227

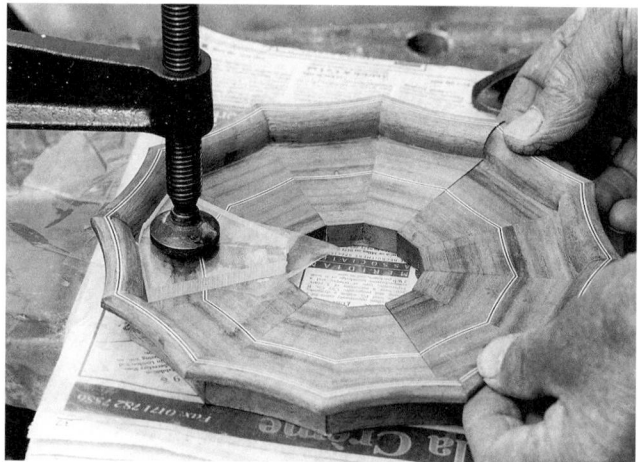

would suggest the use of hand pressure, coupled with cramping both segment sets to a flat surface. I normally manage this task alone, but an extra pair of hands can be a great help. Finally, the remaining 'slice' is fitted by similar means; this is the only time when two joints have to be managed simultaneously (Fig.277).

The foregoing method may seem a trifle odd to some readers. There is a degree of method in the madness however: whilst no overwhelming objection exists regarding assembly of the segments in two groups of six, giving a final straight pair of joints, if cumulative errors creep in, the final result may well take the form illustrated in Fig.278(a). Correction may require a good deal of the larger set to be sanded away and, although the inlays may be persuaded to line up eventually, the loss of area and possibly shape on the two affected segments could well be sufficiently obvious to spoil the piece. Assembly as shown in (b) does at least allow the possibility of some

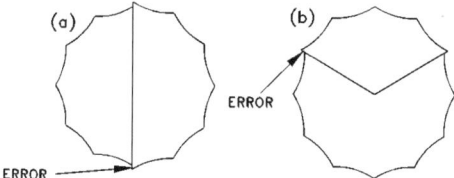

Figure 278

lateral movement as the necessary timber is sanded away; in other words, the smaller set, as drawn, will move inwards, thus tending to correct misalignment without undue timber removal. The reverse is equally possible if the sanding is required on the larger group of segments. Even so, the system is limited in scope and is certainly not a means of escaping the consequences of unduly inaccurate work.

The centre section of the assembly is fitted with a circular stepped plug (Fig.263). Both the plug and its matching recesses may be machined on the Pivot Frame.

The plug should be initially a little proud of the tray surfaces on both sides; this will minimise the amount of sanding necessary for a flush finish.

The piece may be left in this state as a plain tray. Fig.279 shows an additional feature, enabling the tray to be easily lifted and moved around. All three items were actually made on a lathe, the brass centre by means of hand-filing and polishing a revolving length of brass rod. The ebony knob and pedestal could in fact be made on the Pivot Frame, using techniques described in Project 5.

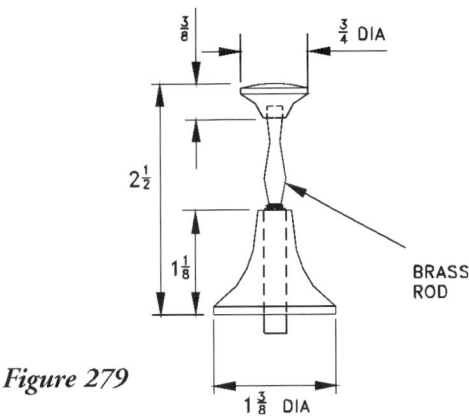

Figure 279

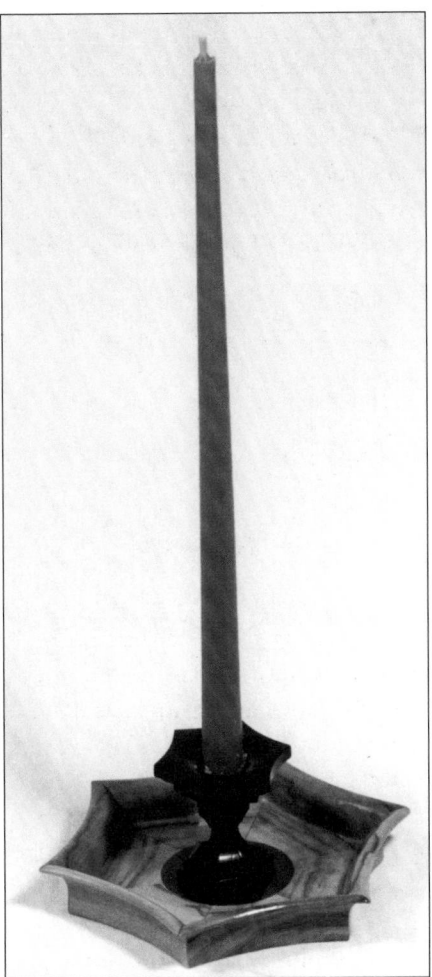

Figure 280

A variation of the project, in the form of a decorative candlestick, is shown in Figs 280 and 281. The general techniques are the same as previously described, with the aid of similar custom-made jigs. It is stressed that the design as shown is strictly for decorative purposes. If desired to use it with lighted candles, the candle holder must feature a suitable metal insert. It is suggested that a project of this nature is attempted as a 'starter', before taking on the more difficult tray.

The scalloped candle holder and pedestal is a two-part assembly, using a central wood dowel $\frac{1}{4}$" diameter to locate and join the parts. Scalloping techniques for small work of this kind are described in Project 5. A complex elevation profile of this kind should not be attempted in one pass, even if a suitable cutter is available; the sideways loading would be too heavy for small work. The inside profile of the holder is machined before the outer, using a combination of straight and ovolo cutters as shown (in principle) in Fig.282. In this case, a $\frac{1}{4}$" diameter hole is drilled through the centre of the blank, allowing it to be aligned with the centre of the

primary disc by means of a suitable bolt or rod (a). The blank is held firmly with double-sided tape *and* hot-melt glue fillets, after which the bolt is removed and the profile machined as shown in (b) and (c). It is preferable to use relatively small-diameter cutters and use the Pivot Frame to effectively increase their diameter; this will reduce loading on the workpiece. The segmented joints are protected with a fitted central disc as illustrated in Figs 281 (b) and (f).

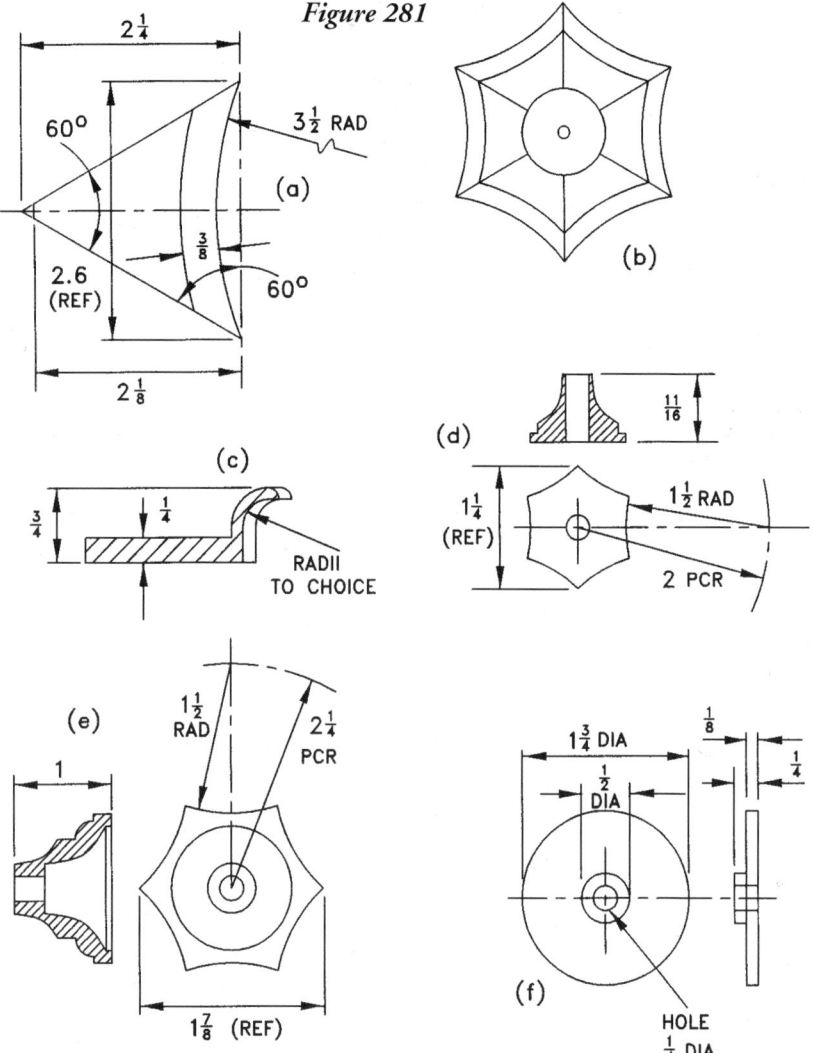

Figure 281

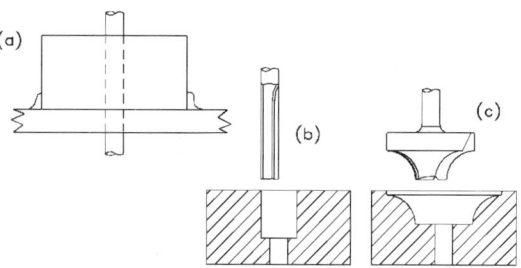

Figure 282

7

ELLIPTICAL SCALLOPED BOX

Figure 283

Throughout this book, I have endeavoured to be as objective as I possibly can about the techniques and particularly the projects I have offered the reader. However, I cannot resist the temptation in the case of this particular project (Figs 283 and 284) to state that it is the one that gives me the greatest personal satisfaction. It was designed specifically as a competition entry and my aim (aside from aesthetic considerations) was to create the impression of great difficulty in its making. Whilst I cannot help but hope that the reader gains this impression at first sight, it has turned out to be the easiest of the three elliptical projects offered (which is why it is also the first). To be sure, it does require a few jigs, but only two of these appear for the first time; the rest are featured in earlier projects.

The Pivot Frame ellipse jig is featured in the illustrations and, given its availability, it is very much the easiest way of cutting the elliptical profiles. However, the jig is positively *not* an essential requirement. All three elliptical components comprising the base and the lid may be generated by any of the geometric means described in Chapter 8, followed by sawing and disc sanding. The decorative coves may be cut to choice using a bearing-guided cutter, and the scalloped features are circular arcs anyway. The shaded veneer fan design on the lid will be recognised as the vehicle for part of Chapter 5, and since this chapter covers the entire process, no further mention of it is necessary here.

Regardless of the method used to actually machine the base and the lid, it will be necessary to draw the

Figure 284

required elliptical profiles and make photocopies as necessary, to enable the positions of the scallops to be determined by trial and error. Since both base and lid are the same overall size and shape, one basic drawing will serve for both. It is necessary, after drawing the outer profile, to generate a second profile $\frac{1}{4}$" inside the first, to produce a reference outline for the scalloped channel in the base. As a minor matter of interest, if an ellipse-drawing jig or geometric construction (of any type) is used for this latter purpose, the inner ellipse will not be parallel to the outer, for reasons given in Chapter 8. The error is quite small in this case however, and may be ignored.

It is necessary to establish the major and minor axes of the drawn ellipses very accurately and to be quite sure that they really are at right-angles to each other, since this is an essential preliminary to drawing the scallops accurately. This will not be a problem for a hand-drawn construction, since the provision of the two axes is an essential preliminary anyway. It is rather less easy if the drawings are made with the Pivot Frame ellipse jig, since it is possible for slight errors to creep in when trying to establish the axes, however careful and cunning the use of the jig. The reader is therefore referred to Chapter 8 (see Fig.183) for a method of establishing the axes by simple drawing. Once this has been satisfactorily done, a couple of photocopies of the drawing are made (there will be a little further 'trial and error' drawing to do).

The first task is to divide the circumference of the inner ellipse on the drawing into sixteen equal parts as shown in Fig.285 (the word 'equal', in relation to the circumference, must be taken with a pinch of salt, since the varying curvature of the ellipse makes this virtually impossible by any manual means). To achieve a practical result, a pair of compasses is set to an appropriate

Figure 285

EQUAL STEPS

9

$\frac{1}{4}$

$\frac{1}{4}$

5

$1\frac{1}{2}$ RAD

$\frac{1}{8}$ WIDE CHANNEL

'B'

JOINT LINE

'B'

SCALLOP CENTRES

'A'

approximate value and stepped around one quarter of the ellipse, between the major and minor axes, and adjusted a little at a time until it will cover the required distance in four equal steps. Once this setting has been found on a photocopy, the same exercise is carried out on the original drawing and the remainder of the ellipse divided up in the same way. Diametrical lines drawn between opposing points should pass through the centre of the ellipse. The reason for using a photocopy for the trial and error process is to avoid defacing the original unduly with abortive attempts. The reason for subsequently returning to the original is that photocopies can 'move' a little during processing and thereby prejudice accuracy (ie. the idea of taking photocopies of photocopies isn't a particularly good one for this type of work).

It is now necessary to choose a suitable machining radius for the scallops, using further photocopies for trials; a suggested profile is given in Fig.285, but that actually chosen will depend upon whether the Pivot Frame or a beam trammel is to be used. The radius is set on the compasses and, with these centred on each of the intersections between the inner ellipse and the radial lines (shown as points 'A' on the drawing), a succession of short arcs are struck to give points 'B'. With these as centres, the actual scallops may be drawn in, and the appearance of the design examined. It may well be that the radius chosen does not present the desired appearance, in which case, the exercise is repeated as necessary. Once a satisfactory result is achieved, the compasses are increased in radius by $^1/_8$" and the inner flanks drawn on the same centres. At this point, it may be noted that the junctions of the pairs of inner and outer scallop arcs produce mitre angles between scallops which are *not* the same as those given by the diametrical lines drawn earlier, as can be seen from Fig.285 (the ellipse throws up quite a few nasty little surprises; this is just one of them). A convenient way of determining these angles, is to use the construction shown in the bottom right hand

quarter of Fig.285 to draw them as accurately as possible. The method is simply to increase the inner flank radius by a considerable amount, and use this to draw the joint lines. Finally, the work is re-done on the original drawing. This may now be regarded as the 'master' from which at least two photocopies are made. The photocopies are cut around the inner ellipse with a sharp craft knife, and put away for the moment; they will eventually be stuck to the base and the underside of the lid.

It is necessary to digress a little at this point, to expand on the method of producing the base and lid in the absence of a Pivot Frame ellipse jig. A further photocopy of the drawing is cut around the *outer* ellipse and stuck to a suitable sheet of ply or MDF, of $\frac{1}{2}$" thickness; this will become the template for the base and lid. My preferred method for sticking paper to wood in this way is to use double-sided adhesive tape, stuck in fairly small pieces around the periphery of the paper. This will permit fairly easy adjustment prior to final adhesion, and in any case, the centre portion of the drawing is not required to be fixed to the timber. The template is then fretsawn fairly close to the elliptical profile, and finally disc sanded down to the drawn line. Note that a 'same size' template of this nature can only be used with a 1:1 bearing-guided cutter, ie. with a bearing of the same diameter as the cutter. If lack of equipment or personal preference dictates the use of a guide bush with a cutter inside it, then an ellipse of the required (reduced) size must be provided on the original drawing and the template made to this outline. Note however, that this will result in the generation of an outer profile which is not quite a true ellipse (see Chapter 8), and it is desirable to use a guide bush of diameter only a little larger than that of the cutter, to minimise errors of this nature. Good dust extraction is highly desirable in such cases, since the relatively small gap between cutter and bush can cause shavings to accumulate. If the ellipse jig is used to cut the base and lid, the inner edge of the cutter is set

Figure 286

Figure 287

walnut. Each piece is made from two small boards of half the required width, biscuit jointed together. They are planed flat and thicknessed using the router in planer mode and then fretsawn to a slightly oversize elliptical profile, using a photocopy stuck to the blank. If the piece is to be machined on the ellipse jig (ie. without an intermediate template), a photocopy of the full scalloped drawing can be stuck to the blank and used to set the jig, although the waste should still be sawn away to spare the cutter. Fig.286 shows a machining operation in progress with a second blank in the foreground. For final work, as distinct from templates, it pays to watch the saw 'rag' as it exits the work; if this is excessive, it can spoil the edges of the work, even after profiling with the router. When using the ellipse jig, it is a fairly simple matter to start each cut at the centre of the long dimension and work both ways towards the ends. This will provide the friendliest grain orientation, and therefore the best overall finish, despite the possibility of slight indentations at the plunge points where the cuts are started. If the blanks are profiled against a template with a bearing or bush guided system in *overhead* mode, much the same procedure may be followed, with the added advantage that the plunge depth can be set off the work and the cutter gently slid sideways into the cut, thereby avoiding indentations. This is shown in Fig.287 in connection with the rather similar task of machining a cove profile. The general mass of the router and ski combination will permit work in either direction, given light depth settings. Spindle moulding is a different matter; the work *must* be fed against cutter rotation in this case. If the work is fed in the climb-milling direction, the relatively low mass of the blank will give rise to snatching. This is dangerous practice, and is to be avoided, despite the possibility of a poorer finish.

The two prepared paper blanks are now stuck to one side of each of the completed base and lid elliptical blanks, taking great care to ensure that they are centrally placed, using major and minor axis lines on both the

to the major and minor axis dimensions. This too, will give rise to a profile which is not quite elliptical but, if the cutter is kept fairly small (say $\frac{1}{4}$" diameter), the error will not be significant. Given the availability of the jig, the task is really very easy.

The base and lid are prepared from stock material to choice. In my own case, these are made from American

drawing and the workpiece. The positions of the scallops on the timber are now clearly and precisely defined by the drawings. Cutting of the scalloped channels is dealt with here in terms of the Pivot Frame jig, since the photographic illustrations show this method. If a beam trammel is used, the only point to watch is that the ski system does not foul the workpiece during operation. It may be noted in passing that the design as dimensioned, and the illustrations of the work in progress, represent the absolute maximum limit of capability of the Pivot Frame fitted with an Elu MOF96 router, and the 500mm. guide rods. The set-up requires a primary disc of $19\frac{3}{4}$" diameter, which will place the Pivot Frame bars at the extreme ends of the rods. It will be found that the position of the workpiece when machining the end scallops will just allow the shoes to pass unimpeded (Fig.288). The workpiece is placed more or less centrally on a secondary disc of suitable size and tacked in place with hot-melt glue fillets *after* placing the central bolt into the central hole in the secondary disc. Incidentally, the disc needs to be slightly smaller than the ellipse major axis, to avoid fouling of the Pivot Frame shoes. In order to prevent unwanted rotation under cutting load, it is also necessary to fit the underside of the disc with three strips of abrasive sheet, held in place with double-sided adhesive tape (Fig.289). It is important to take the strips more or less to the centre as shown. This is not to

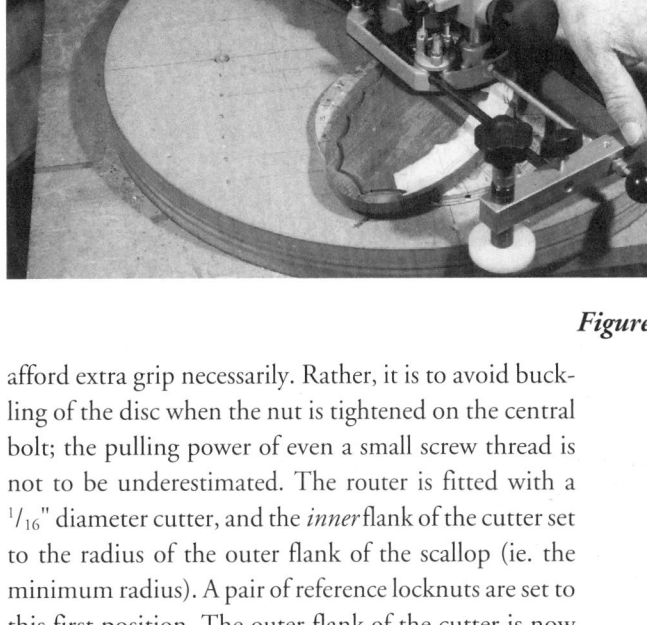

Figure 288

afford extra grip necessarily. Rather, it is to avoid buckling of the disc when the nut is tightened on the central bolt; the pulling power of even a small screw thread is not to be underestimated. The router is fitted with a $\frac{1}{16}$" diameter cutter, and the *inner* flank of the cutter set to the radius of the outer flank of the scallop (ie. the minimum radius). A pair of reference locknuts are set to this first position. The outer flank of the cutter is now set to the radius of the inner flank of the scallop (the maximum radius), and a further pair of locknuts fitted to reference the second position (Fig.290). Note that

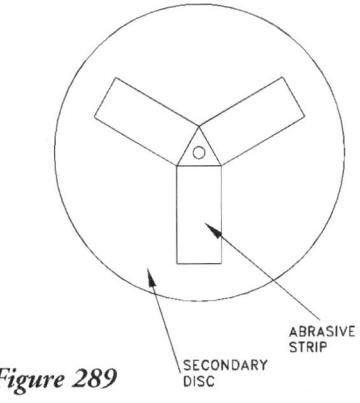

Figure 289

SECONDARY DISC

ABRASIVE STRIP

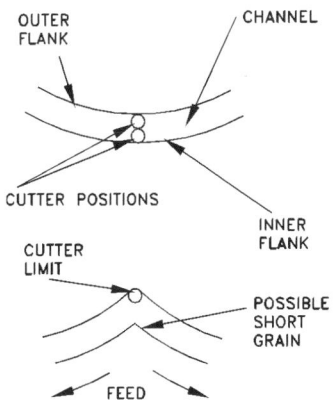

Figure 290

OUTER FLANK

CHANNEL

CUTTER POSITIONS

INNER FLANK

CUTTER LIMIT

POSSIBLE SHORT GRAIN

FEED

the setting of the Pivot Frame cutter radii must be carried out by means of direct measurement from the centre of the primary disc, using the scale drawn directly on the disc (see Fig.21, Chapter 1), or by cutting shallow circular channels in a sacrificial scrap of timber, followed by direct measurement of the result. The aim is to produce a channel of the required radius, and just a little over $\frac{1}{8}$" wide. Once the setting has been completed, the router is slid to its first (minimum radius) position and locked in place. The workpiece on its disc may now be positioned by trial and error until one of the scallops lies directly beneath the cutter, which may be swung backwards and forwards on the Pivot Frame until the outer line on the drawing is followed by the inner edge of the cutter, and the central bolt then firmly tightened. At this point, the depth stop on the router is fixed to cut a channel about $\frac{3}{16}$" deep, and left alone from then on. It will be found that, provided the primary disc has a radial slot to allow horizontal movement of the workpiece as well as rotational movement, any of the scallops can be arranged to sit precisely beneath the cutter path (Fig.288).

It is most important that the cutter is not allowed to swing too far and thus overcut the lateral limits of the scallops, since this will produce a very untidy end result at the outer points. I find that it is preferable to position the cutter at the two extremities in turn, and plunge to full depth; this is followed by a series of *very shallow* passes between the two holes (tiny cutters will not tolerate sideways overloading). Given due care, only a very small radius will remain between pairs of scallops; this can be cleaned up with a chisel or craft knife. Before moving the workpiece however, the router is slid to its second position on the adjuster, and the inner flank machined. In this case, a sharp internal point will be automatically generated without trouble. In view of the inevitable short grain at a few of the internal 'points', it is advisable to work from 'sides to middle' in these cases (Fig.290). There may be just a feather of timber left at

the centre of the channel; this can be dealt with in a single pass, by setting the router position midway between the two pairs of locknuts. I am bound to say that I found this exercise a positive pleasure to carry out, and not at all tedious. Due to the very small radial swing required of the Pivot Frame, it was also possible to do the entire job sitting down; a most welcome situation for elderly folk such as myself. A couple of points need watching very carefully: it is easy to forget to reset the router to the first position when repositioning the workpiece to cut a fresh scallop. It is equally easy to forget to lock the router in position after setting.

The foregoing describes the technique for cutting the scallops in the base. Those in the lid are similarly treated as far as setting-up is concerned, but they are cut as rebates rather than slots (Fig.284). To be honest, my original idea was to cut slots just a little wider than the base slots, to allow the scallops forming the sides of the box to fit neatly into them, but this turned out to be a very difficult exercise, in view of the inevitable slight errors involved in fitting the scallops, as will be seen later. I was therefore obliged to acknowledge my own limitations (a frequent occurrence), and cut a rebate instead. A flat-bottomed cutter of large diameter is required, in order to traverse the entire rebate area for a single scallop without resetting the cutting radius. This will improve the regularity of the machined area. For similar reasons, the timber is removed in a series of shallow cuts, with the depth set *off the workpiece* for each cut; the final cut is of course fixed by the depth stop on the router. The aim is to provide a rebated surface free of steps between scallops since, however tiny, and however carefully sanded afterwards, a high-gloss finish will reveal them as ripples. The *outer* edge of the cutter is initially set to the minimum radius, and referenced with locknuts against the *inner* face of the pivot bar (note that this is different from the base-cutting procedure). This edge is also set against the drawn lines on the photocopy attached to the lid. Prior to cutting however, the radius is increased by about $^3/_{16}$" to ensure that the rebate will sit well inside the base flanks. This setting should also be referenced with locknuts. To repeat an earlier warning, it is very easy indeed to forget to reset the cutting radius between operations. In view of the need to keep the rebated surface dead flat, it is also advisable to ensure that over-depth cutting due to spring in the guide rods is avoided. This can be done with a home-made intermediate ski attachment which is fitted as close to the router base as circumstances permit, as can be seen in Fig.291.

The sixteen scalloped side flanks are machined by the same process as described in Project 5, using a similar jig (see Fig.260). It is quite in order to use the same jig in fact but since I have an inherent dislike of wasting timber, the partially re-dimensioned jig of Fig.292 is offered in its place. This reduces both the length and the thickness of the blanks by 25%. The flanks themselves may be machined in plain contrasting timber, in which case, there is little more to be added to the information given in Project.5. On the other hand, it is possible to add an extra dimension of interest to the design by providing flanks which are inlaid with a small semi-elliptical 'kernel' surrounded by contrasting veneer. In the example illustrated, the kernel is in blackwood, the veneer is sycamore and the remainder mopane.

Actually, the task is not unduly difficult and does, I think, offer a very interesting machining exercise. Readers are warned however, that it is *very* time-consuming, since it involves several operations, which must be repeated many times. It is advisable to make about

Figure 291

twenty blanks, to cater for possible errors, although only sixteen are actually required. A number of plain blanks may also be provided in scrap material, to assist with setting up. To deal with the twenty blanks; the first task is to cut forty pieces of timber to the dimensions shown in Fig.293, ignoring the veneer and cutaway for the moment. These must be machined to the same length,

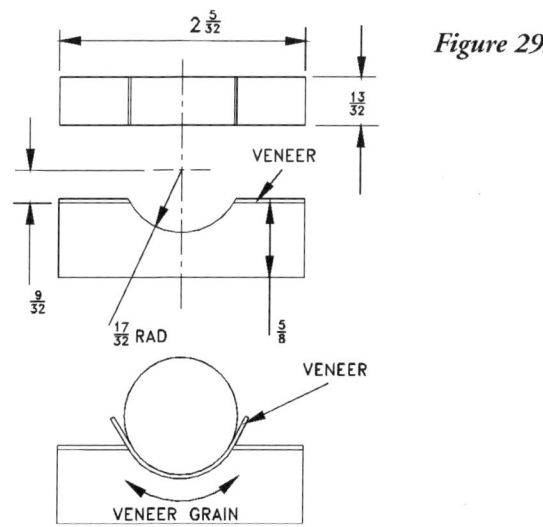

Figure 293

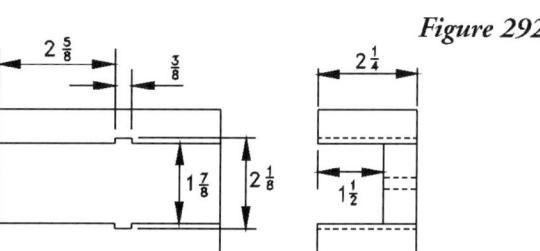

Figure 292

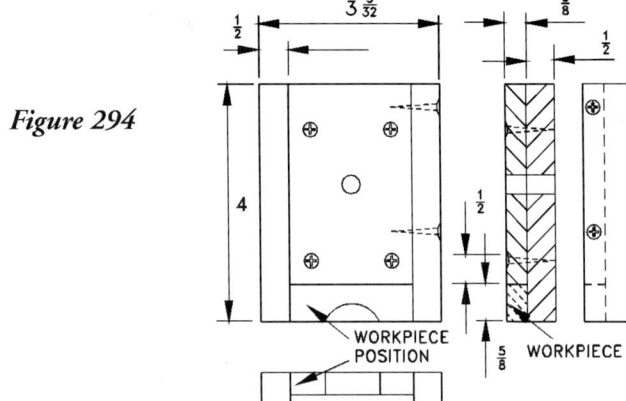

Figure 294

width and thickness. Note however that both the length and the thickness are initially made rather greater than required by the jig of Fig.292. Each blank is faced on one edge only with a strip of veneer. Ideally, the veneer thickness should be half the standard thickness. Thus, when two blanks are finally glued together, the combined veneer thickness of the two halves will revert to the standard value (it improves the appearance somewhat). If the vacuum veneer thicknessing jig described in Chapter 6 is used, this is a simple matter. Otherwise,

Figure 295

each blank must be gently sanded to reduce the veneer thickness a little (this is not a simple matter). Any cold-setting glue that the reader feels happy with may be used. I used superglue, on the grounds that it is both strong and quick-setting. One small snag I have found with superglue however, is that it does appear to give a rather darker joint line than most other glues.

The small circular recesses must be the same for all blanks and a jig is therefore required. This can take the very simple form illustrated in Fig.294. The woodscrews holding one of the side flanks of the jig may be released slightly to allow insertion of the blank, and then tightened to lock it in place, an operation which may be carried out with the jig in position on the Pivot Frame primary disc. Note that the jig as drawn is very slightly different from that illustrated in Fig.295. The latter is not a particularly good design, since the low position of the woodscrews causes the flank to tilt away from the workpiece slightly when they are tightened. The jig is positioned on the primary disc such that the required recess will be cut precisely at the centre, and then fixed with fillets of hot-melt glue. A bolt passing through the jig and the primary disc will aid setting up. Regardless of the fact that all blanks are (or should be) of identical length, they are nevertheless best dealt with in pairs, which must be suitably numbered, and the end which bears against the fixed flank of the jig identified in all cases. This allows for any slight error in lateral position of the recess. Routing may be carried out with a $\frac{1}{4}$" straight cutter in a number of shallow passes and, to provide the best possible finish directly from the cutter (no subsequent sanding is allowed), and to protect the veneer, it is necessary to work from 'sides to middle'. Even this is not quite enough. When machining the left-hand side, the cutter must be lifted clear of the work on the clockwise return stroke of the Pivot Frame, otherwise small pieces of veneer may be torn away (Fig.296). Due to the direction of rotation of the cutter, the right-hand side will take care of itself and it is not necessary to lift on the anticlockwise return stroke.

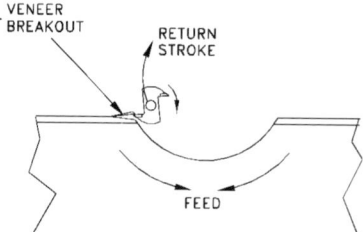

Figure 296

When all blanks have been completed, it is necessary to insert a slip of veneer into the recess, as shown in Figs 293 and 295. The veneer grain must be in the direction illustrated. It would certainly be easier to fit if the grain ran crosswise to the length of the blank, but the eventual visible end-grain would also finish rather muddy-looking, and certainly considerably darker than the straight sections. The snag with fitting the veneer 'long grain' as shown is that it will almost certainly snap if pressed directly into the recess. It must therefore be steamed to shape beforehand, by means of a pair of convex and concave pressure pads ('cauls'). The concave member may conveniently be machined in wood on the Pivot Frame to the same radius as the set of blanks. The convex member must however be of metal (conveniently a short length of rod), since it is required to be heated. Choice of metal is important: under no circumstances should steel be used directly in contact with wood, since it can react chemically in the presence of moisture, to produce deep purple or even black stains in some timbers. It may however, be used safely if a strip of polythene sheet is inserted between metal and timber but, in this case, the caul temperature must be very carefully controlled to ensure that the polythene does not melt. Brass may be used safely, but I find the ideal material is aluminium alloy, since it may be heated and cooled fairly rapidly due to its relatively low thermal mass. At the same time, it stays hot long enough to do the job. It is important that the diameter of the rod matches the curvature taken by the veneer as it is pressed

into the wood caul. Readers with access to metalworking facilities will have no trouble machining the rod to the required diameter, but in the absence of such facilities, a standard diameter (say 1") should be used, and due allowance made for veneer thickness when machining the concave caul and the cutouts in the scallop blanks (hence the rather odd dimension shown for these in Fig.293). The rod may be heated on a hot-plate or upturned domestic electric iron and the veneer pressed into the wood caul and cramped as shown in Fig.297. The veneer should be well damped beforehand, but not allowed to soak, since prolonged immersion may darken the veneer permanently. The temperature of the rod should be sufficient to cause gentle sizzling of the dampened veneer as it makes contact. When cold, the veneer will spring back to a permanent set which is rather less than that required, but sufficient to allow final gluing without cracking. The same metal caul, used cold this time, may be used when gluing the prepared veneer slips into the blanks (Fig.295). When the glue has set, surplus veneer may be trimmed away with a craft knife.

Figure 297

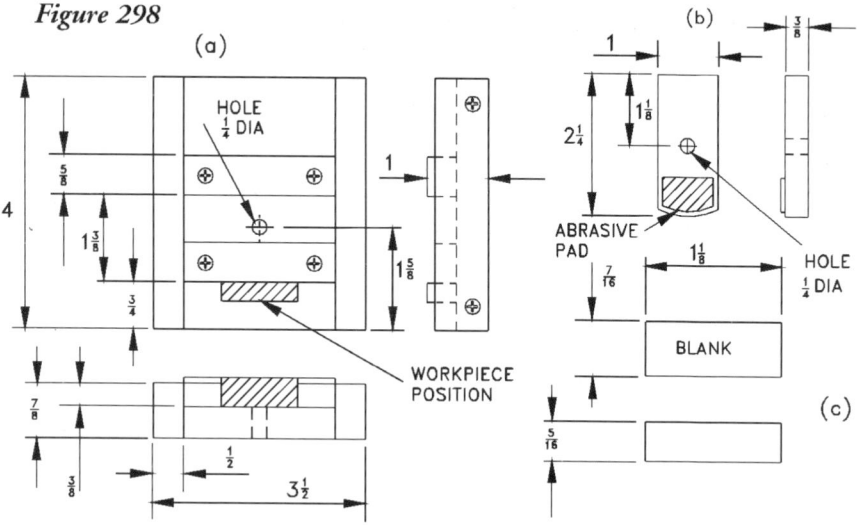

Figure 298

Figure 299

The curved kernels may also be machined without undue wastage, given a further small jig. This takes the form shown in Figs 298 and 299, and allows the use of very tiny scraps of timber as machining blanks. Due to the fact that the jig hasn't a great deal of timber to grip, it is possible for the rotating cutter to send the blank flying across the workshop unless one or two precautions are taken. All the blanks must be made exactly the same thickness, to give the cramping system a fair

chance. The underside of the shaped cramp is fitted with a small piece of abrasive sheet, of about 240 grade, to provide an improved grip on the timber; note that the abrasive is kept well away from the machining line, to avoid blunting the cutter. It is also necessary to arrange the workpiece position such that its final shape is rather as shown in Fig.300(a). This is to avoid the possibility of the cutter catching in the workpiece and moving it, (b). The cutter is plunged in small increments on the right-hand side, starting from a predetermined position, set by a suitable stop against a Pivot Frame shoe, and moved anticlockwise in one pass. This is admittedly somewhat at odds with my previous 'sides to middle' recommendations in terms of machining direction to produce a good finish, but is necessary in this case to avoid the cutter catching in the work as the cut is completed. This will not occur at the left-hand side incidentally, since the cutter rotation is in a 'friendly' direction at this point.

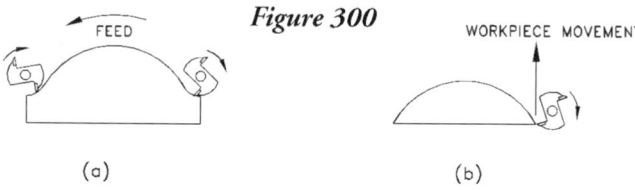

Figure 300

The kernels are easily held by single cramps when they are glued into the main blanks. Excess timber is very carefully sanded off afterwards, to leave a dead flat surface without sanding away any of the veneer on the flat part of the blanks. This implies vary careful setting up of the sander table to an accurate right angle with the disc, and a delicate touch when sanding. To ensure that the blanks lie flat on the sander table, any surplus kernel at the sides of the assemblies must first be sanded away with equal care. Finally, pairs of blanks are glued together to complete the assemblies, making quite sure that the inserts line up accurately. The blanks may now be carefully sanded to the overall length and width that just fits the main profiling jig illustrated in Fig.292 (they were made slightly oversize initially to permit these operations). The fit in the jig must be such as to totally inhibit workpiece movement when the hand nut is tightened. Machining of the blanks to their final curved profile follows the practice described in Project 5. The procedure is further illustrated in Figs 301 and 302.

The flanks are divested of their surplus by sawing away the outer parts. They are then fitted into their curved recesses in the base, one at a time. The mitred joints between adjacent flanks are disc sanded and individually fitted. Since this is essentially a manual operation, it must be done with very great care, with the aid of a further jig, illustrated in Fig.303. The jig is actually nothing more than part of a fairly thick MDF disc, machined with a radius equal to that of the inner face of the flanks, and with its edge dead square to its lower face. The rather awkward handling position illustrated is purely for photographic clarity, and is *not* recommended. The main purpose of the jig is to ensure that the edges of the flanks are maintained square to their bases during the mitring operations, but it will also be found a very convenient means of handling the work.

Figure 302

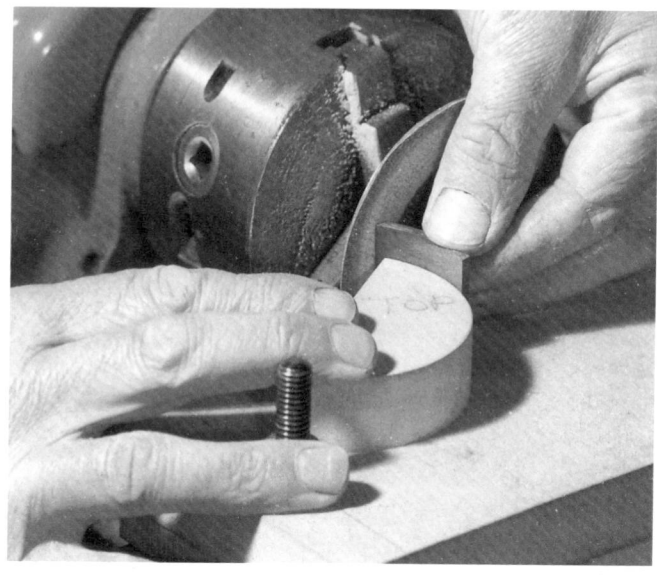

Figure 303

Figure 301

The mitre angle and overall length of each flank piece must be determined visually, with the aid of the original drawing, and also with a good deal of trial fitting along the way. The last piece to be fitted is the most difficult, since this requires two mitred joints to be matched at the same time. I would strongly advise that all pieces are machined and fitted before attempting to glue any of them in place. This implies some form of identification, which can quite easily be effected with small numbered pieces of self-adhesive label. Fitting presents a strong case for superglue, since each piece can be placed and held momentarily by hand. It may well be however, that the necessarily slightly 'easy' fit of the pieces in their base channels allows some slight risk that they may not end up truly square to the base after gluing. For this reason, it is advisable to cramp a small right-angled guide block behind each piece prior to gluing (Fig.304). This will

Figure 304

ensure that the pieces are fitted at right angles to the base, and also that they are pressed firmly against the outer flank of their respective channels. Note from this illustration that both the base and the flanks are finished, including polishing, before assembly. Admittedly, this does demand extra care when sanding and assembling, to ensure that the finish is not damaged. On balance however, it is much better than attempting to finish after assembly; the tight corners would present severe problems. After assembly, the plain single-piece lid may be tried for fit. It should fit easily, with just a little play in all lateral directions. It may well be desired to stop the project at this point, in which case, the lid may be given a finish and fitted with a knob.

The piece is, I think, improved by the addition of a further plinth, made as a separate item, and glued to the main lid. A design embodying a further scalloped rebate is dimensioned in Fig.305. The rebating procedure, based upon this drawing, follows earlier practice and is in fact illustrated in Fig.291. It also features the sand shaded veneering exercise which, if undertaken at all, should be carried out prior to the rebating exercise. I think the appearance is materially improved by allowing a larger rebate area at the ends than at the sides; hence the appearance of the elliptical profile dictating the position of the scallop points in Fig.305.

The lid must of course be fitted with a knob. This can be a plain circular knob made on a lathe, or with the aid of the Pivot Frame, and may even be scalloped if required, as featured in Project 5. In this particular case, the ebony knob illustrated is a blatant piece of 'showing-off', since it is elliptical, small, and heavily undercut (Fig.306). There may well be other jigs capable of carrying out small elliptical work of this nature, but the Pivot Frame ellipse jig is the only one known to me.

The greatest difficulty with this item is keeping it down on the worktable. That illustrated is actually the third; the first two flew off during machining. The problem here is the cove cutter used for the profiling.

Figure 305

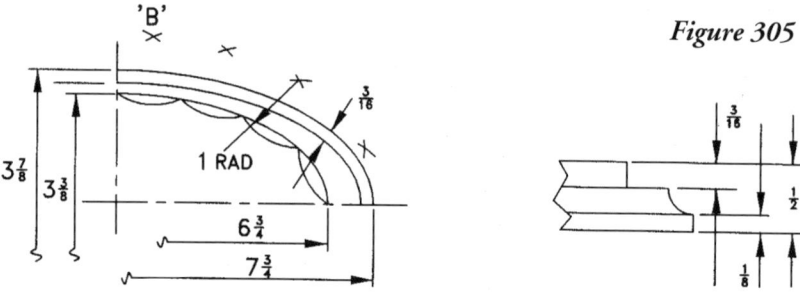

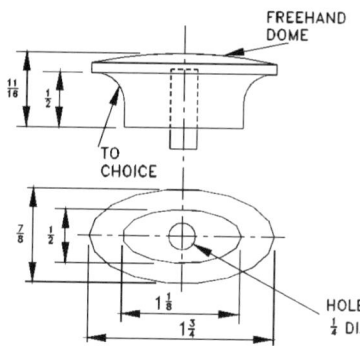

Figure 306

Figure 307

Despite very light settings, the fact that almost the entire length of the cutting edge is presented to the work results in a heavy loading on the hold-down system. Matters are further complicated by the fact that no mechanical fixing aids are possible, since they get in the way. After my first two failures, I settled for the arrangement illustrated in Fig.307, which involves a combination of superglue on the underside and hot-melt glue around the edges. The blank is also appreciably larger than that required by the knob profile. The sacrificial plywood sub-table has to be bandsawn away from the knob after machining.

Initially, the main outer profile is machined to within about $\frac{1}{4}$" of the sub-table, with a $\frac{1}{4}$" straight cutter, and then the surplus timber at the corners chiselled away as shown. This is an important procedure since the succeeding cove cutter is liable to bite savagely into them, disturbing the workpiece. Undercutting is carried out with a cove cutter, used initially at the same jig settings as the straight cutter.

Machining is taken almost to the previously machined depth. The position of the router on the guide rods (ie. the major axis only) is then adjusted inwards, a little at a time, to give a rather longer undercut at the ends than at the sides. At this point, all hot-melt glue is chiselled away from the sides of the workpiece, to avoid

cutter contamination. The superglue will hold the workpiece quite safely for the remaining work. The straight cutter is then replaced, and set to its original cutting line (only the major axis setting needs adjustment), and taken to full workpiece depth. At this point, the top face of the workpiece may be levelled if necessary, with a large diameter cutter. The lateral jig settings may be disturbed for this operation, since they are no longer required. The sub-table is removed from the main worktable, and a $\frac{1}{4}$" hole drilled in the dead-centre of the base of the knob, to a depth of about $\frac{1}{2}$". The sub-table may now be bandsawn away from the workpiece. The knob is fitted with a length of $\frac{1}{4}$" diameter brass rod, which may be used as a convenient handle for the final work, before being sawn off, leaving a short stub to be fitted into a corresponding hole in the plinth. The top of the knob is domed essentially by hand, initially with a disc sander, to remove the bulk of the waste, and then by hand sanding. It is strongly advised that any final finishing process is carried out before sawing the dowel to length. Bun feet may be fitted as an option; in my case, they are made from copper, since this suits the timber colour very well.

8

PEDESTAL TRAY

Figure 308

This project, although not the last in the series is, in one respect, the most difficult. The plain elliptical profiles comprising the base and the outer shape of the tray may be machined either by means of templates or directly by sawing and sanding. However, the scalloped top, comprising thirty-two individually machined segments, represents something of a challenge. The pedestal is also quite tricky, since it presents an elevation profile which requires the elliptical planform to change in both axes from bottom to top. Once again, to my knowledge, the only router jig capable of performing such a task is that designed by me. This particular pedestal design however, was produced solely for the purpose of showing off the capabilities of the jig and can be replaced by other,

simpler designs without sacrificing the appearance of the piece as a whole. For example, a plain circular cross-section pedestal of similar elevation profile can easily be made on a lathe or the Pivot Frame. If this route is adopted, the ellipse jig is not an essential requirement to make the piece. The scallops, inlay and pedestal support on the tray do however, require the Pivot Frame. The completed piece is illustrated in Figs 308 and 309.

With this in mind, it would seem sensible to get the easy parts out of the way first (although they should actually be made last, after satisfactory completion of the tray). The dimensions for both are given in Fig.310. They are made from plain boards which have been planed flat to the required thickness and, since only

Figure 309

outer profiles are required, they can use drawings stuck to one face, followed by rough sawing and disc sanding to the drawn profiles. If preferred, particularly for reasons of eliminating risk to valuable timber, templates may be made in the same way and used with guided cutters to produce the final parts. Whatever the method, it will be necessary to retain (or mark) the major and minor axis lines on both, very accurately, in order to locate the central spigot hole, and also to aid alignment on final assembly. All necessary operations have already been described in earlier projects.

The real 'meat' of the project lies with the top tray. This, I feel, is a particularly interesting exercise, if only for the reason that it demonstrates another aspect of the awkwardness of the ellipse when divided into segments or scallops. Undoubtedly the first and most important task is to produce a master drawing, as in Fig.311. This must be made as accurately as possible, since it will be needed to machine the scallops, and also as a master layout for the final jointing and assembly. Although only partially

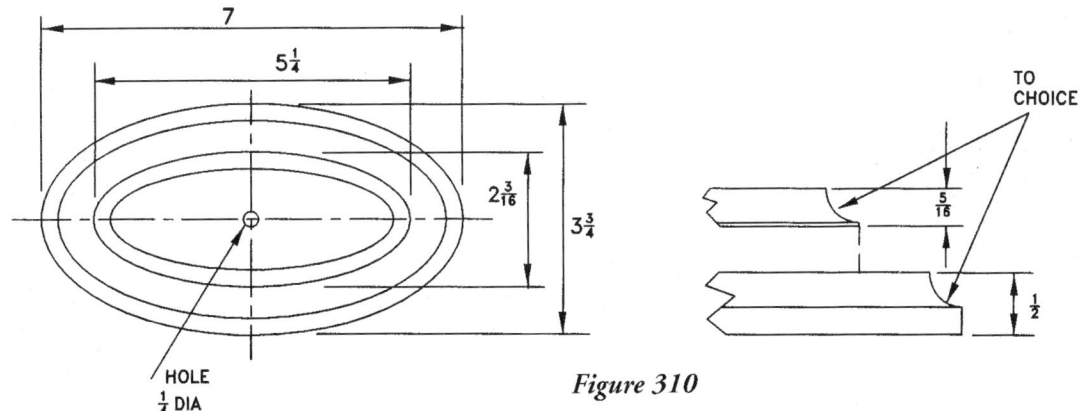

Figure 310

Figure 311

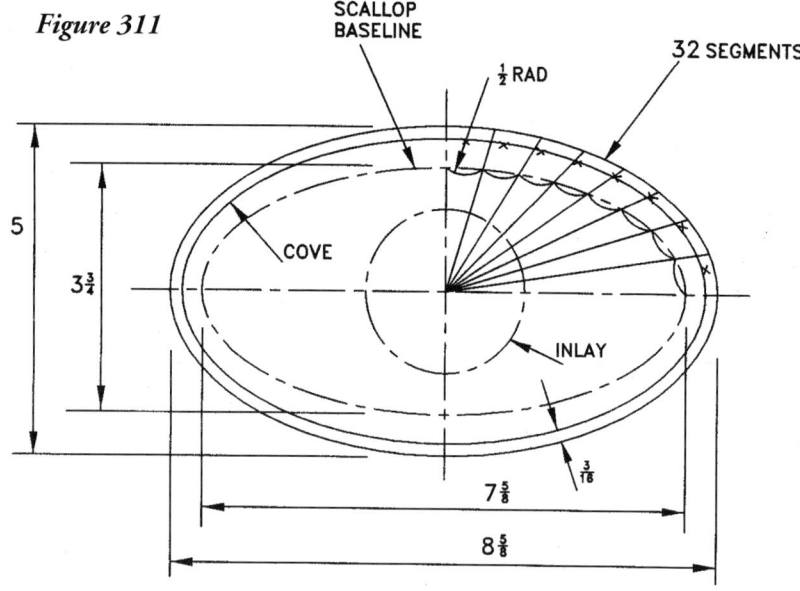

SCALLOP BASELINE

½ RAD

32 SEGMENTS

COVE

INLAY

5

3¾

7⅝

8⅝

³⁄₈

shown on the drawing, the scallops and segment lines should be drawn for the entire ellipse in order to make sure that the drawing is accurate. In passing, the segmented construction is necessary if internal scallops of the kind illustrated are required, since it simply isn't possible with a router to produce flanks curved in both plan and elevation, together with sharp internal corners (not to my knowledge anyway). Even if a plain, internal elliptical profile, rather than a scalloped design, is chosen, this too has its difficulties in the absence of an ellipse jig. The problem here lies with the generation of a suitable template for the internal work. The task is by no means impossible, but the registration of the blank with a suitable internal template would need to be very carefully done.

To begin with, the two master ellipses, representing the outer profile and the scallop baseline are drawn on the same major and minor axes. That representing the cove is not required for the construction. One quarter of the inner ellipse is divided into eight equal parts (ini-

tially on a photocopy), using compasses on a trial and error basis, as described in Project 7. Once the setting is established, the exercise is repeated all round. This, as noted earlier, is essentially for accuracy's sake, but also because the segments are 'handed' in sixteen pairs, It could be argued that the segments could be made in eight sets of 'quads', if it is remembered that two of each set must be regarded as 'upside down' when machining, but at least half the ellipse will be required as an assembly planform. Moreover, with sets of quads, there is plenty of scope for error; it isn't particularly amusing to end up with sets of four identical segments, with two in each set quite useless.

It can be seen from Fig.311 and the photographs of the finished piece, that the segments are not taken right to the centre of the tray. A top inlay disc and an underside pedestal support are fitted, both of which require a fairly large circular cutout at the centre. Regardless of whether the actual inlay design of Fig.312(a) is adopted or not, it is advised that some form of central feature is provided, since it is very difficult indeed to provide perfect alignment of the sharp points formed by the segments at the centre. On the other hand, the segments should be kept at *almost* their full length during manufacture. A small hole at the centre of the final assembly will actually help registration of the segments on the master drawing when they are assembled. Moreover, the longer the segments, the easier it is to judge their angular accuracy.

The segments may be made from a single stock board of constant thickness or from a number of smaller scraps, provided that, in the latter case, these too are of identical thickness. A couple of photocopies of the master drawing are made and cut with a craft knife into segments, which are then stuck with double-sided adhesive tape to rough sawn blanks, cut from the stock timber. Plenty of spare timber should be allowed on the length, to ensure that the final elliptical profile can be machined cleanly. Note also, that the segments are not all of the same length and width. It is strongly advised that several spares are made for experimental purposes; these need not be in the chosen timber, but must be of the same thickness. It is also a good plan to keep a little of the chosen timber (of the right thickness) in reserve; mistakes will be made along the way, depend upon it. The sawn segments are sanded on their flanks, almost to the drawn lines.

The set-up for machining the scallops is essentially the same as that shown in Fig.291, Project 7, with the exception that each segment must be handled individually. The use of the Pivot Frame is assumed for the small radius given in Fig.311; if a beam trammel is used a larger radius will be necessary, and this must be used on the master drawing at the outset. Although not absolutely necessary, it helps a great deal if the segments are prepared (after sanding the flanks), as shown in Fig.313. This reduces the cutter loading and the possibility of movement of the segments during machining (the holding area is not very large). Each segment is attached in turn, with hot-melt glue fillets or double-sided adhesive tape, to some form of base which is provided with a hole to receive a $\frac{1}{4}$" diameter bolt. A secondary disc as used with the Pivot Frame is to be preferred, but more or less

Figure 312

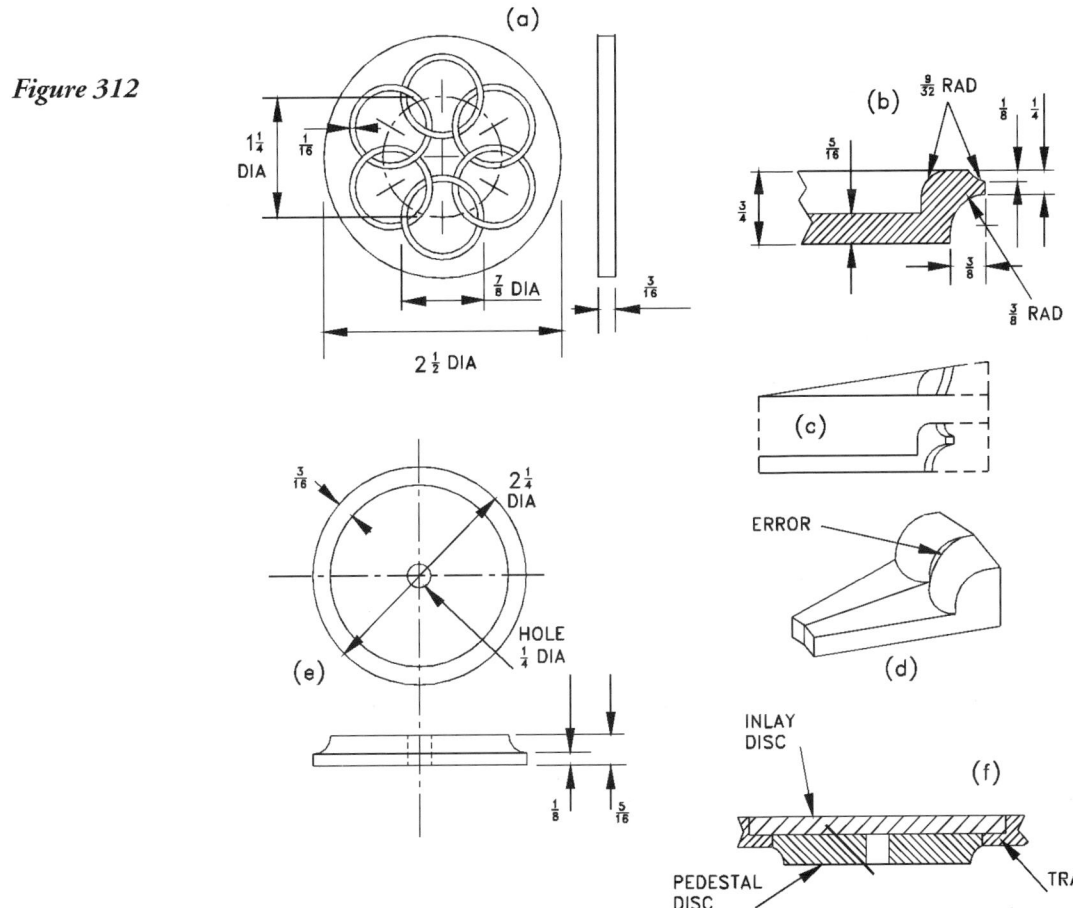

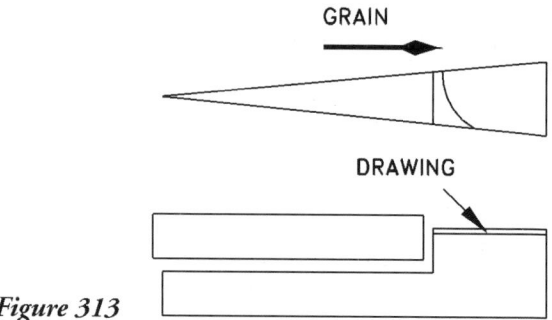

GRAIN

DRAWING

Figure 313

any small flat panel will do. The arrangement permits the assembly to be slid and rotated in a slot in the Pivot Frame primary disc or trammel worktable to place the scallop outline beneath the cutter. It is important that the thickness of the inner portion of each segment (ie. the tray thickness) is constant for all segments. For this reason, an ovolo cutter of suitable radius, but also with a reasonable diameter of flat bottom cut, is used. This enables the scallop radius set on the Pivot Frame or trammel to be locked, and the plunge limit set with the router depth stop. The segments will appear typically as illustrated in Fig.312(c), which is offered simply to give an impression of segment shape but, at this stage, the top and bottom outer coves will not be present on the actual segments; they are not in fact cut until the whole tray has been assembled. The attention of the reader is directed also at the associated drawing (d). As previously mentioned, the ellipse is not a particularly friendly animal where scallops and joints are concerned and, whilst it is possible to arrange for a set of scallops to meet precisely on a given elliptical profile, the centres of the radii forming the scallops will not suit a different size of ellipse, even though it is based on the same major and minor axes. The reader is invited to check the matter with compasses on a photocopy of the master drawing. It will be found that, although the main scallop outlines meet perfectly, different radius settings on the same centres will not meet at the segment joint lines. In this

case, the problem lies with the ovolo cutter, which represents a range of radii (in plan) over its full profile. When machining the scallops, the inner edge of the cutter is set to traverse the drawn scallop lines. If the segment is then fully cut 'right through', then it will actually be seriously overcut at the top surface, due to the larger radius at the top of the cutter. For this reason, each segment is fully machined to one flank, but stopped short of the other, otherwise the error shown in (d) will occur. Dependent upon the position of the segment, the error can be sufficiently large as to render the segment useless. Despite numerous efforts, I find this a very difficult phenomenon to describe in relatively few words, since the cutter behaviour is complex. This is the major reason for the earlier suggestion that a number of experimental pieces are made. These should be dry-assembled into adjacent pairs of segments, with a fully-traversed scallop cut on each, and the mismatch effect studied. The reason for stopping the cut on one flank will then become clear (there's nothing like a little experimentation – that's the way I found out!). Matters cannot however be left here. The un-machined portion of each scallop must be gently taken down with file cards (lengths of abrasive paper stuck to suitable flat thin sticks) until it matches its neighbour. The task isn't particularly difficult, but requires care and plenty of time. There are (for what little it is worth) four positions where a segment does not need to be matched to its neighbour in this way; these occur at the major and minor axes. This task must incidentally, be regarded as simultaneous with that of matching each pair of segments for fit on the master drawing, by gently disc sanding the flanks until the segment joints *and the scallops* fit accurately.

This leaves the problem of ensuring that all the inner parts of the segments (the base of the tray) are of constant thickness. This is easy to manage freehand, given a suitable ski system for the router. A straight $^3/_8$" diameter cutter is used with depth of cut set (and locked) to machine just a whisker of material from the bottom of the cut left by the ovolo cutter. The segments are stuck to a flat worktop, one at a time, or in small groups, with a gap between each as illustrated in Fig.314. In this way it is a simple matter to machine all segments dead flat and to the same thickness. It is also possible to clean up the bottom corners of the scallops, by allowing the cutter to just touch the ovolo flank. This is by no means as risky as it may appear, and it will be found that, despite stopping the cut short when making the ovolo, the bottom of the profile will need little or no attention (again, not easy to explain, but very apparent in practice). The only precaution to be taken is that the cutter is fed *in the climb milling direction*. In the photograph, the router is being pushed, rather than pulled along the scallop line. This is for the reason, explained in Chapter 7, that the cutter will tend to push itself away from the edge, rather than pulling itself into it (see also Fig.151). The task is a very pleasant 'sit-down' job. There isn't even a problem with being too close to the machining dust because there is virtually none to speak of.

Under no circumstances should any attempt be made to sand or finish each individual segment after the foregoing machining process. This will simply give rise to inadvertent dubbing of the edges, and correspondingly poor joints. Rather, the segments are assembled in elliptical 'quarters', my own preference being for aliphatic resin glue. Note that the segments are so small that it is not really a safe business to attempt to biscuit joint or dowel them in any way, as has been described for other projects. One is obliged therefore, to place total reliance upon the glue and the initial stability of the timber.

The assembled quarters are given a preliminary sanding, mainly to ensure that any small differences in level between segments, on the inner flat section, are dealt with, but avoiding dubbing the edges. The quarters are then assembled into two halves and the process repeated at the new joint line. Finally, the complete assembly is glued up, at which point, final sanding is possible on the inside.

Figure 314

The piece may now be turned over and given a fairly rough sanding, largely to make the position of the joint lines on the major and minor axis readily visible, since these must be used to position the drawing of the outer profile. Some assistance is possible here by cutting away the inner portion of the drawing, thus allowing internal alignment of joint lines and drawn axes. The same argument may be applied to a template, if this is the chosen method. The outer profile of the ellipse may now be machined, and the top and bottom coves cut with bearing-guided cutters. The bottom cove, being much the heavier of the two, should be machined first in order to allow the placement of hot-melt glue fillets around the profile. The top cove, being much lighter, may be machined by using a couple of strips of double-sided adhesive tape to hold the work down.

The completed tray is centred and fixed with double-sided adhesive tape over a sacrificial sheet of plywood or MDF which itself is held to the Pivot Frame primary

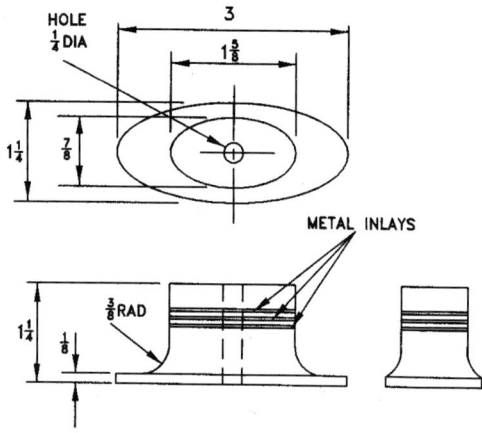

Figure 315

(¹/₁₆″ diameter), and the rings, which need be no more than ¹/₈″ thick inclusive of a generous final sanding allowance, made with a cutter of about ¹/₈″ diameter. No particular difficulty will be encountered in the actual machining of the rings; the Pivot Frame can do far more delicate work than this if need be. Problems may however, arise in subsequent handling. Inadvertent over-pressure with the fingers can snap them quite easily.

Finally, the pedestal. If this is made as in Fig.315, any built-up work with veneer or metal inlays is tackled first, with rough sawn blanks. The blank for the base must be rather generous on size however, to provide plenty of support for the machining which, since a large cove cutter is used, is quite heavy, even with very light feeds. In general, the procedures outlined for making knobs are followed, as described in earlier projects, but the alterations in elliptical aspect ratio with vertical height are made by gradual adjustment of major and minor axes in very small individual steps, with a complete elliptical pass at each step, working from the base profile inwards and upwards to the top. Any slight ripples or 'witness' marks may be sanded away later. All major parts of the piece are shown in Fig.316.

disc. The large holes for the pedestal support and the inlay disc (Fig.312(f)) are then bored and counterbored with a suitable straight cutter. The support disc is a simple exercise. The inlaid top is rather less so but, in principle, it is fashioned in exactly the same way as described in Project 2, but using the drawing of Fig.312(a). The inlay circles are cut with a tiny cutter

Figure 316

ELLIPTICAL PLAIN BOX

Figure 317

This project, illustrated in Figs 317 and 318 is the only one in the series which requires the Pivot Frame ellipse jig as an essential tool. Although I would very much like to be able to describe an alternative means of carrying out the work with, for example, the aid of elliptical templates, I cannot think of a satisfactory answer. The wall of the box is both thin and deep. Any machining method involving bearing-guided cutters would necessarily involve machining at full depth in a single pass, even if the work were brought gradually to final size by means of a series of bearings of reducing diameter. It would, I suppose, be possible to use a combination of cutters and guide bushes; this would at least allow the depth of cut to be kept to sensible increments. In both

cases however, the work would require 'inside' and 'outside' templates which would need to be accurately registered with the workpiece. None of these methods could be fairly described as 'safe'. Even if the operator remains out of danger, the rather flimsy nature of the workpiece places it at considerable risk. In any event, the ellipse jig is used to ensure a good fit between the base and the wall.

The following notes therefore assume the availability of the jig. The basic procedures in terms of arranging and fitting the various components are very similar to those given for the simple circular box featured in Project 4. To avoid unnecessary repetition, the interested reader is therefore referred to that project, since

Figure 318

only those features peculiar to the ellipse jig are covered here. The timbers used for the box and lid are American walnut and sycamore veneer. The (optional) knob offered is somewhat special, since it also involves metal, but the basic timber is ebony.

The main difficulty lies in the making of the elliptical side wall of the box, referred to from now on as the 'ring' for the want of a better word. It is actually made up from three small boards, which may be planed flat to begin with using a ski system as a planer. A veneer layer is placed between each of the two pairs of joints. The boards may be roughly fretsawn slightly oversize into ring blanks, using a paper drawing stuck to the first, as a template. This may then be used to make pencil lines on the remaining two, and also the two veneer sheets, which may be roughly knife-cut to shape. At the same time, a sacrificial panel of MDF is cut to the outer profile only; this is not part of the final assembly; it is used only as an intermediate stage for the trial and error

fitting of the ring to the base. I would not advise the simultaneous gluing of all three blanks with their interleaving veneers, since this would involve gluing, registering and assembling four joints at once. This would, in my view, offer considerable risk of slippage. One joint at a time is far safer. It is also necessary to prepare two further, slightly oversize. boards in a similar way for the base and lid.

The ellipse jig is now used as a drawing device, by placing a pencil in the router collet, rather than a cutter. It is not possible however to use any old pencil. A metal rod, of a diameter which fits the collet is used, with a small hole drilled in one end to receive a length of lead which may be stripped from a pencil stub. The drilling of the hole may admittedly present a little difficulty in the absence of a metalworking lathe, but the job may be done in a pillar drill, along the lines illustrated in Chapter 4 (see Fig.83). The lead is held in place with superglue. It pays to be very careful indeed with such a simple device since, if the lead breaks, the residue must be removed by re-drilling.

A sacrificial sheet of fairly thin plywood is attached to the movable worktable of the ellipse jig, with fillets of hot-melt glue all round. Using the pencil attachment, the elliptical profiles of the inner and outer flanks of the ring are drawn directly on to the plywood, as indicated by the dimensions in Fig.319. The outer profile also serves for the base and the lid. An ellipse is also drawn midway between these two; this serves to indicate the position of the rebate in the base (that for the lid must be dealt with in a slightly different way, as will be seen). A further pair of ellipses are drawn roughly $^1/_8$" inside and outside the main elliptical profiles; these are used to assist location of the workpieces on the plywood. Finally the major and minor axes are drawn in, using the technique described in Chapter 8 (see Fig.183). The router is fitted with a $\frac{1}{4}$" straight cutter of sufficient length to cover the complete depth of the box, including the base, but minus the lid. The ellipse jig is set up such that the outer flank of the cutter traces the rebate line (Fig.320(a)). Reference locknuts are set on the inner face of the pivot bar, and the outer face of the ellipse jig adjuster nut at this position. The jig is then set up so that the outer flank of the cutter traces the inner ring profile (b). This is referenced by means of further pairs of locknuts on the other side of the pivot bar and adjuster nut.

The ring assembly is attached to the plywood panel, using the drawn inner and outer ellipses to position it, and held with several hot-melt glue fillets on the outer flank only. The *inner* profile may now be machined to full depth using very small plunge increments for each pass. The jig is then reset to the stops determining the rebate position to machine the rebate in the top face of the ring. The $\frac{1}{4}$" cutter is then temporarily replaced by one of rather larger diameter (about $^5/_8$" diameter) to skim the top surface dead flat. The ring may now be removed from the plywood panel.

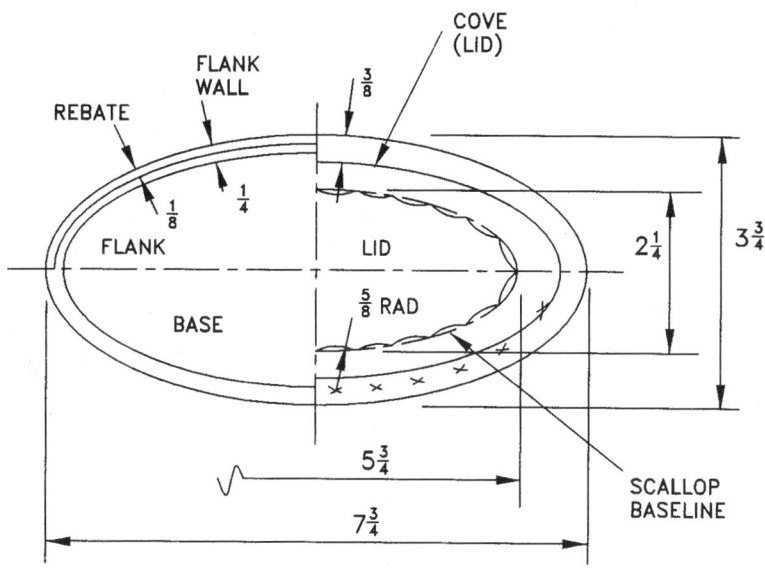

Figure 319

The $\frac{1}{4}$" cutter is replaced, and its inner flank set to trace the outer profile of the ring (c). It is referenced with locknuts as before on the inside of the pivot bar and the outside of the adjuster nut. The jig is then reset such that the inner flank of the cutter traces a path giving a slightly larger ellipse than that given by the rebate line (d). The MDF trial and error panel is fitted to the plywood panel and a rebate cut all round. This will give a slightly oversize setting with regard to the ring rebate. The jig is adjusted inwards on both major and minor axes a little at a time (the cutter position may be judged against the existing rebate), until the ring fits reasonably firmly, with no undue force and certainly with no sloppiness. If things are accidentally overdone, the procedure is repeated with a fresh MDF panel. Once a satisfactory fit is established, the position is referenced with locknuts on the outer face of the pivot bar only; the jig adjuster is left strictly alone from now on. The true base panel is fitted and a rebate cut. The depth setting

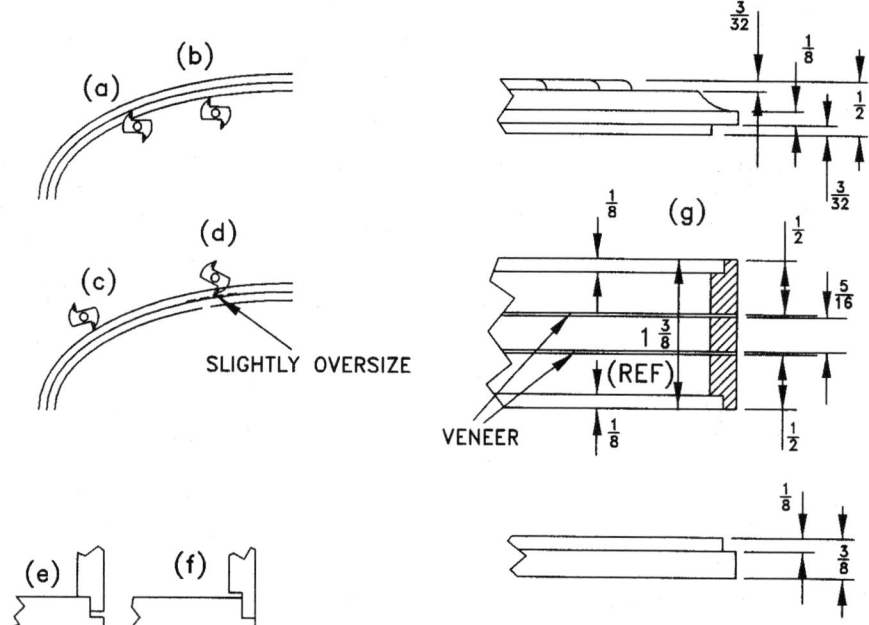

Figure 320

must be approached with care. Too great a depth will cause a gap between ring and base on the outside (e); too little will cause a gap on the inside (f). It is also sensible to set the depth with the router slid outwards to the locknuts on the Pivot Frame only. The cut is started from one of the major axis ends, and slid inwards, and the router controlled from the pivot bars to avoid overcutting on depth due to spring in the rods.

The base is left on the jig and the elliptical ring fitted, ensuring that it seats closely all round. The ring is fixed firmly to the base with hot-melt glue fillets, applied on the inside only. The outer profile of the complete assembly is now machined lightly to establish the cutting profile; the ring is then removed and the base cut almost to full depth. It will not be possible to machine to full depth, since the original glue fillets attaching the base to the panel will still be required. Any residual timber will need to be chiselled and/or sanded away as part of the final finishing process. The ring is replaced, and held lightly with glue fillets, and its top surface

skimmed dead flat with a large diameter cutter as before. The $\frac{1}{4}$" diameter cutter is then replaced to cut the top rebate to receive the lid. Since there is no direct access to the drawn lines on the plywood panel at this point, the major and minor jigs settings for the rebate must be made with direct reference to the top of the ring. This is not a difficult task in itself but, after cutting the rebate, the opposite flank of the cutter is set about $\frac{1}{16}$" inside the cut rebate line on both axes, to establish an 'easy fit' cutter position for the corresponding lid rebate. This is referenced with locknuts and then the inner flank of the cutter is set to the outer profile of the ring, and again referenced with locknuts. The entire assembly may now be removed and replaced by the lid blank, and the lid rebate machined. The jig is reset to the position previously established by the locknuts and the outer profile machined. Once again, to ensure that the lid sits dead flat on the ring, the cutter depth for the rebate is set off the workpiece.

At this stage, the piece may be turned over and fixed

to a plain worktop with double-sided adhesive tape, in order to machine the rim cove with a bearing-guided cutter. Matters may be left at this stage if so desired, but an optional further decoration in the form of a scalloped rebate is offered in Fig.319 (note that this design features twenty-four scallops). If the edges of the scallops are allowed to be simply square with the base, then the task may be very simply handled with a straight cutter of fairly large diameter, as described in Project 7 (see Fig.288). If the top edge is to be rounded as shown in Fig.320(g), it is unlikely that an ovolo cutter which provides the necessary small radius will also have a sufficiently large flat base to cover the entire rebate in a single sweep, particularly at the ends of the ellipse. In this case, the *maximum* radius of the Pivot Frame or trammel is set by means of locknuts, allowing the router to slide on the guide rods, away from the scallop, to cover the entire rebate area as necessary. When finishing the piece, it is strongly advised that the inside surface of both the base and the ring are fully sanded and polished before final assembly and gluing. Major components of the piece are illustrated in Fig.321.

The lid will of course require a knob. This may be made to individual choice. Other projects describe techniques for making circular, elliptical and scalloped knobs, and the reader is referred to the appropriate portions of these projects. A design which might be tackled by the more adventurous reader (using previously described

techniques), is illustrated in Fig.322. This features layers of copper and silver, alternating with ebony. Provided the metal surfaces are given a slight 'tooth' with fine emery (around 800 grit), and are washed clean in non-greasy detergent, they may be fixed quite reliably with either epoxy resin or superglue. As an added precaution, a copper spigot (which is needed anyway, for attachment to the lid) is taken right through the assembly, and allowed to break through the top, where it is domed flush and polished along with the rest of the knob. There is no particular difficulty in cutting soft metals with a router. Tungsten carbide cutters in particular, will go through them easily without ill effect on the cutters. Cutting should be fairly light however, since copper, in particular, may snatch a little if the cut is too heavy. It is also of the utmost importance to wear eye and respiratory protection, since the metal swarf is produced in the form of very fine slivers, which can actually float in the air like wood dust. Knobs of this type are actually much easier to make on a lathe, if available.

Finally, it will be noted that the finished piece as illustrated, is fitted with a copper plate beneath the knob, and four copper bun feet. These require a metal-working lathe, since they may not, in my view, be safely produced with a router.

Figure 322

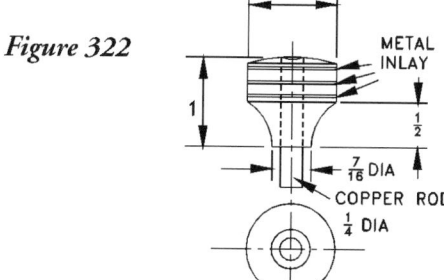

INDEX